TEXAS HERITAGE SERIES

Frank X. Tolbert

THE DAY
OF
SAN JACINTO

THE PEMBERTON PRESS

Jenkins Publishing Company
Austin and New York

To L. R. Bryan, Jr., Louis Kemp, Sam Houston Dixon,
and Clarence Wharton

and all others who have kept the story of the
day of San Jacinto alive
through the years

Contents

Illustrations

Maps

THE DAY
OF
SAN JACINTO

Introduction

SO WHAT? I say to myself—another book on the glorious fighting breed that made up the Republic of Texas. Like so many other people who have reason to revere Texas, I lose patience with the unbalanced approach to Texas history and tradition, with the attempt to make it seem as if 99 percent of all that was worth-while in her story happened in the 10 years of revolution and republic and that what went on before, and more especially, what has gone on since is of transient importance and academic interest only.

To me the story of the revolution against Mexico and the decade of travail that followed is a chapter in the history of Texas. But only a chapter, not the whole book, with the briefest of prologues and epilogues.

The period of the 1830's and the 1840's are the glamor years; the period of the 1870's and since are the formative years when Texas tried to come up to date and to recover the social, political, and intellectual sophistication she lost with the departure of such men as Houston, Austin, and Lamar. We started with giants and devolved and, happily, now and then evolved, with pygmies—it has been a long, tortured, and tortuous road to resurrection; and it is that road that needs chronicling.

And so I pick up Frank X. Tolbert's "The Day of San Jacinto" with a ho-hum attitude, thinking that here is an inevitable commercial offering from the publishing mileau that has spelled financial success for such nice people as Walter Lord, Jim Bishop and my own colleague, Eddie Weems.

I know the proliferous Mr. Tolbert. I respect him as a journalist of taste, high good humor, and a way with an anecdote. I expect his book to be lively and superficial, to sell well.

Well, he has written a good book. Sure, it's lively, but it's not superficial. And it is absolutely absorbing. Working without the elegaic qualities which inhered in Lon Tinkle's *Thirteen Days to Glory*, in which Tinkle could organize the fall of the Alamo into a magnificently gloomy Greek epic of inexorable tragedy, Tolbert has caught up the spirit of San Jacinto in a book that deserves to be read by anyone interested in Texas or military confusion or political ineptness.

Texas had no business winning the Texas Revolution, and more particularly, the battle of San Jacinto. But the Mexicans deserved to win even less. Sam Houston had the quality of leadership, but he had little to lead. And he had a civilian populace without patience for anything but immediate victories, and a government more interested in self-preservation than in constructive planning. And the solid people, with money and slaves and influence, were too comfortable to want to disturb the status quo. They just wished the whole jumbled mess would somehow go away.

(Lest we seem to condemn the landholders and merchants too easily, I might add that theirs was a good case—Mexico had been a generous host, and even in 1835-1836 there were handfuls of people who felt gratitude. But the proportion was no greater then than in 1969).

On the other hand, Santa Anna couldn't leave his opium alone, he couldn't leave off wenching even on the afternoon of battle, and he couldn't believe that he was fallible or tolerate advice from subordinates. And so he caught the Texans in an indefensible position, but he was indefensible too.

As a professional historian I am bound by union rules to find something to quibble about. Usually I point out archival collections not consulted, new interpretations not elicited, or, if I can find nothing else, a proof error on page 927. In this instance my chief complaint is that the book is interesting, which violates rule number one of the historians' code.

The story of San Jacinto has been told many times, accurately and inaccurately, sketchily and completely, dully and more dully. Only in the sources—Santa Anna's account, Ramon Caro's astringent *Verdadera Idea*, Sam Houston's battle reports, or Robert Coleman's "Houston Displayed"—has this lusty campaign heretofore been narrated so lustily.

But now Tolbert has told a story that is good Texas, and he has told it to be read. If there is anything he has left out, it doesn't matter. San Jacinto has its biographer, and he shows balance, skill, and good humor. The latter is a particularly needed quality, for San Jacinto is essentially a picaresque adventure.

Joe B. Frantz

Prologue

The Texas Revolution couldn't possibly have hap-
pened, yet happen it did. There never will be another
Alamo, so futilely heroic, apparently; another Go-
liad, so futilely tragic, apparently; or another San Ja-
cinto, so triumphant and important, apparently.

—Dr. Samuel E. Asbury of Texas A&M

O N MARCH 2, 1836, the Mexican subprovince of
Texas declared itself an independent nation. This
was an impudent thing to do, for there were only
about thirty thousand Texas colonists and they shared the
land with more than twenty thousand Indians. At least half of
these Indians were unfriendly.

Mexico was then a nation of eight million and was under an
absolute military dictatorship. In contrast, the Texas rebels
of 1836 were often confused by provisional government
leaders who quarreled among themselves like schoolboys. Also,
many of the thirty thousand colonists were satisfied, in varying
degrees, with the City of Mexico government, which was not
only far away but had been generous with its public lands
and had taxed not at all in the 1820s and lightly in the 1830s.

Most of these 1836 Texans were from the United States.
In 1821 a Virginian named Stephen Fuller Austin was given
permission to bring the first Anglo-American settlers into the
easternmost regions of the subprovince. For the most part

1

Austin's settlers were families who came with the simple hope of bettering their fortunes in a wilderness where land was almost free. But there were speculators, too, among them, and smugglers. Slave trading flourished. Debtors and fugitives from justice found the careless Mexican rule comfortable. Men and women ruined by scandals or overwhelmed by personal tragedies moved to the sparsely settled subprovince to make new starts. The medical doctors, lawyers and other highly trained men seemed almost as numerous as the crude frontiersmen and other rustics. Many of the men who were to run the government and the army of the new Republic were trained in the law or in medicine. Adventurers, soldiers of fortune, gamblers, and pirates seemed just as land-hungry as hard-working, honest farmers and ranchers.

And there was plenty of land. In those days, Texas sprawled across the western part of the continent. The southwest and western borders followed the Rio Grande to its headwaters in Colorado and beyond up into Wyoming. One northern boundary in the west was the Arkansas River, and another northern boundary in the east was the Red River. An eastern boundary line, flowing south between Texas and the United States into the Gulf of Mexico, was the Sabine River.

In 1836 sizable parts of the present-day states of New Mexico, Colorado, Wyoming, Kansas, and Oklahoma lay within Texas. Yet most of the colonists were in the comparatively snug and very fertile southeast reaches of the subprovince as defined by three great river systems, the Colorado, the Brazos, and the Trinity. All of these rise in northwestern highlands and flow in generally southeasterly patterns to the Gulf. The Brazos, central stream of the settled region, was the Main Street of Texas. Steamboats and other large craft could ascend more than a hundred miles up what the Spanish explorers called The River of the Arms of God.

In 1836, the Texas colonists were surrounded by Indians. Even over across the border in the United States some southern tribes were on the warpath and sometimes interrupted mail service to Texas. Along the coast were the Karankawas and related tribes, giant men and ritualistic cannibals. The Karanks had fought against Austin's colonists some years before, but the tall tribesmen actually helped the settlers during the Texas Revolution. Generally, the Indians along the Gulf and in East Texas were more friendly with the whites than those on the western and northern frontiers. The Cherokees in East Texas were well-armed, semicivilized fellows who were mainly interested in securing title to their East Texas farms. The savage Comanches, Kiowas, and Apaches, who rode in from the west or north, were much occupied in stealing horses and women and lifting an occasional scalp. There was no general Indian war in 1836 yet raids were commonplace and settlers on outlying farms and ranches led dangerous lives.

At first, Stephen F. Austin was given complete civil and military authority over his foundation colony. He used this power wisely. In the decade after 1822 his settlement grew from an original three hundred families to more than eight thousand persons, and these Anglo-Americans began to figure heavily in the politics of the gigantic Mexican state of Coahuila y Texas.

Austin's colony, as well as others in Texas, had a lot to offer. Heads of families got 4,605 acres of lands and other inducements. Times were very bad in the United States in the 1820s and many Texas pioneers left unpaid bills back in the states. Stephen Austin had a law passed which closed the courts for twelve years against people from outside of Texas who were trying to collect debts. And all of a Texan's land, tools, and stock were permanently exempt from seizure even if a debt suit was won by the plaintiff after the twelve-year period. Also, a federal act of 1823 exempted the colonists from import duties for seven-year periods. Austin was even thinking some of basing "the credit system on moral character alone . . . to avoid unjust retroactive effects."

In the late 1820s the liberal, democratic government that had suited Austin and the other Texas colonists so well was undermined gradually. And in the early 1830s a military dictatorship took its place.

Leaders in the City of Mexico, who wanted a highly centralized form of government, fretted over the fast growth of the Anglo-American settlements in Texas. A "Law of April 6, 1830" was aimed at stopping any more colonization by people from the United States. Although Austin got his colony and that of Green DeWitt exempt from the Law of April 6, he still continued to try to get this law repealed. His colony capital, San Felipe de Austin on the Brazos, was the scene of a series of conventions held to protest this unpopular legislation.

When the import duties exemptions ran out, unwise attempts were made by Mexican officials to try and collect these tariffs by force. Mexican soldiers, many of them ex-convicts, were garrisoned in Texas ports and several skirmishes took place between them and the colonists in the early 1830s.

Austin's policy was to remain aloof from Mexican politics, to take no sides in the numerous revolutions and counter-revolutions centered in the City of Mexico. As the Texans' grievances increased, Austin found it harder and harder to maintain this aloofness. Finally, in late 1833, he visited the City of Mexico and warned that if the Texas troubles weren't attended to the colonists would "take matters into their own hands and tranquility would be disturbed." He asked that

Texas be made a separate state of Mexico, that the April 6, 1830, law (or rather its eleventh article) be abrogated, and that a more convenient system of courts be established. He even asked for more mail routes between principal Texas towns and those in other northern Mexico regions. Austin did get the clause in the Law of April 6 repealed and the promise of other reforms. The Mexican leaders wouldn't approve changing the status of Coahuila y Texas, though.

Although Austin's mission seemed fairly successful, while returning home he was arrested on the suspicion that he planned "to incite an insurrection" and was thrown into a Mexican prison. No formal charges were filed against him but he was detained until July, 1835.

In Texas, Austin had been the leader of the "Peace Party" consisting of those who had no intention of breaking away from Mexico or starting armed rebellions. During his absence the tension mounted in the colonies and the "War Party" clamored for revolution if that were necessary to bring separation from Mexico.

In January, 1835, the customs house at Anahuac, the principal port of Galveston Bay, was reestablished. The new customs collector was a Capt. Antonio Tenorio and he brought with him forty soldiers. His job was to force the Texans to pay duties and to try to stop a traffic in what the new laws defined as smuggled goods. Tenorio was on dangerous ground. Anahuac had been the scene of an armed uprising against another Mexican tax collector in '32.

In June of 1835, Tenorio arrested two prominent colonists, Andrew Briscoe and DeWitt Clinton Harris. Briscoe was an Anahuac merchant who liked to play practical jokes on the Mexican soldiers. Harris, whose family founded a big Texas town, Harrisburg, had been dealing with Briscoe in goods on which no duties had been paid. Harris was soon released but Briscoe was detained. Harris went back to Harrisburg, where he recounted what had happened. About twenty men, all settlers, formed into a company and elected a young lawyer named William Barret Travis as their captain.

The Travis company mounted a 6-pound cannon on truck wheels normally used to haul logs, rolled the artillery aboard the sloop *Ohio*, and sailed for Anahuac. There they caught the Mexican garrison completely by surprise, and Tenorio surrendered after a bloodless siege of the town. This is Travis's report on the affair:

> We landed at Anahuac on June 29 and on the morning of the 30th the troops capitulated, delivering to us 64 stands of muskets and bayonets. They agreed to leave Texas immediately under parole, never to serve against the people of Texas. I sent them bag and baggage aboard the sloop, and they are now [after crossing Galveston and San Jacinto Bays] on the march to La Bahia without arms.

Briscoe was of course released. The clash between Tenorio and Travis must have been rather good-natured, for Tenorio was entertained at a barbecue before he boarded the *Ohio*. Peace Party meetings all over Texas condemned Travis's action, but the War Party gained adherents when the colonists intercepted a courier bearing a message, intended for Tenorio, from Gen. Martin Perfecto de Cos, a brother-in-law of the dictator of Mexico. The message announced that more troops would be sent to Anahuac and other Texas centers: "In a very short time the affairs of Texas will be settled, definitely, for which purpose the government has ordered to take up the line of march a strong division composed of troops which were in Zacatecas. These Texans will be ground down."

Cos had been busy that spring in Texas's sister subprovince, Coahuila. The General, whose title was commandant of the eastern internal provinces, had gone to the capital, Monclova, and had dissolved—it turned out forever—the legislature of the State of Coahuila and Texas. Cos said he did this because some of the legislators had been involved in fraudulent sales of Texas lands. This was true. However, dissolving state legislatures was a part of the dictatorship's policy since the liberal Mexican Constitution of 1824 had been abolished.

In August of 1835, Stephen F. Austin returned to Texas from his Mexican imprisonment. Austin was honored at a huge dinner and he told the colonists that war with the centralist Mexican government now seemed inevitable. He still hoped that there would be uprisings against the dictator all over Mexico, and Texas could stay within the nation. "We are defending our constitutional rights against military usurption," he said.

There was fighting near the town of Gonzales, about seventy miles east of San Antonio, in the autumn of 1835. Again a hastily organized band of Texans subjected the government forces to humiliating defeat. In San Antonio itself, in December of the same year, the rebels once more drove off a vastly superior Mexican army—the "strong division" promised by General Cos and under his command. But despite all the fighting and the rebel victories that took place in 1835, Austin and many other powerful leaders continued to oppose the idea of undertaking a war of aggression, or even a war for independence. Most Texans still considered themselves Mexican citizens when, in February of 1836, a massive expeditionary force from Mexico crossed the Rio Grande.

Members of the old War and Peace Parties were about equally divided on March 2, 1836, when the colonists held a convention and declared Texas independent of Mexico. The

Texans didn't have $200 in the treasury. What small armies they had were scattered throughout faraway West Texas, and most of them were soon to be overwhelmed by the hosts from the Mexican interior. Even while the convention was in progress, the battle of the Alamo, the most famous fight of the Revolution, was going on at San Antonio, a hundred fifty miles southeast of the convention site on the Brazos River.

A much more important battle took place less than two months later on a pleasant-looking ranch near the southeast corner of Texas, where the dark waters of the San Jacinto River meet a broad, deep waterway called Buffalo Bayou and both are lost in the salt of San Jacinto Bay. In the Southwest, San Jacinto is pronounced "san juh SIN tuh," even when spoken in Spanish, and it means St. Hyacinth.

What follows is the story of the battle of San Jacinto, told by soldiers who were there at this unlikely climax to the unique and very complex revolution that decided, directly or indirectly, the ownership of almost a million square miles of the American West.

The Napoleon of the West

Santa Anna assigned General Cos to the post of honor, of greatest danger, as the leader of the assault [against the Alamo]. To himself, he [Santa Anna] assigned the post of greatest safety, to command the reserve.

FROM THE DIARY OF COL. JUAN ALMONTE

ALTHOUGH the expeditionary force that entered Texas in the spring of 1836 was called the Mexican army, it did not have the full support of the Mexican nation. Moreover, many of its members were not Mexican citizens at all but European and American soldiers of fortune. Its best sniper, for example, was an Illinois rifleman named Memory Johnson. The commander of this army was Gen. Don Antonio Lopez de Santa Anna y Perez de Lebron, President of Mexico. His soldiers, like his political supporters, were called Santanistas.

Santa Anna had assumed the Presidency of Mexico in 1833. Despite the fact that until then he had been a loud champion of the liberal Mexican Constitution of 1824, and that his title had a democratic sound, his authority was absolute. Soon after he became President he abolished the 1824 Constitution and put Mexico under a military dictatorship, explaining when he did so that the majority of the people weren't advanced enough to live under democratic rule. What Mexico needed, he said, was despotism, and he would try to be a good despot.

In 1836 the President was forty-two and a handsome, manly-looking fellow. That same year the wife of a European diplomat in the City of Mexico described him as a "tall and romantic-looking" man. Tall he was for a Mexican, 5 feet 10 inches, and he had a spare, wide-shouldered build. His grand, medal-laden uniforms and Napoleon-style hats accentuated his theatrical good looks. He sat handsome horses on gold-stamped saddles which had saddle horns in the shape of golden eagle heads.

Santa Anna was a man of complex character. Perhaps because he was addicted to opium, his personality could change radically from one moment to the next. There are many well-documented stories attesting to his courage and even recklessness in the face of danger, yet at times he was so cowardly it was comical. As a rule he was so dishonest that it's hard to see how he could have trusted himself, yet he could display a keenly developed awareness of honor. He was a vain man and surrounded himself with luxuries that were almost effeminate, but he loved such violent pastimes as cockfights and bullfights, and once arranged for a match between a bull and a Bengal tiger. This particular contest (which the bull won) served two purposes. It gratified Santa Anna's taste for violent sport, and it pleased one of his mistresses. Women, especially beautiful ones, were another of his hobbies.

The President was immensely popular in Mexico, both with the masses and with the privileged military and church men. President Andrew Jackson once described him as "the pride of all Mexican soldiers and the idol of the priesthood." *El Presidente* was an engaging man, and a most effective speaker. Though he had help in preparing formal speeches, his extemporaneous talks were impressive. Yet basically he was ig-

norant in political matters, and couldn't have defined either
the political philosophies he opposed or those that at various
times he endorsed. He was a shameless egotist, and the philos-
ophy that actually guided his career was nothing more than
opportunism.

Throughout his life, Santa Anna showed scant loyalty to
the causes he espoused. Trouble between political parties con-
tributed to his personal success, and he was not above stirring
it up deliberately. Often while he claimed to be a member of
one political party, he would secretly conspire with the opposing party to undermine his own. Among the victims of such
maneuvers was an honest politican named Gomez Farias.
Farias, elected Vice-president under Santa Anna in 1833, was
a true democrat and shared none of the President's lust for
wealth and glory. Bancroft's *History of Mexico* comments:

> Gomez Farias was ever disposed to serve his country. The
> privileged classes received some hard blows from Farias,
> who maintained energetically that the civil authority
> should always be above the military. And he endeavored
> to prevent interference on the part of the clergy in
> secular affairs.

Obviously such a man could become a stumbling block to
Santa Anna. But the resourceful President found ways to use
Farias's integrity to his own advantage and, at the same time,
to undermine his Vice-president. From time to time, on some
such pretext as illness, Santa Anna would temporarily turn
the government over to his Vice-president. Farias would courageously try to effect reforms and would soon be butting
heads with the military and the church leaders. Santa Anna,
claiming all the while to be Farias's friend, would often spend
his alleged vacation plotting with the generals and the bishops.
As soon as Farias's battles with his political enemies had

caused sufficient confusion in the government, the President would return to his job and would obtain the wider powers he claimed he needed to straighten things out.

Gradually, it became apparent that Santa Anna was in reality the leader of the privileged classes, and these elements sought to give him unrestricted powers. Farias had the support of most congressmen and of the men in the large state militia forces. Santa Anna took care of this by ordering the state militias to be reduced to one man for each five hundred citizens—a trifling size—and by chipping away most of the Congress's powers. Farias put up a good fight for the Constitution of 1824, which to some degree was patterned after the United States Constitution. But by 1835 he had lost his post and been sent into exile. When Santa Anna began to call himself "The Napoleon of the West," the title was not as extravagant as it sounds. Mexico owned millions of miles in the West, and Santa Anna owned Mexico.

Like Napoleon, Santa Anna went to war when he was very young. During the Mexican Revolution against Spain, when Santa Anna was seventeen, he was a cadet in the Spanish Royalist army in Mexico. He received his first wound in this war. He was later a Spanish army officer, a revolutionist and, frequently, a counterrevolutionist. When in 1822 a Mexican named Augustin de Iturbide set himself up as Emperor of the new country, Santa Anna was one of his chief supporters. But Iturbide failed to give Santa Anna a job he wanted in the · government, so at an opportune time Santa Anna denounced the Emperor and came out for a republic. In the ensuing revolution Iturbide was run out of Mexico. Santa Anna was a busy combat general during most of the 1820s, frequently switching sides in Mexico's ceaseless civil wars.

In 1829, some 3,000 Spaniards under a General Isador

Barradas landed in Mexico on Cabo Rojo, about thirty-five miles south of Tampico. Their intention was to reconquer Mexico for Spain, and their landing met no immediate opposition. However, a resisting army of about two thousand Mexicans was raised, and Santa Anna was appointed its commander. Although there were several encounters between Barradas and Santa Anna, the Spaniards suffered more from insects and fever than they did from Mexican guns. Finally, Barradas surrendered to Santa Anna on condition that he and his army would be permitted to take ship out of the mosquito-ridden country. The terms were granted.

Santa Anna emerged from this campaign with a new title, "The Hero of Tampico." He was hailed as his country's savior. One cynical Mexican biographer of Santa Anna claimed that Barradas actually defeated The Hero of Tampico twice in battles. According to this source, Barradas had been given $1,500,000 in expense money by the king of Spain and had some of this money hidden in another country. Disgusted with his mosquito-bitten invasion, he had simply decided to get away and enjoy his profits.

Often throughout his career Santa Anna owed his success to such good luck as this Tampico affair. Even after his several military reverses, he could present himself to the Mexican people with such persuasive salesmanship that he would seem admirable even in defeat.

Santa Anna was unusually confident when in February of 1836 he led his seven thousand troops into Texas, for the previous year he had smashed a similar revolution in the province of Zacatecas, and in the process, he had displayed a talent he considered truly Napoleonic.

The Zacatecans, like the Texans, were unhappy because of the abolition of the 1824 Constitution, but it was the order reducing the militia of all Mexican states that really brought on the Zacatecan rebellion. The powerful militias maintained by the Mexican frontier states were intended primarily for protection against wild Indians, but these militias were also effective brakes on the ambitions of centralists in the City of Mexico. Santa Anna's decree that each militia should have only one man for each five hundred residents of the state and that the frontier states would be protected mostly by the federal troops was calculated to put the states at the mercy of City of Mexico militarists. So in 1835 about five thousand Zacatecan militia, led by the Governor of the province, marched themselves against an army of four thousand professional soldiers led by *El Presidente*. Santa Anna was the skillful general that day and he had far better equipment. He won easily and took two thousand seven hundred fifty prisoners. He executed hundreds of the captives and allowed his troops to plunder and rape in the beautiful ravine city of Zacatecas.

The brutality of Santa Anna's behavior toward his vanquished enemies may have been quite spontaneous, but he had seen such merciless tactics employed after battle when he was a young boy, and in all probability that early experience did influence him. It was in 1813, when Santa Anna was nineteen years old and was serving as a sublieutenant of fusiliers in a Spanish Royalist army led by a ruthless and bloodthirsty general named Joaquin de Arredondo. At this time, the Spanish army was doing battle with some thousand Texas Latins, Anglo-Americans, and Indians who, calling themselves "The Army of the North," had undertaken a war against Mexico. Arredondo used Texans who were secret royalists to lure the rebels into a trap on the Medina River, just west of San Antonio. The Spanish General then almost annihilated the republicans. (Arredondo would have hanged his pupil if he'd known that Santa Anna was making love to one Miss Pia Quinta, the commander in chief's mistress. The enterprising young sublieutenant did, by some accounts, get caught forging the General's name on checks.) Among Santa Anna's trophies of this campaign was a grim witticism of Arredondo's: "If you execute your enemies it saves you the trouble of having to forgive them." If Santa Anna learned about merciless warfare from Arredondo, his teacher would have been proud of the President's performance in Zacatecas.

It was while Santa Anna was busy slaughtering Zacatecans that the Texas colonists rose up and ran all the Mexican garrisons out of the province. Santa Anna was angered at what the Texans had done, especially so over the fate of his garrison at San Antonio where, in December of 1835, some four hundred Texas militia stormed the town and took the surrender of the twelve hundred federal troops that were stationed there under the President's brother-in-law Gen. Martin Perfecto de Cos. The colonists confiscated most of the army's weapons and sent Cos and his men back across the Rio Grande on what they called a parole. That is, the Mexican General and his soldiers were made to swear that they'd never take up arms against the Constitution of 1824 again.

Santa Anna, at the head of his great expeditionary force, met the whipped Cos column near the Rio Grande in February of 1836. The dictator rearmed his brother-in-law's brigade and made them wheel around and head back for San Antonio. To Cos's credit, he told Santa Anna he didn't want to fight the colonists again after their chivalrous treatment of his army in defeat, but this scruple only got him a tongue-lashing from the President.

El Presidente sent out printed circulars to the Texas colonists announcing that he intended to restore an old Spanish policy of not letting even a bird flying across the Sabine River pass without a challenge. The Sabine, now part of the Texas–Louisiana boundary, was then generally considered an eastern border of Mexico, although Santa Anna was fond of saying that he believed his empire really extended eastward all the way to the Mississippi.

Late in February, 1836, Santa Anna's armies crossed the Rio Grande and marched to San Antonio, where for the first time they encountered Texas resistance. The rebels were in a church-fortress in San Antonio called the Alamo.

During the winter of 1835–36 the provisional government of Texas had repeatedly ordered the Alamo destroyed and its cannon carried away. Two of the Texan officers who were given this command were William Barret Travis and the famous frontiersman Jim Bowie. Travis and Bowie disobeyed these orders and they were both in the Alamo when the Mexican army appeared. The rebels had barricaded themselves in the old mission with fourteen cannon left there by Cos's men the previous December.

When Santa Anna reached San Antonio, there were about a hundred and fifty men behind the thick walls of the Alamo, including the celebrated Davy Crockett and a handful of his Tennessee sharpshooters. On February 23, Santa Anna and some five hundred men arrived in San Antonio. Within days, the main body of the Santanistas, perhaps five thousand men, caught up with the General. They quickly surrounded the church-fortress and laid siege. Within a few days some thirty men from the nearby town of Gonzales managed to slip through the Mexican lines. They were the first and last reinforcements to enter the Alamo.

Santa Anna loved quick, cheap victories like the one in Zacatecas. After such triumphs, he could watch the firing squads at work. He was immensely annoyed that a hundred eighty Texas artillerymen and riflemen should hold up the parade of his thousands of veteran soldiers across the rebellious province. While his army, commanded in effect by several other generals and a number of lower-ranking officers, besieged the Alamo for thirteen days, Santa Anna himself grew bored.

Married to a very homely woman, the President had dozens of lovely mistresses and sometimes he would take one of them along on military campaigns. Apparently he found a pretty girl the best cure for boredom. But this trip he didn't seem to have fetched one with him to Texas.

However, he had heard one of his staff, Maj. Gen. Manuel Fernandez Castrillon, speak of the beauty of a seventeen-year-old San Antonio girl named Melchora Iniega Barrera. Since *El Presidente* knew that Castrillon was a connoisseur of female charm, he enthusiastically asked the Major General to bring Miss Barrera to the commander in chief's quarters. Castrillon, a cultivated native of Spain, apparently despised the Creole President, but until Santa Anna suggested that he act as his commander's procurer, he had managed to keep his dislike a secret. Now Castrillon refused to comply with Santa Anna's offensive suggestion, and his refusal is said to have started ill feelings between the two men that were to become more intense as the Texas campaign wore on.

The President got someone else to introduce him to Melchora Iniega Barrera. Antonio Menchaca, a prominent citizen of San Antonio who later fought with the rebels, said that Melchora was from one of San Antonio's best families. She lived with her widowed mother in a dwelling that was, for that crude frontier village, fairly impressive. The main house, which was made of heavy timbers and limestone blocks, had three big rooms, and there were several smaller adobe houses in the compound. Menchaca said that Santa Anna moved in with the Barreras several days before the Alamo battle reached its bloody conclusion.

Mother Barrera must have known that her illustrious boarder was a married man. The poor woman also knew that she was dealing with a tyrant, and perhaps she felt that her daughter might even be better off as the well-cared-for mistress of Santa Anna than she could be in San Antonio, then a dangerous crossroad for contending armies and a favorite target of fierce Indians. Santa Anna was reputed to be generous with his womenfolk—except for his wife, whom he sometimes publicly scolded. He even gave estates to his favorite ladies, and at least one mistress had lasted long enough to become very wealthy. Nonetheless Mrs. Barrera courageously demanded that the President either marry Melchora or give up courting her.

Santa Anna had on his staff a young sergeant who had been an actor and had studied Latin. This fellow, soon to have commissioned rank, played the role of priest, said Menchaca, as Santa Anna took Melchora Barrera in a mock marriage. His Excellency was in the midst of his honeymoon on March 6 when, at the cost of hundreds of Mexican lives, his army finally overwhelmed the Texans in the Alamo.

General Castrillon was said to have been the "soul of the assault" on the Alamo. Bridegroom Santa Anna stayed back with the musicians and a part of his staff

> until he supposed the place was nearly mastered, when he moved up with that escort towards the Alamo, but returned again upon being greeted by a few rifle balls from the upper windows of the church. He entered the area towards the close of the battle and directed some of the last details of the butchery.

Not one of the fighting men in the Alamo had survived the battle. A few women and children and two Negro slaves who had been in the fortress were spared. Although there were no prisoners to shoot, Santa Anna remained true to his barbaric principles. He had the bodies of all the slain Texans heaped together on a mass pyre, soaked with oil, and burned without further ceremony.

Within a few days after the fall of the Alamo, Santa Anna paraded his troops through the streets of San Antonio. This parade was intended especially for the eyes of a Texas girl named Mrs. Suzanna Dickenson. Her husband had been a lieutenant of artillery in the Alamo and was, of course, slain in the massacre. The young matron and her eighteen-month-old child, Angelina, had been in the mission throughout the siege. Mrs. Dickenson had been wounded slightly. After the battle she had been taken prisoner and led to Santa Anna.

By all accounts she was a very attractive woman. So she must have made an appealing figure, holding her blond baby, and standing defiantly before the Mexican President. Santa Anna was impressed by both mother and child. Only a few hours before he'd caused the death of Angelina's father, yet he asked Mrs. Dickenson if he could adopt the baby. He got a negative answer.

Santa Anna put on a parade for this poor, grief-stricken woman because he wanted to impress her with his strength. Afterward, he sent her East as messenger to the Texas rebels. It must have been quite a parade, for Mrs. Dickenson always insisted that Santa Anna had around ten thousand troops on the Alamo assault. He probably had about half this many surrounding San Antonio, and about two thousand five hundred actually attacked the Alamo walls.

While the parade was going on Santa Anna's English-speaking aide, Colonel Almonte, was busy writing warnings in English to the Texas rebels. These told of Santa Anna's nine-point program for his expeditionary forces in Texas:

1. Drive out of Texas all persons who had taken part in the rebellion.

2. Drive out all settlers living near the Gulf of Mexico or the United States border.

3. Move into the interior those settlers (North Americans not included) who had not taken part in the war.

4. Vacate all land grants made to nonresidents.

5. Remove from the province all those who were not colonists. (This is not precisely worded. It was explained that it really meant that Santa Anna's armies would slay all adventurers found in Texas.)

6. Allot lands to Mexican soldiers.

7. Permit no Anglo-Americans to live in Texas.

8. Insure that the expenses of the war were paid by Texas.

9. Liberate all Negro slaves.

Mrs. Dickenson was given a horse and supplies and told to find the leaders of the insurrection and give them the written warnings. She carried baby Angelina in her arms. A young Negro slave named Joe, a small fellow "of excellent countenance," accompanied her. Joe had been the body servant of the Texan officer Colonel Travis, and, like Suzanna Dickenson, he had been in the Alamo throughout the siege.

According to some accounts, another Negro—the former servant of Santa Anna's aide, Almonte—also traveled with Mrs. Dickenson. In 1829 a Mexican Congressional decree had emancipated all slaves, and Almonte was aware that ostentatious compliance with this order might raise sympathy for the Mexican cause in the northern part of the United States. Some Texas slave holders had ignored the law, while others had evaded its intention by freeing their slaves and then simply indenturing them for ninety-nine years. That spring in Washington John Quincy Adams told his fellow congressmen: "If war breaks out between the United States and Mexico the Mexicans will be waving banners of freedom while your banners will be those of slavery." Perhaps Almonte deliberately selected two Negroes to send with Mrs. Dickenson and told them to spread the word among Texas slaves that they would soon be liberated.

Mrs. Dickenson left San Antonio on March 11. The same day about eight hundred soldiers under Brig. Gen. Joaquin Ramirez y Sesma, also at San Antonio, started for East Texas. Mrs. Dickenson did not leave with these troops, and it seems that no Mexican observers were near when, on March 13, she was found by three Texas army scouts about fifty miles east of San Antonio.

Meanwhile, Santa Anna dictated his report of the Alamo battle to his civilian secretary, Ramon Caro, and had it dispatched to the City of Mexico. The President's story had it that six hundred rebels had been killed in an Alamo which Santa Anna described as being strong as Gibraltar. Like many of *El Presidente's* subordinates, Caro later had a falling out with Santa Anna. Thereafter the secretary was so brash as to write that only one hundred eighty-three Texans were killed, and that the Alamo was a "mere corral and nothing more." Certainly, he said, it was not a strong fortress. Santa Anna told the folks back home that he lost only seventy men taking the Alamo. Secretary Caro said that six hundred Santanistas fell in the actual assault and many more died from neglect of their wounds. Caro further charged that Santa Anna had failed to bring a proper hospital corps to Texas, "only a few medical students and not more than three hundred pesos' worth of drugs." (He must have discounted Santa Anna's large personal supply of opium in this three-hundred-peso estimate.)

According to Caro, Santa Anna was niggardly with government funds in Texas because he was robbing his own war chest. Without Congressional supervision, Santa Anna had arranged late in 1835 for a 400,000–peso loan to finance the Texas expedition. Among the securities pledged for the loan were the import and export duties of several Mexican ports, including that of Matamoros, at the mouth of the Rio Grande. According to Caro, half of this loan was in silver and the rest in bonds, and after the Alamo victory Santa Anna started sending both bonds and chests of silver back to the City of Mexico for deposit to his own account.

While Santa Anna's main force conquered the Alamo at heavy cost, a Mexican division of about twelve hundred men under a brilliant general named Jose Francisco Urrea was driving eastward along the Texas coast. On March 19 on Perdido Creek, near a town called Goliad or Mission La Bahia, Urrea overtook some four hundred well-armed rebels, most of them young recruits from the United States. Their commander was a West Point officer named James Walker Fannin. On March 14, Fannin received orders from Sam Houston, commander in chief of all Texas forces, to blow up the fortress at Goliad and retreat beyond a stream called Coleto Creek to the town of Victoria on the Guadalupe. When these orders had reached him, his command had been divided because he had previously sent troops to the aid of refugees in a nearby town. Fannin had felt obliged to wait for the absent men, and did not begin his retreat until March 19. He was three miles west of the Coleto when the Urrea forces trapped him and pinned him down. Fannin could have tried to shoot his way out of the trap, for his troops had five hundred spare muskets and nine brass cannon. But he stayed where he was, and his men soon ran out of water. Meanwhile reinforcements, some of them fresh from the Alamo, joined Urrea, so that the force surrounding the rebels numbered about two thousand. Fannin surrendered, after killing about two hundred fifty Santanistas, according to his account. Urrea set Mexican casualties at one hundred, killed and wounded.

Urrea was a humane officer, and he had no intention of murdering his prisoners. He left a Col. Jose Nicolas de la Portilla with a couple of battalions in charge of the captives at Goliad, and rode on eastward at the head of his main forces. Santa Anna was furious when he heard that Urrea hadn't executed the Texans on the spot. On March 26 at Goliad, Portilla got two sets of orders. The first, from Santa Anna, told him to kill the "perfidious foreigners." The second, from Urrea, told him "to employ the prisoners in rebuilding the town of Goliad and see that they are treated well." Portilla spent a sleepless night. Then he decided to obey the President. On March 27, which was Palm Sunday, 342 Texan prisoners were shot. Twenty-eight men escaped under fire during the executions and about twenty medical doctors, mechanics, blacksmiths, and other men with specialized abilities were spared because the Mexicans needed their services.

By March 24, Santa Anna had approximately three thousand men on the march scouring Texas from the northernmost settlements to the more populous Gulf Coast regions. The northern column consisted of about eight hundred men with one 24-pound cannon. It was commanded by Gen. Antonio Gaona. His orders were to destroy all settlements in his way and push on to the big town of Nacogdoches, near the Louisiana border. General Ramirez y Sesma's eight hundred were in advance of the main or middle drive, aimed at the towns of Gonzales on the Guadalupe River and San Felipe de

Austin on the Brazos. Urrea's task force of two thousand was to drive about a hundred fifty miles along the coast, with the island of Galveston as its objective.

At this stage apparently boredom again overtook Santa Anna. He regarded the balance of the campaign as nothing but mopping-up operations and a lot of business for his firing squads. So he decided to take his "bride" and head for the City of Mexico, leaving the Texas expedition to a suave Italian general named Vicente Filisola. Filisola, who had been second-in-command throughout the campaign, was a professional officer. He was a cautious man by nature, and he knew that he had everything to lose and nothing to gain by taking over the expedition. Moreover he disliked having the armies divided into three columns. Messages from Sesma sent around March 14 indicated that a Texas force of about four hundred men had just retreated from the town called Gonzales. Sesma, who was then on the Guadalupe River about seventy miles west of San Antonio, also reported that the Guadalupe was alarmingly swollen from spring rains. Filisola had little respect for the Texas rebels, but he did fear the prospect of taking a divided expedition through the vast Texas wilderness, especially during spring floods.

Santa Anna's favorite aide, Colonel Almonte, also opposed the President's departure. The two of them persuaded His Excellency to stay in Texas long enough "to plant your banners on the Louisiana border in person." Heavy reinforcements were sent to Sesma, who seemed to be nearest to the rebel forces.

Santa Anna left San Antonio to follow Sesma's column on March 31, 1836. He and Melchora Barrera rode in a luxurious coach pulled by six white mules and escorted by fifty splendidly uniformed dragoons. General Filisola, Caro, and one or two other subordinates followed in a lesser coach. *El Presidente's* camping gear, which included a big silk-and-canvas tent and heavy carpets, crates of champagne, medicine chests full of opium, and crates of fighting cocks, had to be carried by long strings of pack mules. The cocks were, like women, a hobby that Santa Anna often indulged in while he was on expeditions.

His Excellency was so sure that the Texas Revolution was virtually over by March 31 that he had already ordered Gen. Pedro Andrade's cavalry brigade, together with a lot of artillery, supply wagons, and other properties, back to San Luis Potosi, Mexico, where he'd rented the wagons. But Sesma and others on the General's staff opposed this move, pointing out that the Texas prairies were so muddy and the rivers so swollen that wagons and artillery would have very rough going. Soon after they left San Antonio, Filisola and Almonte prevailed on the President to send back an express rider canceling his order.

Santa Anna's train reached the Guadalupe River on April 2. One look at the swollen river told the President that he could go no farther in his coach. On the morning of April 3 he started the coach back to Mexico with a cargo consisting of Melchora Barrera and a trunk full of silver from his Texas expedition expense money.

A Capt. Domingo Badillo commanded the little escort of dragoons that guarded the coach on the return trip. Badillo had the double responsibility of depositing the silver to Santa Anna's account and installing the President's new mistress in quarters in the City of Mexico. According to Tony Menchaca, the San Antonio chronicler, Melchora was later married legally to the young man who had acted the priest at the fake marriage. Whether Santa Anna ordered this marriage is not known. In any case, it is rumored that Melchora later bore Santa Anna a child.

After a tender farewell to Melchora on that April 3, 1836, The Napoleon of the West ate a piece of opium. Then he was ferried over the Guadalupe, mounted a big black horse, and rode off eastward, toward the Brazos River and San Felipe de Austin.

---·◆·⊰ 2 ⊱·◆·---

Senor God Damn

The conquest of Texas should be classed, properly,
with conquests like those of the Norse sea rovers.
The great Texan hero, Samuel Houston, drank hard
and fought hard. Indeed, his career was as pictur-
esque and romantic as that of Harold Haardraade,
himself, and was much more important in its results.

—Theodore Roosevelt

IF THE ARMY that was called Mexican was in reality a
motley assortment of soldiers from all over the world, the
Texan force was even more varied in composition. The
only native Texans in its ranks were about thirty youths of
Spanish, Canary Island, Corsican, and Mexican ancestry, all of
whom had been born in or near San Antonio.

Because of the colorfully blasphemous language the men
of the miserable little Texas army regularly employed, the
Santanistas had nicknamed them *"Soldados God Dammes."*
A single Texan was *"Senor God Damn."* Once during the
Revolution a Texan, under a flag of truce, met a Santanista on
a sidewalk in Matamoros. The Mexican greeted him: *"Senor*
God Damn, tomorrow we may be shooting at each other.
Now, while there is time, let us go into that cantina and
vamose a little whiskey."

As Noah Smithwick, a member of a ranging company

27

loosely connected with the army, described it, the Texan fighting force

> bore little resemblance to the army of my childhood dreams. Buckskin breeches were the nearest approach to a uniform. And there was a wide diversity even there, some being new and soft and yellow, while others from long familiarity with rain and grease and dirt, had become hard and black and shiny. Some, from having passed through the process of wetting and drying on the wearer while he sat on the ground or on a chunk before the camp fire, had assumed an advance position at the knee, followed by a corresponding shortening of the lower front length, exposing skins as guiltless of socks as a Kansas Senator's. Some wore moccasins and some wore shoes. Here a broad-brimmed sombrero overshadowed the military cap by its side. There a tall beegum [stovepipe hat] was worn familiarly beside a coonskin cap. In lieu of a canteen many men carried a Spanish gourd, a curious specimen of the gourd family having two round bowls, each holding a quart and connected by a short neck. A strap could be adjusted about the neck of the gourd canteen.

The quartermaster of this army, old Valentine Bennett, was once, years later, asked about the uniform of the Texas forces in April of 1836. "Rags were our uniform, sire!" replied Major Bennett. "Nine out of ten of them was in rags. And it was a fighting uniform."

The Texan General Sam Houston dressed appropriately to lead these ragmen. He wore a slouch hat creased almost into the shape of the three-cornered headgear that was in style in George Washington's time, a mud-splattered black frock coat, a velvet vest, and snuff-colored pantaloons. On important occasions he wore high black boots, but since they were about to give out, he often substituted Indian moccasins. Sam Houston was an appropriate leader for the *Soldados God Dammes* in other respects too. For example, he was at least as much given to swearing as any man under him.

Houston had been a boy hero of the War of 1812, a Congressman from Tennessee for two terms and Governor of that state for two years. He had come to Texas in December, 1832. Because Mexican law required two Christian names for legal documents, Houston signed himself "Don Samuel Pablo Houston" in his land titles and on the rolls of the Roman Catholic Church of Nacogdoches. He never explained why he picked "Pablo."

In 1836 Houston was in his forty-third year. By then he had already been a citizen of the United States, the Cherokee Nation, and Mexico—and a leader in each one of them. He was grand in looks and manner. He was 6 feet 2 inches tall and he weighed a trim 235 pounds. He had a 48-inch chest and a 34-inch waist. His powerful hands were big as bunches of bananas. The General was a good blacksmith and gunsmith and would help out when the Texas army's smiths were behind in their work.

Houston had an extraordinary and forceful personality. One Texan of the time, who'd been both his friend and his political enemy and ultimately viewed the General dispassionately, said: "Old Sam was a man commissioned for leadership by God. He needed no gewgaws or artificial decorations of rank." Houston's voice was a booming baritone and he had a rich gift for language, although he was mostly self-educated. He had memorized long passages of classical literature, including most of Alexander Pope's translation of *The Iliad,* and he was fond of quoting from literary works.

Houston had lived for many years among the Cherokee Indians, and he had learned much from this great tribe. "It's cunning, Indian cunning that makes Houston so successful," wrote one of his political enemies. The accusation was prompted by envy, but perhaps it was not altogether unjust. Although the Cherokees were his special friends, Houston was on good terms with all Indians. He kept his word in his dealings with them, and as a result they respected him. It was undoubtedly his influence that kept the East Texas clans of the Cherokee Nation from siding with the Santanistas in 1836. The understanding that Houston had of Indians was no accident, for when he was a child in eastern Tennessee the Cherokees were his neighbors. As a young boy he had run away from home and lived among these friendly Indians for about three years. He was eighteen when he returned to white civilization, and on his first job he took part of his pay in gay calico cloth, which he gave to Cherokee girl friends.

The only fighting Houston saw in the War of 1812 was the Battle of Tohopeka (Horse Shoe Bend) in Alabama, which took place on March 27, 1814. General Andrew Jackson commanded the American forces in this battle, which was part of a campaign against the Creek Indians, who were British allies. Early in the battle a barbed arrow stuck in Houston's thigh. Sam kept on fighting with saber and pistol until the Creeks were driven back. Ensign Houston had a lieutenant of his company pull out the arrow, which left a huge wound. When General Jackson rode past, he paused to order the boy to the rear for medical care, then continued on his way. Houston quickly got away from the surgeons and back into the fight. When Jackson returned and called for volunteers to storm a ravine where the Creeks had a strong position, Sam dashed forward, calling for his platoon to follow. Down in the ravine the young officer fell after being shot twice in one shoulder and once in the upper part of his right arm. His daring inspired the American forces and they went on to rout the Creeks. At Horse Shoe Bend, Houston earned the attention and admiration of Andrew Jackson, and the relationship between the two that began there had a great influence on Sam's life.

While he was still a United States Army officer, Sam once appeared in Washington in the buckskins and feathers of a Cherokee warrior. John C. Calhoun, then Secretary of War, undertook to reprimand the high-spirited young officer, and Houston and Calhoun became bitter enemies. In later years it may have been Congressman Houston's influence that was decisive in keeping Calhoun out of the White House. In politics, as in war, Houston was Jackson's protégé. From 1823 to '27 Sam was a Congressman, and from '27 to '29 he was Governor of Tennessee. His career was so promising that he was mentioned as a Presidential possibility.

But in 1829 a personal misfortune put an end to the Governor's progress. Early in that year Houston was married to a young Tennessee belle, Eliza Allen. After a few months of marriage Eliza left Houston and returned to live with her parents. Not long afterward Houston left Tennessee forever. Neither Sam nor Eliza ever publicly explained this separation. One popular hypothesis is that after her parents forced her to marry the thirty-six-year-old Governor Eliza told her husband she was still in love with a former suitor of her own age, and Houston, with his immense vanity, was enraged. So she left. There have been other guesses at Eliza's motives. From the Indians, Sam had picked up the habit of going nude when he was at home. He himself was absolutely lacking in self-consciousness when he did this, but Eliza seems to have been a very sensitive girl, and this uninhibited behavior may have upset her. Another speculation is that Eliza might have been offended by her husband's extreme hairiness. Houston's powerful body was matted with chestnut-colored hair which he seems to have been rather proud of. When he made political speeches on hot summer days, he liked to take off his shirt and stand on the stump stripped to his waist. Whatever the difficulties were between Houston and his wife, he announced publicly before he left Tennessee that they were his fault. He said that Mrs. Houston was blameless and if he heard that any man spoke ill of Eliza he would return and kill the fellow.

Coming from Houston, this was not an empty threat. Some years before Houston had fought a duel with a Gen. William White in Simpson County, Kentucky, and General White had been severely wounded. To others the outcome of the duel was obviously the result of Sam's skill, but he himself attributed it at least in part to good fortune. The morning of the duel, he had been awakened early by the barking of a bulldog. He got up and began molding bullets for use in the fight. Just as the first bullet fell from the mold, a gamecock crowed. Houston took these sounds as good omens, and marked the bullet on one side for the dog, on the other for the cock. It was the same bullet that wounded General White. After the duel, Houston commemorated the event and his good luck by carving the figure of a bulldog on one of his pistols and that of a gamecock on the other.

It was in April of 1829 that Houston resigned as Governor of Tennessee. Immediately, he went to live with his Cherokee friends, who by this time had been pushed far to the west into Indian Territory. Near what is now Fort Gibson, Oklahoma, he settled down as a trader and planter. Soon he was married under Cherokee terms to an Indian girl named Tiana Rogers, a distant relative of the humorist Will Rogers. Tiana must have loved Houston very much or she wouldn't have put up with him. He had taken along a wagonload of whiskey, most of it for his own use, and he drank almost continuously. In advanced stages of intoxication, he would seek fist and gun fights. His Cherokee friends kindly humored him and sometimes even protected him. On one occasion, when he got into a drunken duel, they took the lead out of the pistols so he could be allowed to fight without endangering himself or his opponent. The Cherokees gave him the nickname which was to haunt him the rest of his life. They called him Big Drunk.

One traveler to the territory reported that a giant white man in buckskins, followed by about four hundred Cherokee warriors, was going around conferring with other Indian leaders. In Washington, Jackson heard that Houston was planning on "carving out a little two-horse Republic" made up of a confederacy of Indian tribes. Jackson rebuked his friend for having such ideas, but in 1832 the President was glad enough to make use of Houston's talent for getting along with Indians. Many Indian tribes, among them the Comanches, were still very troublesome to settlers on the frontiers, so in 1832 Jackson gave Houston $500 expense money and commissioned him to go to Texas to make treaties with the more hostile tribes there.

There is a story among the Cherokees that Sam wanted Tiana to go with him to Texas, but she refused. Whether this is true or not, Tiana did stay at their big plantation house, called *Wigwam Neoshe*. She had land and slaves. Houston took nothing but his expense money. Apparently, she was well provided for.

Houston rode over much of settled Texas, but his first report to Jackson was not on the Texas Indians. He knew that Jackson had been trying to buy Texas from Mexico and had been unsuccessful. Houston's first message to the President was that the Mexican province was ripe for revolution.

Did Houston come to Texas with the idea of leading a rebellion? No definite answer can be given, but he had probably thought of it, and so had others. A letter written by a leader of the War Party, Col. John A. Wharton, virtually invited Houston to lead a revolution. The War Party, which remained in the minority up to the eve of the 1836 rebellion, wanted separation from Mexico. The letter Wharton had written to Houston read in part:

> Dr. Branch T. Archer of Virginia has been in Texas for upwards of 12 months. He is of opinion there will be some fighting in Texas next fall and a fine country will be gained without much bloodshed. He is very desirous that you should come to Texas, believes you can be of more service than any man. Texas does, undoubtedly, present a fine field for fame.

Texas certainly impressed the Houston of 1832. He wrote Andrew Jackson that the province would be his "abiding place." He settled down in bachelor quarters in Nacogdoches, a town in a pine forest near the Louisiana border. Years before he'd passed the bar examinations in Tennessee, so he began the practice of law in Texas. He was very popular in East Texas, especially with the ladies. Mrs. Augustus Sterne, wife of a leading Nacogdoches merchant, guided him into the Roman Catholic Church, which under Mexican law he had to join before he could own land in Texas. Mrs. Sterne called herself Houston's godmother. Miss Ann Raguet, the accomplished young daughter of another prominent Nacogdoches businessman, gave Sam Spanish lessons. In actual fact, Houston continued to travel around a good deal for the next three years, and was not able to spend more than occasional short periods of time in his new home. Nonetheless, this phase was a relatively calm interlude in his life.

In 1835 a Consultation of Texas leaders was held, and in November of that year the Consultation issued a declaration that the province "would defend with arms the republican principles of the Constitution of 1824 against the centralizing encroachments of Santa Anna." On November 12, 1835, the Consultation elected Houston commander in chief of the regular army—a force that he was supposed to raise—with the rank of major general. He was not given control over the volunteers. A rabble of colonists, the group that ousted Cos in December, had already gone off to San Antonio, but these men were not a part of Houston's command. Even if they had been, he was elected too late to get into the campaign against Cos.

The Consultation organized a legislative body called the General Council, presided over by a Provisional Governor, Henry Smith. Although the General Council still considered Texas a part of the Mexican federal union, in January of 1836 it authorized several small expeditions against Matamoros, the busy Mexican harbor city at the mouth of the Rio Grande. Houston was supposed to go to the far southwest of Texas where volunteer armies prepared to march on Matamoros were to be waiting for him at Goliad, the town that was later occupied by the unfortunate Fannin, and nearby Refugio. But when Houston got to his army, he found his troops, most of whom were fresh recruits from the United States, unprepared and in confusion. The weak and disorganized condition of the Texan forces he found at Refugio and Goliad convinced Houston that the proposed Matamoros expeditions would be failures, and he made a number of speeches at Refugio vigorously opposing the venture. Then he returned to San Felipe in Central Texas, where Governor Smith had his headquarters, and reported to the General Council that he'd made an effort to stop the puny expeditions. Smith agreed that they should be thinking only in terms of defense until they got more men and guns.

In February Smith sent the General to East Texas on an urgent mission. Mexican agents there were stirring up the Cherokees against the Anglo-American settlers, and Houston, a Cherokee chief, was of course the ideal ambassador for the Texans. His mission was successful. The Cherokees agreed to remain neutral, in return for which Houston promised them that when Texas became a nation it would give the Indians white-man-style title to their East Texas lands.

While Houston was negotiating this agreement, the provisional Texas government was growing increasingly disorganized. Governor Smith had incurred the anger of many eager rebel leaders, and his authority over the rebellious Texans dwindled rapidly. At best, Smith had little talent for getting along with his colleagues, and the political atmosphere in Texas was so tense because of the personal ambitions and avarice of many members of the War Party that a more diplomatic man than Smith might well have foundered. During Houston's visit with the Cherokees, Smith was actually impeached. The Governor, however, maintained that his enemies had no right to deprive him of his authority and continued to consider himself Governor. Houston remained loyal to Smith.

Fortunately, before Smith's government dissolved altogether, the Council had arranged for a Convention to be held at Washington-on-the-Brazos on March 1. Despite the conflicts that had virtually paralyzed the provisional government, the delegates arrived for this Convention on schedule.

When Houston's business with the Cherokees was settled, the big man got on a little buckskin pony and, with his feet almost dragging the earth, he rode to Washington-on-the-Brazos. Houston must have made quite an impression on

Refugio citizens with his opposition to the Matamoros expedition, for this community had elected him a delegate to the Washington Convention even though he'd never lived there.

The only building available in Washington for the delegates to meet in was a crude shelter owned by a gunsmith and part-time Baptist preacher named Noah Byars. This building wasn't Byars's shop. It was simply an unfinished structure in the business section of the town, with cloth instead of glass in the windows. Somebody promised Byars some rent, he said, but he never managed to collect it.

On March 2, the Convention approved a Declaration of Independence from Mexico. This well-written document complained that Texans had suffered "the most intolerable tyranny, the combined despotism of the sword and the priesthood." The only trouble with this eloquent pronouncement was that many of the delegates hadn't lived under the Mexican government long enough to know whether it was really tyrannical or not. Only ten of the fifty-nine had lived in Texas more than six years. The author of the Declaration, a moody lawyer named George Campbell Childress, had arrived in Texas only a few weeks before. And he may well have written the Texas Declaration in Nashville, Tennessee, and brought it to the colony in his saddlebags.

Author Childress made his strongest point in the Declaration when he wrote that the Mexican government

hath now a large mercenary army advancing to carry on against us a war of extermination. It hath, through its emissaries, encited the merciless savage, with tomahawk and scalping knife, to massacre the inhabitants of our defenseless frontier. It hath been, during the whole time of our connection with it, the contemptible sport and victim of successive military revolutions, and hath continually exhibited every characteristic of a weak, corrupt and tyrannical government. These and other grievances were patiently borne by the people of Texas until they reached that point at which forebearance ceases to be a virtue. We then took up arms in defense of the National Constitution.

At Washington, an ad interim government was established to take the place of the provisional government. David Gouverneur Burnet, a forty-seven-year-old native of New Jersey, was elected President. Burnet was a stocky man with brown sea-captain-style whiskers. He carried a double-barreled pistol in one pocket of his black frock coat and a Bible in the other. He looked like a parson. No one would have guessed from his appearance, speech, or behavior that he'd led almost as colorful a life as had Houston.

Burnet's experience as a revolutionary leader had begun in 1810 when he supported Francisco Miranda in an unsuccessful attempt to liberate Venezuela from Spain. On this expedition Burnet commanded a launch which he claimed fired the first shot for South American independence. After Miranda's defeat, Burnet escaped from Venezuela and set out for Texas, but his health was broken. Not long after he arrived in the new colony, he developed tuberculosis. For some incomprehensible reason, he then rode out alone into the hunting grounds of the savage Comanches. The Indians took in the ailing stranger, and he lived among them for two years. By the time he left, he had regained his health. Apparently the Comanches had treated him very kindly, yet inexplicably in later years Burnet was intolerant and suspicious in his dealings with all Indians.

One of the vices the pious new President detested was blasphemy. If he heard the Lord's name taken in vain, he would often angrily denounce the offender in the most outraged terms. This kept him pretty busy around that talented swearer, General Houston, and his army of *Soldados God Dammes*. According to his political adversaries, old Davy nipped in secret at French brandy, but Burnet represented himself as a teetotaler and he took a public stand against the drinking of spirits. It is easy to believe that Burnet actually despised liquor as much as he did profanity. There is certainly no question as to Houston's habits in the matter, for he had never tried to conceal the steady and heavy drinking he'd been doing ever since his wife left him in 1829. Washington Irving, who once visited Houston in Indian Territory, later described Sam as "always two drinks scant." Poor Burnet complained that it was hard to sleep during the Washington Convention because of the nightly drunken revels of Sam Houston, Dr. Branch T. Archer, Secretary of War Thomas Jefferson Rusk, and other delegates. This accusation was supported by other witnesses, too. A Virginia real estate man named Fairfax Gray, who was at Washington while the delegates were meeting, said that the Convention was "run by besotted minds."

From the beginning, Burnet had his troubles dealing with the tough, hard-bitten frontiersmen who were his subordinates, and his new authority, together with the problems he faced, had an unfortunate effect on this courageous little man. He became imperious and unyielding. At best he had no sense of humor, and he was very sensitive to criticism.

Don Justiniano Lorenzo De Zavala, a native of Yucatan, a medical doctor, author of a travel book on the United States, and one of the founders of the Mexican republic, was elected Vice-president at Washington-on-the-Brazos. Dr. De Zavala was a political liberal. During the struggle for Mexican independence, he had been kept in chains in a Spanish Royalist dungeon for three years. As long as Santa Anna had appeared to support the Constitution of 1824, De Zavala had supported Santa Anna. But the Mexican President knew that a man of De Zavala's influence and integrity could be dangerous in the City of Mexico, so he sent the doctor to France as Mexican minister. Gradually, as De Zavala realized that Santa Anna was eliminating most of the democratic processes in Mexico, he became disgusted with the dictator, quit his diplomatic job, and retired with his cultured, New Orleans-born wife to a Texas plantation on the San Jacinto River.

Santa Anna considered De Zavala one of the main instigators of the Texas disturbances of late 1835, so the dictator sent word to the colonists that he would not ride into Texas at the head of a punitive force if he were sent the head of the "traitor, Don Lorenzo De Zavala." "If I knew my death would assure the liberation of Texas," said De Zavala in a speech to other Texas leaders, "I would not live another hour. Yet I am certain it is not myself alone but my republican views that the tyrant, Santa Anna, desires to kill."

One of the first actions of the Convention was to elect Sam Houston commander in chief of the Texas army with the rank of major general. In this capacity he exercised more power than he had the year before under the General Council, for now his command included the militia and volunteer forces rather than just the regular army. In effect, he was now in charge of all forces in the field.

Burnet and Houston had had dealings before in real estate transactions, and there is no record of trouble between them before the Convention. At Washington, though, a great animosity developed between these two strong yet utterly different personalities. Burnet was a rather shy man, and no doubt he envied the giant, profane, hard-drinking orator-general. Burnet had been elected President, yet Houston was the dominant personality of the Convention. To make matters worse, the irreverent General made light of Burnet's intensity. Probably under the influence of whiskey, Houston gave Burnet the nickname of "Wetumpka," a Cherokee word meaning a hog thief. The new President would have been enraged by the familiarity of even a complimentary nickname. Under the new pressures to which Burnet was subjected, his resentment of Houston quickly developed into adamant hatred.

De Zavala also quarreled with Burnet at the Convention. He too had dealt with Burnet in real estate matters, and they had had no troubles. But President Burnet lost no time before making it clear that he needed no advice from his Vice-president. De Zavala remarked to a fellow Latin delegate, Antonio Navarro of San Antonio, that never before had such an incompetent person as Burnet been named to such high office. He called Burnet a "mere clerk" and after the Convention he never tried to conceal his dislike for the President.

Burnet's closest associate in the new cabinet was the Secretary of the Navy, Robert Potter. This thirty-six-year-old North Carolinian was a truly enigmatic man. His qualification for the job of Secretary of the Texas Navy was the fact that he had once been a junior officer in the United States Navy. Like many of the other rebel leaders, Robert Potter had left a domestic tragedy back in the United States. He was described by one Reuben M. Potter, an acquaintance but not a relative, as "one in whom unusual powers of brain and tongue were perverted by evil impulses."

In North Carolina some years before, Robert Potter had suspected his wife of having sexual relations with two of her cousins. One, the family minister, was a fellow of fifty-five; the other was a seventeen-year-old boy. All the evidence is that Mrs. Potter was a woman of good character and that the two suspects were innocent. Robert Potter laid separate ambushes for the two cousins, "sprang like a tiger" on them, stunned them, and castrated both with a big, sharp knife. He then gave both victims emergency medical treatment, probably just because if they died, he would have to face murder charges.

Both of the poor cousins survived. Mrs. Potter left her husband. Her father took a shot at Robert but missed. Potter was sent to jail for the crime, which in parts of the South is still called "Potterizing." After he had served his jail sentence, this brilliant orator got himself elected to the State Legislature, but in 1835 he was invited to leave by that narrow-minded organization for cheating at cards. He came to Texas and was elected a Nacogdoches delegate to the Washington Convention. The majority of the voters who elected him were soldiers who'd just arrived in Texas. At the convention, Potter conceived a slumbering dislike for Secretary of War Rusk, and he became the implacable enemy of General Houston.

Writer Reuben Potter referred to Robert Potter as a

namesake but not a relation, one of the most gifted and most pestilent disturbers at the Washington-on-the-Brazos convention. His disorganizing propensities proved a serious bar to business until Rusk checked him in the only way which, with him, was effective.

Reuben Potter didn't explain just what Tom Rusk did to restrain the Secretary of the Navy, but Rusk's enthusiasm for democratic procedure often prompted him to emphatic and usually effective gestures. At another political convention years later, for example, Rusk held a Bowie knife at the heart of a rude participant and said in an unemotional tone: "If you don't follow parliamentary rules I will start carving."

Rusk was a large, blue-eyed, sandy-haired man, muscular and yet inclined to flesh. He was thirty-two years old and he came from South Carolina. His father had worked as a stonecutter on the plantation of John C. Calhoun, and when Tom was a boy the great statesman had become fond of him and sponsored his law studies. Gradually, Rusk became Calhoun's protégé. But despite the animosity between Houston and Calhoun, Rusk got along well with the Texas General.

Rusk had come to Texas on the trail of some men who'd swindled him and some of his friends in a mining venture. He'd caught his men and chastised them, but they'd already lost all the money in games of chance. Rusk liked Nacogdoches and stayed on.

The Secretary of War was a lyrical speaker. He kept his talks brief. Like Houston, Rusk was well aware that two forced marches by Santa Anna's dragoons could have brought the enemy troops to Washington-on-the-Brazos. He frequently reminded the Convention that it must hasten about its business, and he discouraged windy speeches by the delegates. Lorenzo De Zavala often "cited ancient examples" when he was talking. At the Convention he started off a sentence with: "A Roman philosopher once said . . . ," and Rusk interrupted: "Dr. De Zavala, I should like to hear sometime when I have more leisure what that Roman philosopher said. Right now we'd better think and talk about live Santanistas instead of dead philosophers so we can finish up our work in time for a good sleep before we have to run." De Zavala said: "I agree."

During the Convention, two major political factions developed, with Burnet and Potter as the leaders of one group and Houston and De Zavala on the other side. Tom Rusk managed to stay friendly with everyone except Potter. And the Secretary of War often acted as peacemaker between choleric delegates. When two men were shouting angrily at one another, Rusk would interrupt with this suggestion: "Let's take a scoop of whiskey until tempers cool." Rusk was as fond of liquor as Houston, but he couldn't hold it nearly so well. It was said that at one time during the Convention Rusk proposed that "we all take one more drink of whiskey and then saddle up and go to the rescue of the boys in the Alamo."

If this story is true, the suggestion was probably made after many drinks and after the courier from the Alamo, John W. Smith, brought to the Convention a courageous report from Colonel Travis. Travis informed his government that:

> At least two hundred shells have fallen inside of our works without having injured a single man; indeed, we have been so fortunate as not to lose a man from any cause, and we have killed many of the enemy. The spirits of the men are still high though they have had much to depress them.

On the subject of outside aid, Travis concluded: "Unless it arrives soon, I shall have to fight the enemy on his own terms."

For once at the Convention Burnet and Houston were in agreement. They both thought the delegates should stay in Washington and organize the government. Both believed that the "grand error" of the colonists so far had been investing in small offensive actions and trying to defend isolated, vulnerable West Texas forts like the Alamo.

However, the Convention did not intend to leave the Alamo to its fate. Orders went to Fannin, then in Goliad, to make ready to help Travis and his men. At that time another force of about four hundred volunteers was on the march to Gonzales, a town about seventy miles east of San Antonio. When his function at the Convention was completed, Houston was to ride to Gonzales and take command of this force. Fannin was to rendezvous with Houston on the west bank of the

Cibolo, a creek near San Antonio. Then Houston was to command an operation against the Mexicans surrounding the Alamo.

Houston left the Convention on March 6 with only three aides. They arrived in Gonzales on March 11. By then rumors of the fall of the Alamo had reached that town, and Houston believed the rumors. But he was afraid a general panic would break out if he admitted that Travis had probably been defeated before Houston's own force was even organized, so he affected to disbelieve the news. He did, however, send an express rider to Fannin instructing that Colonel to disregard their earlier plan to rendezvous near San Antonio and instead to retreat past Coleto Creek to a town called Victoria Guadalupe (now simply Victoria, Texas). These were the orders that Fannin was belatedly executing when Urrea overtook him.

At Gonzales Houston took command of an army consisting of "374 effective men." While he waited for definite news from the Alamo and word from Fannin, he organized his force into a regiment, the First Texas Volunteers, with Edward Burleson, a famous Indian fighter, as Colonel. Houston also sent three scouts, Henry Wax Karnes, Erasmus (Deaf) Smith, and one Col. Robert Eden Handy, a young man from Philadelphia who was called "The Handsomest Man in the Texas Army," out on the road to San Antonio on the morning of March 13. These were the men who found Mrs. Dickenson. According to Karnes, he took Almonte's dispatches from Mrs. Dickenson and galloped with them to Houston in Gonzales while the other scouts, the lady and child, and the Negro followed at a slower pace. Mrs. Dickenson and her escort arrived in Gonzales around twilight on the thirteenth. Her report that the Alamo had fallen and that a division of Mexicans under Ramirez y Sesma was advancing on the town "threw both army and colonists into the greatest consternation."

Twenty-five soldiers deserted, said Houston, "and carried panic with them to the eastern section of the country, as far as the Sabine, by announcing the fall of the Alamo and the massacre that followed."

The thirty reinforcements that had joined Travis only two weeks before had all been from Gonzales, and some of the women who greeted Mrs. Dickenson when she arrived had also lost husbands in the battle. They asked so many questions that finally Mrs. Dickenson had to include the brutal details of the siege—how the last few wounded defenders had been shot in cold blood, and how after the battle Mexican soldiers had amused themselves tossing the bodies of Texan soldiers into the air and catching them on the points of their bayonets.

Houston did not meet Mrs. Dickenson when she arrived, but when he heard of the fall of the Alamo, he thought at once of the widows of the defenders. He had only about $300 with him, but he gave most of that to the distraught women. He also gave three of the army's four baggage wagons to civilians who were preparing to evacuate the town. He threw two small cannon, his only artillery, into the Guadalupe River, for the spring rains were still coming down and the prairies were so muddy "they would almost bog a saddle blanket." Houston didn't have enough teams to drag the cannon along on the retreat, which started on the night of the thirteenth.

The next morning fifteen miles east of Gonzales, the army met a reinforcement of about a hundred twenty-five men, but twenty-five of these volunteers deserted when they heard what the Mexicans had done in San Antonio. These were trying days for Houston. Some of the recruits wanted to stop and fight the Mexicans, while others would desert on hearing bad news from

the west. There was little sleep for anyone during the first
three days of the retreat.

A soldier named J. H. Kuykendall described one incident
that took place during these days that shows how hectic the
retreat must have been.

A young man by the name of Rhodes was found asleep on
his sentinel's post. Gen'l. Houston swore he would have
Rhodes shot. During the next day's [March 15] march,
Rhodes, who was under arrest, stopped in the middle of
a creek to drink. This caused men to the rear to halt for a
moment. Gen'l. Houston rode up and on being informed
what was causing the delay, cried aloud: "Knock him
down, God damn him! Knock him down! Standing there
holding up the whole army! God damn him! Knock him
down." Frightened by these imprecations, Rhodes in-
stantly cleared the way and there was no necessity to fell
him. After we camped in the evening, the general repri-
manded Rhodes and ordered his release.

Early the following morning, before Houston had broken
camp, the army was joined by about fifty mounted Texans
who, without asking anyone, turned their horses loose to graze
within the line of sentinels. Houston angrily cursed the newcomers for this, and told them that if they stayed with the
army they would be foot soldiers and their horses would be
used for draft animals. Some mounted their horses and left,
"which they could do with impunity since they were careful
not to attach themselves to any organized companies." But
others let themselves be converted into infantry, and as Kuykendall said, "Considering that our people were as much
attached and accustomed to mounted service as the Cossack
or Comanche, the voluntary relinquishment of their horses
was a strong manifestation of patriotism." Kuykendall said

that Houston didn't want many horses with the army because there was no grain to feed them, and it would have slowed the army's progress to have to stop and graze them.

Infantrymen could always be fed in a land that teemed with horned cattle and game, but the fare Houston's hard-pressed army had was limited. Whenever the troops halted, the General placed a third of the force on guard duty, and this restriction on his men's activities, together with a shortage of ammunition, prevented them from doing much hunting. As a result, the troops had to settle for boiled or roasted beef. When they stopped long enough, the meat was cut in strips and smoke-dried over campfires. Each mess had at least one portable corn grinder and each man was rationed one ear of corn a day. Some of the soldiers also had with them a bread substitute called *penole,* which was a mixture of coarsely ground corn-meal and dried wild berries, with sometimes a little sugar. Coffee was in scant supply. The only commodity the Commissary General ever seemed to have enough of was chewing tobacco. Houston, who chewed tobacco almost constantly, must have seen to that.

For the most part, though, Houston himself was no better provisioned than his men. The only foodstuffs among his personal supplies were some ears of corn he carried in his saddle-bags. He also carried along his lucky double-barreled pistols, decorated with his own dog and rooster carvings. In his saddle-bags, along with the corn, were battered copies of *Gullivers' Travels* and the *Commentaries* of Julius Caesar and some crude maps of Texas. A young friend of Houston's named Mary Bowles, the granddaughter of the Cherokee chieftain John Bowles, had made more than one contribution to the General's gear. It was she who had made the Indian moccasins Houston wore when he wanted to spare his boots—or his feet—and she had also given him a vial of ammoniacal spirits made by distilling liquid from the shavings of deer horns. Houston believed this ammonia prevented colds, and he carried the vial in his breast pocket and applied the spirits to his nostrils regularly. Perhaps his confidence in Mary Bowles's concoction was not altogether misplaced, for he got no colds despite the uncertain spring weather and the fact that among the luxuries he lacked was a bed blanket. He slept on his saddle blanket, with his saddle for a pillow. In any case, the habit of putting his vial of spirits to his nostrils became a nervous gesture, and may have given rise to a report made by a hostile subordinate some time later to Secretary of the Navy Potter to the effect that Houston was eating opium.

Houston's soldiers, their reluctance to travel on foot notwithstanding, made pretty good time. While they marched, Houston rode around roaring for them to hurry as if he were driving a bunch of cattle. By March 17, they were on the Colorado River and in the vicinity of the present town of La Grange. Houston waited at the Colorado until all civilian fugitives had crossed the river. As he later said: "I permitted none of the colonists to remain behind and be exposed to the ruthless enemy."

The army crossed the Colorado River on March 20. The next day, General Sesma's division arrived at the west bank of the river and camped about two miles upstream from the rebels, and the two armies maintained their positions for six days. While Sesma was waiting for the main column to come up, Houston seems to have been planning to cross the river at night and spring on the Mexicans. However, the news of Fannin's surrender drove the idea of attacking Sesma out of Houston's mind. He was haunted by the possibility that he might make the same rash mistakes that Fannin's really well-equipped division had made. Moreover, Sesma had two pieces of artillery while the Texans had none.

Houston later estimated that at that time he had about eight hundred effectives, or able-bodied soldiers, under his discipline. His political adversaries claimed that he had had twice that many men on the Colorado, but they may have included civilian hangers-on, as well as volunteers who belonged to no organized companies. Houston admitted that his force on the Colorado was "respectable" and that he probably could have whipped Sesma despite the Mexican cannon, but Sesma was not the only Santanista general. What Houston feared was that as soon as he'd finished fighting the advance Mexican column, even assuming that the Texans won fairly easily, fresh Santanista armies would have time to come up before his men would have had a chance to recover from the battle. In such circumstances the victory over Sesma would have done them more harm than good.

Though old Sam was cautious, he was by no means a craven. His personality was a strange mixture of the qualities of a superstitious, cunning, occasionally ruthless Indian war chief and a warm, kindly, courtly, humorous, civilized gentleman. He took his job as commander in chief of the small, ill-equipped rabble that was the Texas army very much to heart, and he weighed his decisions with all the shrewdness, foresight, and subtlety at his command. He knew if he wasn't careful the Santanistas could easily surround him, and if they did he, like Fannin, could be annihilated by the sheer weight of numbers. In the General's papers, there is this evaluation of the situation:

While in camp on the Colorado it was learned that Fannin's regiment had been captured and that Sesma, across the river from us, was in communication with Urrea and Gaona. Urrea could, therefore, cross the Colorado at Wharton, about 40 miles below the Texan camp, with his 1500 men and attack the [our] left flank. Gaona with his force of about 750 could cross the Colorado at Bastrop, about 60 miles above the Texan camp, and attack the right flank, while Sesma could attack the front.

Houston was forced to base his estimate of Urrea's and Gaona's strength on insubstantial rumors, but he was certain that the combined forces of the three Santanista armies around him were substantial, and his position was obviously not well suited for a defensive battle. So on the evening of March 26, despite the clamors of his offensive-minded officers, Houston had his army falling back to the Brazos.

One company commander estimated that between two and three hundred men left the army, some getting furloughs to take care of their families and some deserting, during the journey from the Colorado to the Brazos. For the first time, though by no means the last, there was talk of naming a new general. Had there been in the army a man of strong personality with more military experience than Houston, Sam would almost certainly have been relieved of his command when he turned his back on the Colorado. There were many candidates for Sam's job, but none were really qualified. They all lacked experience or training, or both.

The Texans got to San Felipe on March 28 and stayed overnight. There was real dissatisfaction in the ranks the next day when Houston led those who would follow him northward up the Brazos, naming as his destination the plantation headquarters of the region's richest man, Jared Groce. Groce's was about twenty miles from San Felipe, and Houston explained that his reason for going to the plantation was that they would find food supplies there. Moreover, Houston knew that the 160-foot-long steamer *Yellowstone* was then at Groce's.

At that time the ship was calmly taking on a cotton cargo as if the war were hundreds of miles away.

David Burnet and certain members of his cabinet had fled from Washington-on-the-Brazos, a few miles upstream from Groce's, to Harrisburg, where they stopped for a while. Harrisburg was southeast of Washington, and it was the head of navigation on Buffalo Bayou and the old town is now within the city of Houston. Burnet complained vigorously in dispatches to Houston that the army should have come downstream to protect the new temporary capital.

Two company commanders, Wily Martin and Moseley Baker, refused to follow the General to Groce's. Baker asked permission to guard the San Felipe crossing of the Brazos. Martin wanted to move downstream about twenty-five miles from San Felipe and protect the crossing near Fort Bend or Old Fort (now Richmond, Fort Bend County). Houston had no time to deal with mutineers, so he simply gave Baker and Martin the permission they asked for.

When Houston headed up the river on that March 29 he was followed by only about five hundred men. As Private Kuykendall described the march:

Late in the afternoon we arrived at a creek. Ere the army had crossed this stream it began to rain in torrents. As we foundered through mud and water, pelted by the storm, General Houston rode slowly close my company. He wore a black cloth dress coat, somewhat threadbare. He complained of having no blanket. He said he'd had a good one but some scoundrel had stolen it. He then said: "My friends, I am told that evilly disposed persons have told you I am going to march you to the Redlands [the Nacogdoches country near the Louisiana border]. This is false. I'm going to lead you into the Brazos bottom

near Groce's to a position where you can whip the enemy
even if he comes ten to one, and where we can get an
abundant supply of corn.

Kuykendall does not say whether he was reassured by these
words, but if he was then satisfied to serve with Houston,
others were not. The frustration of the men, which first became a problem during the retreat from San Felipe, was to
plague Houston throughout the campaign.

—◆•⊰ 3 ⊱•◆—

The Runaway Scrape

It was hell on women and oxen.

—PRIVATE NOAH SMITHWICK

HOUSTON'S men were not the only ones who needed
reassurance when Houston withdrew from the Colorado. The settlers too reacted with considerable
alarm. After the fall of the Alamo and the Goliad tragedy, all
Texans expected Houston to retreat to the Colorado. But most
of the colonists wanted him to make a stand at the Colorado
and save the fertile and comparatively populous country between that river and the Brazos. When Houston's army retreated to the Brazos and failed to make a stand at San Felipe,
the majority of the colonists believed that the rebels' cause was
hopeless. Only a few hundred civilians had fled West Texas
after the fall of the Alamo, but Houston's retreats and the
ad interim government's flight to Harrisburg caused a panic
that began around the Colorado and spread into the Brazos
and Trinity valleys. The mad scramble of the colonists to get
out of the way of Santa Anna's armies became known as "The
Runaway Scrape." Most Santa Anna sympathizers among the
colonists joined in The Runaway Scrape, for after the Goliad
and Alamo massacres, they were afraid of the Mexican President.

Families broke up. In many cases, the older men, the

women, and the children gathered up what was portable and
struck out for the Sabine River. This trek to the Louisiana
boundary was called "taking the Sabine chute." Many of the
younger men hiked off to join the army. In the confusion
domestic misunderstandings were inevitable, but most families
met the crisis with courage and dignity. For example, Dr.
Johnson Hunter's family of Fort Bend County, just west of
what is now Houston, was one that certainly didn't panic.
After the fall of the Alamo, members of the family took their
several ways with a kind of casual bravery. Led by Dr. Johnson, the older folks and the children started driving over five
hundred head of cattle toward the United States by way of the
ferry over the San Jacinto River.

Dr. Hunter's sons, Robert and John, went to join the army.
And Robert Hunter, a keen observer if not a very literate lad,
described the scene when he left his family like this:

I had been in the fite at San Antonio in December, 1825.
After we whipt General Coss [Cos] we ware dischard &
come home. A short time [later] Sant Anna come to San
Antonio & Colonel W. B. Travis, commander of the
Alamo, sent a dispatch to Sanphilop [San Felipe] &
Brazoria for help, that he would hold the Alamo. A
currer [courier] come to our place on the Brazzos in
Fort Bend Co. He shoed his dispach, stating that Colonel
Travis wanted men to defend the Alamo. Brother John,
Robert McAnnella and his brother Pleasant McAnnella
& I and Merdeth [Meredith] Tunget was on top the ginn
house nailing on shingles. Father said Well Boys who of
you is going to Travis? I said, I am one, & the balance
all said I with you. The currer said Capt. John Bird was
making up a company at Sanphilop. This was bout 4 in
the evening & we had to go bout 30 miles. We got our

horses & extry clothes & some grub & guns & left for
Sanphilop. We got thare about 2 in the morning.

Private Hunter's company was about fifteen miles east of
Gonzales

when we seen a currer coming from Peach Creek the Capt
said Well Boys we wate & see who that is, it may that we
got some news. Currer come up and he said what company is this & then he handed a dispach to Bird & he red
it and he said Boys Bad News, the Alamo has fallen, this
dispatch is from General Sam Houston at Gonzales.

While waiting for Houston's retreating army to reach them,
Bird's company saw a lot of pitiful civilians. Private Hunter
described one bunch like this:

That same morning [March 14] we seen two women with
five children with bundles of clothing on thare heads. The
Capt [Bird] ast theme which way are you going? We are
trying to git a way from the Mexicans. Thare husbands
was kild in the Alamo. The Capt ast theme, why are you
walking don't you have no waggons? They said yes but
our horses was out on the prire & we could not finde
theme. We left our supper on the table, we took what little
clothing we could carry & our children & left afoot. The
Capt. had his own waggon & team. Colonel Knight &
White of Sanphilop had put 2 large boxes of tobacco in
our waggon. The Capt told Leuitenant McCallister to
throw them tobacco boxes out of the waggon & giv room
for the women & children. Why Capt that tobacco was giv
'o the company [said Lieutenant McAllister]. I was sitting
on the waggon tong and the Capt said to me Bob giv me
that ax. He taken the ax and chopt the boxes to peaces
& threw them on the ground & cald his men to come &

get thare tobacco. They took what they wanted. Bout this time General Houstons army come a long & the Capt haled them, Boys don't you want some tobacco. They holloid yes. Here help yourselves [said Captain Bird] and they taken all the tobacco. That giv room for the women & children so we got them all abord. General Houstons army past on, and we fell in as rear gard.

Dr. Pleasant W. Rose and his eleven-year-old daughter, Dilue, were better spellers than Bob Hunter, and they wrote just as vividly about The Runaway Scrape. Their narratives were blended later by Dilue Rose into one chronicle.

That 1836 spring Dr. Rose and his wife and five children lived on a big farm near the east bank of the Brazos about fifteen miles south of Dr. Hunter's home. They were in the path of Santa Anna's main or middle column. The Rose family had been misinformed. They had heard that Houston was going to meet the Santanistas at the head of ten thousand men. They didn't leave their farm until about a week before Santa Anna reached the Brazos.

The Roses were happy in Texas. They'd never suffered any indignities from the Mexican government. Dr. Rose had been a United States Army surgeon during the War of 1812. Before the family moved to Texas in 1832, he had practiced in St. Louis. Times were hard in the United States, where the government wasn't at all generous with its public lands. Dr. Rose wanted to combine farming with his medical practice, and he'd heard that in the Mexican subprovince of Texas the head of a family could get more than a league (4,428 acres) of land almost free. Moreover, when they gave away this land the Mexicans weren't even too careful about keeping their records of the transactions. For instance, Sam Houston, who had arrived in Texas around the same time as the Rose family, had obtained a piece of land in one survey as the head of the family and another, smaller free spread in another survey as a bachelor.

Under Mexican government the colonists were exempt from taxation and from the payment of import duties for varying periods after settlement, sometimes as long as seven years. Between 1829 and 1835, a tax collector was almost as much of a curiosity as a live mastodon, said one colonist.

On the way to their new home, the Rose family had been shipwrecked on the Texas coast, but none of them sustained any injuries and all their belongings survived intact. They lived first at Harrisburg on Buffalo Bayou.

"Everything in Harrisburg was different from what we'd been accustomed to," wrote Miss Dilue Rose. "No churches, no preachers, no schoolhouses, no courthouses. They had no use for a jail; everybody [was] honest." First they rented a new frame house. "When we got to the house, the kind ladies of Harrisburg had sent meal, butter, eggs, milk and honey, and had the house in order and supper ready," said Miss Dilue.

Soon they moved to the Brazos farm fifteen miles west of Harrisburg. Dr. Rose brought in a big stock of medicines, dry goods, and groceries from New Orleans duty free. He had yet to pay a cent in taxes when The Runaway Scrape began.

Rose seemed to appreciate the generosity of the Mexican government. Other Texans didn't. As a scholarly Mexican statesman named Jose Maria Tornel said, most of the colonists

enjoyed a privilege which gradually became a habit of not contributing in any way to the national burden. We gave away lands in Texas that are a paradise. Then the colonists reacted like the asp of the fable after we took them to our bosoms. The most trivial duty imposed on them by our laws was scarcely respected. They imported goods duty free, which were far beyond the needs of an infant colony, and included much contraband which was sold in all departments of the Mexican republic.

Dr. Rose had heard that President Santa Anna was developing into a tyrant, but the dictator's regime had no immediate effect on the family by the Brazos. Dr. Rose seemed to be willing to go along if the majority of the colonists wanted to cut connections with Mexico, but he was by no means a hot-headed rebel. Dr. Eugene Barker, a leading Texas historian, had men of Rose's type in mind when he said that

the Texas revolution was not a spontaneous outburst of patriotic indignation against Mexican oppression. Few of the colonists were satisfied with all features of Mexican rule but few also were ready to go to the length of armed rebellion. A small party of Texas radicals and Latin distrust of Anglo-Saxon forced the war.

Miss Dilue was probably quoting her father when she said that their friend William B. Travis had "precipitated" the Revolution when he led the Texan party that ran Tenorio's garrison out of the port of Anahuac in 1835.

Dr. Rose came to Texas with a fair supply of money and goods. Most colonists were less prosperous, and the Mexican government had made Texas a haven for people who'd been caught in the harsh credit systems of the United States and other countries at that time. In the United States in 1836, there were still debtors' prisons in many states. Under the Mexican government's laws, it was almost impossible for foreign creditors, including those in the United States, to collect debts owed by the Texas colonists. So a fellow who was hopelessly in debt in New York or Georgia could step over onto Texas soil and almost overnight became a big landowner without an obligation to anyone or anything in the world except the faraway City of Mexico government.

The Rose family was Protestant. As the Spanish rulers had before them, the City of Mexico government required colonists to at least profess Roman Catholicism. The Rose family, like Sam Houston, became "Muldoon Catholics." Father Miguel Muldoon, the "Friar Tuck" of the Texas Revolution, was the chaplain of the Stephen F. Austin colony. The good Father made all the colonists "Catholics" on an assembly-line basis. Muldoon was a big, red-faced man, well-educated, golden-hearted, pugnacious, and often drunken. For a while he was the only Texan east of the Colorado River who could perform a marriage ceremony. He is known to have made a solitary trip among the savage Comanche Indians to rescue a white woman captive, and it is thought that he performed such exploits more than once.

Muldoon never required Texans to attend religious services, although Dilue Rose reports that he did close a Protestant Sunday School in San Felipe de Austin. Although Muldoon was sympathetic to the rebels, he was never with the Texas army. Early in the Revolution, he saved one young Texan from a Santa Anna firing squad. He later rescued another Texan from the Santanista prison at Matamoros.

The Roses had lost their only Bible on the trip to Texas, and Mrs. Rose once asked their friend William Barret Travis to see if he could buy a new Bible for them. Apparently there wasn't one in the whole province, for Travis, who before the Revolution practiced law in courts all over Texas, couldn't find one. But he did find some illustrated Sunday School books which he gave to Dilue, her nine-year-old sister, Ella, and her thirteen-year-old brother, Granville.

Like the majority of Texas colonists, the Rose family owned no slaves. So they had no reason to quarrel with the Mexican government's emancipation proclamation of 1829. Even those Texans who did own slaves were not troubled by the decree. They either ignored it altogether or, if it seemed advisable, obeyed the law technically while continuing to disobey it in spirit. The Mexicans really made little effort to enforce the law freeing slaves in Texas, but they did capitalize on their position in relation to slavery in their dealings with the United States.

In 1833 Santa Anna's aide, Colonel Almonte, passed by the Rose farm on an inspection tour. With the persuasive, English-speaking Almonte was an Abolitionist leader from the United States, Benjamin Lundy. This was Lundy's second tour of Texas under Almonte's guidance. Lundy suspected that slave-holding interests in the South wanted to add Texas to the United States, by purchase or conquest, and carve it up into five or six slave-holding states. Almonte encouraged Lundy's suspicions and showed him how the Texans were still holding hundreds of slaves in defiance of the Mexican emancipation order. When Lundy got back to New Jersey he published two pamphlets, "The Origin and True Cause of the Texas Insurrection" and "The War in Texas." In these he said the Southern "slave trust" had agents working to foment the rebellion. He called the colonists a bunch of "thieves and brigands."

Actually, many of the Texas leaders had distaste for slavery. Stephen Austin had a plan for making Texas free soil "as soon as the old slaves die off." However, the best evidence that the slave interests had little or no part in the uprising of 1836 is the fact that many of the big slave owners were either sympathetic to Santa Anna's government or neutral. William H. Wharton, one of the guiding spirits of the Texas War Party, commented on the fact that most of the big land holders (and slave owners) were absent from the combat rolls of the Revolution:

In glancing over the list [of those who fought in the Battle of San Jacinto] I am surprised and mortified to find that very few men of property had any part in the perils of that glorious day [April 21, 1836]. I do not see on the roster a single one of the wealthy merchants of Matagorda or the opulent planters of Old Caney. . . . The planters were taking care of their cattle and slaves and the merchants were minding their goods . . .

Neighbors of the Rose family had a number of slaves, some of them wild creatures fresh from Africa. Once while Dr. Rose was away on a sick call, Mrs. Rose and the children had a terrifying encounter with an escaped giant slave who was called The Wild Man of the Navidad. This huge Negro besieged the Rose family, shouting African gibberish while he tried to break into the house. Finally, after eating a raw chicken, he went away. He was never captured, said Dilue.

One of the fears of the colonists, which was expressed in the Rose chronicles, was that Santa Anna's approach might stir up a revolt among the Texas slaves, so many of whom were still virtually savages.

The Rose family began making serious preparations to leave for the United States after they heard that Colonel Travis and all his men had been slain in the Alamo. Miss Dilue wrote: "Colonel Travis was headstrong and precipitated the war with Mexico, but he died at his post defending San Antonio." Dilue and her sister Ella got out the pretty Sunday School books that Travis had given them, and they wept most of one day in grief for the chivalrous Colonel.

A courier came by with a dispatch from Houston "which told the people to leave [their homes]. Houston's army was retreating to the Brazos and President Burnet and his cabinet had fled to Harrisburg."

Miss Dilue said the weather was most abnormal that spring. Fierce rainstorms had filled the Brazos to flood stage. It would be winter chill one day and summer hot the next. Tornadoes cruised the troubled skies. The buffalos behaved crazily, and perhaps because of the movements of the armies across Texas, buffalo herds drifted further south than usual. One day, between three and four thousand buffalos came out of the bottom and stampeded right by the Rose farmhouse. The family, thinking that Mexicans or Indians were behind the herd, was terribly frightened. Miss Dilue reported that the "buffalo passed and went on to the coast and the prairie looked afterwards as if it had been plowed. We had been several days without news from the Texas army and did not know but that our men had been massacred."

The sad news about the Alamo caused Mrs. Rose's bachelor brother, a rugged young fellow named James Wells, to decide to join Houston's army. Wells seemed to have had little thought of fighting until he heard of the fate of friends in the Alamo. Dilue said her mother

made Uncle James two striped hickory shirts and bags to carry provisions. I spent the day melting lead in a pot, dipping it up with a spoon, and moulding bullets. Father finished planting corn. He hid part of our furniture, books and other things in the bottom. Mother packed what bedding, clothes and provisions she could, ready to leave at a moment's warning. We would have to haul these ten miles on the sled to a Mr. Bundick's. Father had made arrangements for Mr. Bundick to haul our family in his cart.

Uncle James mounted his horse one morning in late March and set out to the north in search of the Texas army. That same day the Rose family left home at sunset, hauling clothes, bedding and provisions on the sled pulled by one yoke of oxen. . . . We camped the first night near Harrisburg. Next day we crossed Vince's Bridge and arrived at San Jacinto in the night. There were fully 5,000 people at the ferry. The planters from Brazoria and Columbia, with their slaves, were crossing. We waited three days before we were allowed to cross.

Part of the confusion at the ferry was caused by the businesslike attitude of the owner, Nathaniel Lynch, who was charging high tolls. When President Burnet at Harrisburg heard about this, he galloped to the ferry and threatened to press the ferry into government service if Lynch refused anyone passage because of inability to pay. Thereafter, ferry service across the San Jacinto River improved.

Mrs. Rose was an intelligent woman with a good sense of humor. While she walked along at the start of The Runaway Scrape, carrying an ailing child in her arms, she reminded the children of some of the trials the family had been through since being shipwrecked on the Texas shore. They had been attacked by packs of wolves, had visits at the lonely farmhouse from giant, half-hostile coast Indians, and had turned back the siege of The Wild Man of the Navidad. So, she told her children, they weren't going to be frightened by the prospect of a hundred-mile journey with a lot of company. Father Rose and thirteen-year-old brother Granville often had to leave the line of march to herd cattle. The first time Granville did this, Dilue said: "Ella and I had been grieving over Colonel Travis and now we had a big cry when brother left us."

The evening the party of five families to which the Roses were attached reached the Trinity River men who'd been with the army began to rejoin their families. I know they have been blamed for this, but what else could they have done? The Texas army was retreating and the Mexican army was crossing the Colorado. Colonel Fannin and his men were prisoners. There were more Negroes than whites in our party and many of the slaves were wild Africans. There was a large tribe of Indians on the Trinity as well as the Cherokee Indians in [upper] Eastern Texas, and there were Tories, both Mexicans and Americans, in the country. It was the intention of our men to see their families across the Sabine River and then return and fight the Mexicans. I must say for the Negroes there was no insubordination among them; they were loyal to their owners. . . . At the Trinity the river was rising and there was a struggle to see who should cross first.

One of Dilue's small sisters, the ailing child Mrs. Rose had carried from their farm, had a high fever. As the family was crossing the Trinity in a boat, the child had convulsions. The river was out of its banks and rushing so swiftly that it took eight men to control the boat. When they reached the other side in darkness, the Rose family's only possessions were two good saddle horses, the clothes they had on and a rifle. Brother Granville was fording the Trinity at another place with the livestock.

When we landed on the east side of the Trinity the lowlands were flooded and everyone was rushing for the prairie. Father carried the sick child on his horse. Sister Ella and I rode behind mother. Mother carried the baby and father's gun in her arms.

Even sadder days were ahead for the Rose family.

4

Santa Anna Turns Commando

The so-called President, Vice President and other rebels of authority had set out at midday from Harrisburg in a steamboat for the Island of Galveston. General Houston was at the Pass of Gross with 800 men and two 4-pound guns [del calibre de a cuatro].

—SANTA ANNA'S INTELLIGENCE REPORT OF APRIL 15, 1836

ON APRIL 7, 1836, Santa Anna rode into the burned town of San Felipe de Austin. San Felipe is on the west bank of the Brazos River, about a hundred and fifty miles east of San Antonio and about the same distance west of the United States border. When the President reached the town, he was on the point of about fourteen hundred troops.

Baker's company, one of the two that had refused to retreat to Groce's with Houston, had burned the town and crossed to the east bank of the river. There they had dug trenches and installed themselves. The Texans had also very efficiently moved all the boats and rafts in the vicinity to hiding places on the eastern shore. Some hours before the Mexicans arrived, Baker sent three men in a canoe back to San Felipe as pickets to warn him of the Santanistas' approach. They must have been a very sleepy trio, for Santa Anna's clattering column surprised them. Two of the Texans escaped in the canoe; the third, a man named Bill Simpson, was caught. He told Santa Anna that Houston, with around five hundred followers, was only twenty miles upstream, at Groce's. Simpson also told the Mexicans that the Texas army was still on the west side of the Brazos.

It is hard to understand why Santa Anna, with his fourteen hundred men, didn't ignore Baker and ride upstream after the diminishing main body of the rebels. However, the Mexican President did send new orders from San Felipe to the Urrea and Gaona divisions. Urrea was to halt his sweep along the Gulf Coast, and Gaona was to abandon the northernmost reaches of settled Texas; their two forces were then to join Santa Anna's army at the seat of Austin's colony. From San Felipe "the campaign would be carried to its conclusion with a united army," said His Excellency.

Meanwhile, Santa Anna brought up two cannon and started shelling Baker's trenches on the other shore. Between the cannon shot and the rifle fire of Mexican sharpshooters Baker's men were busy. One of them, Pvt. John Bricker, was the first Texan to die in action in the San Jacinto campaign. He was hit in the head by a small copper ball on April 8.

Mexican carpenters went to work and built two flatboats, but Baker kept his fire so hot that the Santanistas couldn't launch the boats. Santa Anna grew impatient and began riding up and down the Brazos, looking for several miles in both directions for an easier crossing.

On April 9, *El Presidente* left Sesma and about eight hundred fifty troops to deal with Baker and wait for the other columns under Filisola, Urrea, and Gaona. In a near-freezing norther Santa Anna, with five hundred grenadiers and fifty dragoons, rode down the west bank of the Brazos. On the night of April 10 they stopped at a tavern near the Brazos operated by a Mrs. Elizabeth Powell. Although Mrs. Powell hadn't joined The Runaway Scrape, she was loyal to the rebel cause, and she entertained the Mexican President only because she was forced to. The next day, Santa Anna started on down the Brazos toward Thompson's Ferry near Fort Bend, where Wily Martin's company was guarding the crossing. The President arrived at the ferry early on April 12. From the west bank of the river, the Mexican advance guard could see a Negro ferryman on the opposite shore. Santa Anna and some of his staff hid themselves in brush, and Almonte called in his good English to lure the Negro to the west bank. It was said that when the ferryman was on shore Santa Anna himself leaped from ambush and wrestled with the Negro. At about the same time, Wily Martin realized that he didn't have enough men to defend the crossings around Fort Bend, and he fell back from the river.

From Thompson's Ferry, Santa Anna sent word to Sesma that he'd captured a boat, and he ordered Sesma, Filisola, Gaona, and Urrea to join him at Fort Bend. The fast-moving Sesma reached Fort Bend on April 13. Sesma reported that Filisola and Gaona, whose movements had been slow throughout the campaign, hadn't reached San Felipe when he left the place.

At Fort Bend Santa Anna learned from captured civilians that the unguarded and uneasy seat of the rebel government was at Harrisburg, less than thirty miles east of Fort Bend. On April 14 *El Presidente* crossed the Brazos with a train of about a thousand, including around seven hundred fifty of his best grenadiers, his staff and cavalry escort, muleskinners, and women camp followers. His first destination was, of course, Harrisburg, where he hoped to catch Burnet and his old political enemy, Vice-president Lorenzo De Zavala. He did not reveal his plans for Burnet, but he said he would hang De Zavala.

Santa Anna knew that the towering "Don Samuel Houston was the land grabbers' so-called general." Except for Houston, De Zavala, Austin, and one or two others, the Mexican President's information about Texas leaders was vague. He thought that David Burnet was a "Mr. I. Bonnen." Even after he'd ordered the execution of Col. James Fannin's men at Goliad, His Excellency continued to call the unfortunate Fannin "Colonel Fancy."

Civilian secretary Caro reports that Santa Anna was also very dim about Texas geography, and thought that the rivers were at flood-tide "because of snow melting in the mountains." Of this Caro commented, referring indirectly to the President's addiction to opium: "Only His Excellency has seen snow-capped mountains in the deserts of Texas."

Santa Anna's task force passed through the country between Fort Bend and Harrisburg speedily, executing a series of quick raids on the way. As the column drew close to Harrisburg on April 14, it was confronted by a narrow, deep creek. A large fallen tree formed a crude bridge over the creek. According to Caro, Santa Anna had a morbid fear of water. The secretary implied that this terror affected his conduct of the campaign. For example, it was one of the reasons he had allowed Baker's few riflemen to prevent him from crossing the broad Brazos.

When they came to the creek, Santa Anna dismounted and very cautiously inched his way over the log on foot, while a dragoon swam the President's horse across. Then Santa Anna remounted and promptly became the confident, impatient leader again. The ammunition was passed over the log by hand, and the only thing on wheels in the column, a twelve-pound cannon, was floated over laboriously on heavy logs.

This gun, medium of barrel and mounted with brass, was called *The Golden Standard*. Santa Anna was so eager to get to Harrisburg that he didn't take the time to protect the commissary supplies on the backs of his two hundred mules against water damage. He ordered his men to swim the animals across the deep creek with the stores still in the packs.

Among the members of Santa Anna's staff who witnessed this crossing was a Lt. Col. Pedro Francisco Delgado, one of the President's aides. Delgado was a cultured, intelligent officer, and he seriously considered Santa Anna a maniac. As he described the scene at the creek:

> The banks [of the creek] were steep and slippery and water was soon over the packsaddles. Several officers and dragoons fell in the water. There was a terrible confusion, shouts and curses. Stores were badly damaged. Two mules drowned. His Excellency witnessed all this with hearty laughter.

Santa Anna was in one of his daring moods on the night of April 15. He and one officer took fifteen dragoons and rode up within a mile of Harrisburg at about 11 P.M. They dismounted and sneaked into the town, hoping to catch "the so-called government of the filibusters." But Burnet had already fled. The only Texans Santa Anna found were three printers busy putting out Texas's only newspaper, *The Telegraph and Texas Register*. The printers didn't withhold any information. As they told the Mexicans, Gail Borden, Jr., one of the paper's two editors, had left town just an hour before. Burnet, De Zavala, and the others of the cabinet had left Harrisburg the previous morning on the steamboat *Cayuga*. The printers believed that the rebel government was moving to New Washington (now Morgan's Point) on a peninsula where the San Jacinto Bay joined Galveston Bay. New Washington

was about twenty miles east of Harrisburg, but the steamboat
would have to make a long and devious voyage by way of
Buffalo Bayou and the San Jacinto River and Bay.

The printers also told Santa Anna where they thought
Houston's army was and how many men he had. According
to them, Houston and his force of about eight hundred had
left Groce's plantation on the Brazos after camping there for
two weeks, and were that night about fifty miles northwest of
Harrisburg near the present town of Hockley. The printers
believed that Houston was going to San Jacinto, where he
hoped to control the ferry over the San Jacinto River to the
town of Lynchburg. Perhaps, they speculated, he intended to
retreat to the Trinity River, twenty miles to the east of Lynchburg.

Santa Anna was dreadfully disappointed at his failure to
catch the rebel government leaders in Harrisburg. He burned
the town. He threw Gail Borden's presses into the bayou. The
Mexican President now had two major objectives: first, to
catch the fugitive Texas government at New Washington; and
second, to intercept Houston's army at Lynch's Ferry.

Santa Anna claimed to have found in Burnet's quarters at
Harrisburg a letter from Houston which had arrived the day
before and said in part: "The catastrophes of the Alamo and
Goliad with the deplorable loss of the brave Travis and Fancy
[Fannin] have discouraged my men and they are deserting in
platoons, believing the cause of Texas lost." However, this
certainly doesn't sound like a letter Houston would have
written to the already antagonistic Burnet.

On the morning of April 16 Santa Anna sent fifty dragoons
under Almonte in pursuit of the Texas government leaders.
On the way to New Washington, Almonte encountered a
young Texas horseman named Mike McCormick. Mike was

the son of a forty-nine-year-old Irish widow named Mrs. Peggy McCormick, who owned a ranch between the San Jacinto River and Bay. When Almonte saw Mike, the boy was on a mission as courier between Houston's army and President Burnet. The Mexicans followed Mike to New Washington. McCormick knew he was leading the enemy, but they were headed in that direction anyway and the Texan had a fast horse. He rode into New Washington about a thousand yards ahead of Almonte's posse.

Apparently, Burnet had gone as far as Lynchburg on the steamboat *Cayuga.* At Lynchburg, for some reason, he and Mrs. Burnet, along with several members of the cabinet, took horses. They crossed the San Jacinto on the ferry and rode the ten miles to New Washington. There they found a flatboat, which was hauling supplies from the warehouses of the James Morgan plantation out to the Texas schooner *Flash,* about a quarter of a mile out in Galveston Bay. The Texan supervising the loading of supplies into the flatboat had some hard words with Burnet, for the President wanted to commandeer the boat to take his party, including the horses, across Galveston Bay to the town of Anahuac and when the loading supervisor refused to give up his boat, Burnet flew into a tantrum. They finally came to a compromise when the man agreed to have the cabinet taken to the Texan schooner in the flatboat.

The boat had just returned from a loading trip to the *Flash* and was ready to transport President and Mrs. Burnet when McCormick came galloping into New Washington shouting that the Mexicans were coming. Burnet had gone into a warehouse, and when McCormick arrived he sprinted out and had a quick conference with the courier. Apparently Burnet thought there was no longer time to use the unwieldy flatboat, so he and Mrs. Burnet and two or three others got into a rowboat and set out for the *Flash.* One story is that the first Mexican dragoons reached the shore just as the rowboat shoved off and one cavalryman touched Burnet with his lance but didn't wound the Texas President. McCormick turned his horse off into heavy woods and escaped.

Thanks to Almonte's chivalry, Mr. and Mrs. Burnet and their party made it to the *Flash*. When the Mexican Colonel reached the water's edge the Burnet rowboat was within easy musket range, and Almonte could certainly have blasted the boat out of the water and captured or killed the Texas President. Had Santa Anna been there himself, he undoubtedly would have done so. But Almonte ordered his dragoons not to fire because there was a lady in the enemy rowboat. Almonte, said to be the product of an unorthodox mating between a priest and an Indian girl, was a very civilized fellow.

Even though the Texas President got away, Almonte's trip to New Washington was profitable. Capturing the Morgan warehouses, which still contained large food stocks, meant a lot to the Mexicans, who were running short of some supplies. Almonte sent a message to Santa Anna suggesting that the President hurry up with the rest of his task forces, since Almonte's fifty dragoons "were exposed to danger from enemy ships." What Almonte really feared was that the Texas ships might land men in an effort to recapture the food supplies at New Washington.

It took Santa Anna until noon on April 18 to reach New Washington. The time he spent on the trip was not entirely wasted, for on the morning of April 18, before he reached New Washington, the army made one acquisition the General must have believed would be an advantage later on. Not far from the little town and quite close to Peggy McCormick's ranch at San Jacinto, there was a large and prosperous spread owned by one William Vince. Vince had fled before the Mexican army, but his housekeeper, a British widow named Mrs. James K. Brown, had refused to join The Runaway Scrape, so she and her thirteen-year-old son, Jimmy, remained at the ranch house. As she said: "I'm a British subject. And I'll tell either of these dirty armies a thing or two if they try to bother Jimmy and I."

Jimmy Brown, who later became a prominent Galveston businessman, was large for thirteen. When Santa Anna's division passed the Vince home on the road between the Brazos and the San Jacinto, Mrs. Brown watched from the front of the double loghouse, but young Jimmy, a brash sort of boy, wanted a closer look. Before his mother could stop him, he got on a big-boned, black, half-thoroughbred stallion called Old Whip and rode bareback toward the point of the army's column. Col. Juan Bringas, one of Santa Anna's aides, seems to have taken the tall lad for a grown-up Texan, for he hit Jimmy with the flat of his saber, and the boy tumbled off the sleek back of Old Whip.

Mrs. Brown came running. She cried that Bringas was mistreating a child, and a British child at that! At this time, Santa Anna either realized that General Urrea and others on his staff who believed that it would be wise to treat Texas noncombatants reasonably well were right, or was simply feeling generous. He assured Mrs. Brown that no further harm would come to her son. Instead of molesting the woman and boy, the President cursed Colonel Bringas and made him dismount and help the lad to his feet.

However, Santa Anna did let Bringas keep the coal-black stud horse. This famous sire belonged to Allen Vince. Why Old Whip was left at William Vince's in the path of the Mexican army is a mystery. Perhaps his master had been taken by surprise at the approach of Santa Anna's column and had to get away on foot. In any case, Old Whip joined Santa Anna's train on the morning of the eighteenth on the road to New Washington.

Bringas was not the only officer who ran afoul of Santa Anna's unpredictable temper that morning. General Castrillon, whose sensitivity on the subject of Melchora Barrera had displeased His Excellency, apparently offended the President again when during this long march Santa Anna invited himself to share the services of Castrillon's cook. Santa Anna had chronic digestive trouble, and Castrillon's chef could prepare food so that it was both bland and appetizing. Castrillon is said to have been so impudent as to reject Santa Anna's proposal.

Santa Anna must have been still brooding over this fresh display of antagonism on Castrillon's part when, near Allen Vince's ranch, the army reached a stout cedar bridge over a tributary of Buffalo Bayou called Vince's Bayou. Vince's Bayou runs about four miles due south from Buffalo Bayou. Usually it is a tame little stream, but in the unusually rainy April of 1836 it was swollen far beyond its normal proportions. The Vince brothers, who worked several ranches besides the Allen Vince place in San Jacinto County, had built the cedar bridge only a few months earlier. When the half-broken mules pulling *The Golden Standard* came to Vince's Bayou, they refused to venture across the bridge with the heavy artillery. Santa Anna thereupon placed Castrillon, an astute and invaluable major general, in command of a single company, and ordered the General to escort the artillery around the head of Vince's Bayou while the rest of the army proceeded to New Washington by the direct route over Vince's Bridge. In heading the bayou, Castrillon had to travel about nine miles over boggy, high-grassed prairie.

When Santa Anna reached Morgan's plantation, he shared Almonte's interest in Colonel Morgan's belongings, but His Excellency's attention took a less practical direction. Among Morgan's servants, who were still working there, the observant President noticed a decorative long-haired mulatto girl. Her name was Emily, and she was said to be a very comely "Latin looking" woman of about twenty.

Although he was from Philadelphia Colonel Morgan, who was De Zavala's partner in the real estate business, had acquired a number of slaves in the South before coming to Texas. Possibly to quiet his Pennsylvania conscience, Morgan was one of the Mexican settlers who had complied with the 1829 emancipation decree to the extent of freeing his slaves and making them indentured servants for ninety-nine years. On that April 18, Morgan was on Galveston Island commanding a small force of soldiers who were guarding some thousand Texas refugees there. Emily, along with others of Morgan's servants, had been helping load the flatboat when the Mexicans rode up. Emily found favor in the President's eyes, and she was assigned to be a servant in his marquee.

Santa Anna tarried at New Washington until the morning of April 20. Apparently his scouting system was working poorly at the time, for he didn't seem to know until the twentieth that a large body of Texans was in the neighborhood.

Perhaps the President's ignorance on this point resulted at least in part from inattention to the campaign at hand, for he spent the nineteenth of April trying to arrange passage back to Mexico aboard a German schooner which was then lying off Morgan's plantation. By this time, the President had more than his undoubtedly intense boredom with the Texas expedition to make him want to go home. He had worries too, about the political situation in his capital.

Before he took up the march for Texas one of his most

obedient stooges, Vice-president Miguel Barragan, had been named acting President. Barragan died on March 1, 1836, of putrid fever. The Mexican chamber of deputies chose Jose Justo Corro as acting President. Of course, Santa Anna was still President and dictator, but he'd seen dictators upset before in Mexican politics. He must have felt that it would be a good idea to go home and assert his authority over this Corro fellow. Santa Anna was always finding parallels between his career and that of Napoleon Bonaparte, and of his Texas campaign he said that his enemies in the City of Mexico hoped that it "would be as great a disaster for me as Russia was for the Corsican hero."

So Santa Anna had a conference on shore with the German schooner captain, in which it was arranged that he would board the German vessel on the night of April 19. The schooner would take him to Copano Bay on the Texas Gulf Coast, where a Mexican man-of-war, *El Bravo,* would be waiting. He would then take the *El Bravo* to Vera Cruz and from there make one of his conqueror's entries into the City of Mexico. The command of his own advanced task force in New Washington would fall to the thoroughly competent General Castrillon, despite Santa Anna's dislike of that officer. The overall direction of the armies would be given to Filisola.

Santa Anna reckoned without the Texas Navy. Possibly he didn't even know there was a Texas Navy until April 19. On the afternoon of that day an armed schooner appeared off New Washington and attacked and burned the German ship before *El Presidente's* eyes. This Texan warship was one of the four mobilized at Galveston by Robert Potter. Despite Potter's peculiar personal traits and his scant experience, he turned out to be a very efficient Secretary of Navy. The *Flash* must have notified the Texas warship that the Mexicans were at New Washington, and perhaps the warship's officers had been watching through glasses when Santa Anna and the German captain met on shore. With his seagoing transportation destroyed, His Excellency must have reflected that it would take a long horseback ride to get him home to the City of Mexico, for he abandoned the plan to leave.

There is no record as to whether or not Santa Anna knew that Almonte had spared the life of the Texas President when he could have shot Burnet out of the water, but he certainly knew that "I. Bonnen" had made it out to the *Flash*. And Santa Anna may have been displeased with the man who was usually his favorite aide, for on the night of April 19, when *El Presidente* sent out fifty dragoons to look for the Texas army, Almonte was not commanding them. Their officer was a young captain named Marcos Barragan.

Meanwhile, on April 19 when all the supplies had been taken from the warehouses, Santa Anna had burned New Washington. At 8 A.M. on the twentieth, when the Mexicans were packed and ready to leave the town, an excited young Barragan came galloping into the smoldering town with forty-six dragoons. He was shouting: "Houston is close on our rear and his troops have captured some of our stragglers and killed them."

Santa Anna's aide, Colonel Delgado, described the reaction to Barragan's news:

We were then in a dense wood through which ran a lane very narrow and about a league in length. The lane allowed passage for pack mules in single file only and to mounted men in double file. The lane was filled with hundreds of men and hundreds of pack mules. On hearing Barragan's report, His Excellency got on his horse and galloped off at full speed through this lane crowded with men and mules. He knocked over two men and shouted: "The enemy is coming! The enemy is coming!" The excitement of the general-in-chief had such a terrifying effect that order could no longer be preserved. Every man thought of flight, or of finding a hiding place, and [they] gave up all idea of fighting.

After he'd knocked over two infantrymen and banged into a few pack mules, Santa Anna regained partial control of himself.

"A column of attack was formed with trepidation and confusion, amidst incoherent and contradictory orders," said Delgado. Santa Anna ordered the men to drop their knapsacks to the ground, without breaking formation. He was still determined to intercept the Texans, if possible, before they could gain control of the crossing over the San Jacinto, so he had the men march in that direction.

All of the horsemen, including the President, dismounted and went forward afoot, leading the horses. The weather was overcast, and masses of dark clouds moved swiftly overhead. The Santanistas left the woods and marched out over a grassy plain. The grass was up to the flanks of the horses. On both horizons were dense forests of live oaks draped in Spanish moss, with a few tall pines among them. Flankers went on reluctant exploratory trips into these forbidding forests.

Santa Anna must have munched on his opium during the hike, for when at about 2 P.M. on April 20 he established a position on a plain that was part of Peggy McCormick's ranch near the San Jacinto, he was again the confident general, and ready for a fight with the despised *Soldados God Dammes.*

Reading *El Presidente's* Mail

Santa Anna is a base, unprincipled, bloody monster whose avowed intention is to excite the Indians and Negroes and crimson the waters of the Mississippi and make it the eastern boundary of Mexico.

—STEPHEN F. AUSTIN, WRITING TO ANDREW JACKSON

A SERIES of impulsive decisions had led the President of Mexico to Peggy McCormick's ranch by the river named by early explorers in honor of St. Hyacinth of Cracow. In contrast, Sam Houston approached the same country so deliberately that President Burnet repeatedly accused his General of cowardice. When, after leaving San Felipe, Houston had begun his march upstream toward Groce's while most of his officers clamored for him to take his rabble downstream to seek out the Mexican army, he had written to Tom Rusk, then at Harrisburg: "If I'd followed all the advice I got about going up or down the Brazos I would have been like the ass between the two stacks of hay. I consulted none. I held no council of war. If I err, the blame is mine."

The march to Groce's would have been a difficult one at best, and with the spring floods that then prevailed it was exceedingly arduous. But for that very reason, Groce's was, as Houston had told Private Kuykendall during the march, an excellent position. Surrounded by flooding creeks and very hard to approach from the west, south, or north, Groce's was almost like an island, as the Texans realized when it took them two days to cover eighteen miles on the way to their camp. Moreover, Private Kuykendall reported that when, on April 7, Santa Anna began to cannonade Baker's position near San Felipe twenty miles downstream, "every shot they fired was distinctly heard at our camp." With his scouts and spies out, Houston wasn't in much danger of being surprised at Groce's.

For two weeks, while it rained almost continuously, the army camped in the bottom near Groce's. The fastidious and anxious Burnet referred to this position as "the foul and turbid lagoons of the Brazos bottom." Throughout Houston's sojourn at Groce's, soldiers and government officials showed increasing dissatisfaction with him. A day or so after the men had heard shots exchanged between Baker and the Santanistas, Kuykendall wrote:

Col. Somervill [Lt. Col. Alexander Somervell, second-in-command of the First Regiment] returned to Groce's from a visit to Capt. Baker's camp. He came to the tents of my company and talked with the men, expressing himself strongly in disapprobation of the commander-in-chief's retreating policy. He said he was in favor of depriving Houston of the command and supplying a more belligerent leader if Houston persisted in avoiding conflict with the enemy and continued to march the army eastward, as it was generally believed he intended to do. Somervill wished to know whether our company favored such a course and would *take it* should it become necessary. He was assured by both our officers and men he could rely on their cooperation. I doubt not that Somervill and other officers sounded the whole army on this subject and received the same responses. There was no injunction of secrecy—and Gen'l Houston could not have been ignorant of what was in agitation.

As Kuykendall suspected, Houston was by no means in ignorance of what was in agitation, nor was he unaware of the feelings of his men. But the General was a very busy man during those two weeks at Groce's. At no time prior to his arrival at the Brazos had Houston had adequate time for organizational work. At Groce's, he began the immense task of forming his command into some semblance of an army.

Discipline was the first problem. The raw troops in Houston's army had little experience with military regulations. Some of the men, including Capt. Bob Calder and a Viennese rifleman named Pvt. George Erath, believed that Houston was deliberately trying to shake unruly elements of the army when he led the way to Groce's. As Erath observed:

> We had been marched from the Guadalupe [Gonzales] in a zig zag way through swamps and bogs. We had been subjected to all military discipline and practice. We stood guard 24 hours out of each 48 and were not allowed to go to sleep even at the guard fires. The delay at Groce's had good effect in disciplining us and in giving us information on military tactics.

The General did give last-minute pardons to at least two soldiers who had been sleeping while they were supposed to be on watch, but he showed the army that he could be firm when four men were caught robbing and raping women refugees. The four were hanged.

Another of the chores Houston undertook at Groce's was the organization of an effective scout and spy service. Henry Wax Karnes, Colonel Handy, Deaf Smith, Washington and John Secrest, Dilue Rose's uncle, Jim Wells, and a free Negro from San Antonio named Hendrick Arnold were the most prominent members of the spy company. These men would hang around the edges of Santa Anna's camps, and then come back with information for Houston. There are stories, but no documentary evidence, that Deaf Smith and his close friend, Hendrick Arnold, often went into the Mexican camps. As Miss Dilue said, "Mr. Smith looked like a Mexican," and the legend is that in the Santanista camps he assumed the role of an elderly and simple-minded Latin. Hendrick Arnold played the part of a fugitive slave, it was said, and he may have been one of those Negroes Santa Anna used to send insulting and challenging messages to Houston.

Houston also devoted some time at Groce's to the formation of a medical staff. The necessity for such a body was particularly pressing during that spring of 1836, for the Revolution had drawn together frontiersmen who had previously led isolated lives and been exposed to few contagious diseases. Houston's army was plagued by such childhood diseases as whooping cough, mumps, measles, and pink eye. Measles were epidemic. Bad food and worse water caused dysentery. Alexander Ewing, a twenty-seven-year-old who had studied medicine in Edinburgh, Scotland, was made the chief of staff of seven or eight physicians whose duty it was to cope with these problems.

The small arms of this army were as various as those of a pirate crew. Groce's plantation had fairly well-equipped shops, and much time during the rebels' fortnight there was given to weapons repair. Although Houston was aloof with his officers, his behavior with the men was quite the opposite. When the regular gunsmiths were overbusy, he would pitch in and help with the repair of rifles. One day a very young volunteer from the United States arrived in camp. He told a veteran Texas soldier that his rifle wasn't in good working order "and where can I find a blacksmith?" The mischievous older soldier pointed at Houston and said: "See that big fellow in the dirty clothes? He's the smith." The newcomer didn't know the General. He strode over to Houston and said: "Fix my rifle, mister. It won't stand locked." "Set her down, son, and call back in an hour," said Houston. An hour later the new soldier returned, somewhat fearful, for he'd found out who this smith was. Houston was snapping the lock on the rifle. "She's fixed now, son," said the General.

Houston said that "mutiny and sedition was rife" among his own officers. He used two of his loyal spies, Deaf Smith and Karnes, to find out what was going on among his discontented staff members. As the result of a Karnes investigation, Houston placed one of his aides, Col. James H. Perry, under arrest. Perry was in correspondence with Secretary Potter down at Galveston, and it was he who reported that Houston "do eat opium to excess." Houston intercepted this letter. However, Perry was under only limited arrest. He fought at San Jacinto and no charges were pressed against him. Perry had also written in the same letter to Potter that the "Big Drunk" wasn't drinking. Apparently, the Texan General, who had made heavy use of liquor for so many years, drank only from the water canteen strapped to his saddle during the campaign. None of his envious and ambitious officers reported him under the influence of liquor at any time during the campaign, though many, like Perry, deliberately spied on him.

While Houston at Groce's organized his men, Burnet at Harrisburg was enraged at the army's delay. On April 1, when the Texan President received word that Houston had gone up the Brazos to Groce's instead of coming down to protect Harrisburg and the neighboring towns, he decided to send Secretary of War Tom Rusk to join the army and take over the command if Houston continued to postpone engaging the enemy. Rusk left Harrisburg on April 2 and reached Groce's on April 4. He brought a letter from the President to Houston which read: "The enemy is laughing you to scorn. You must retreat no more. The country expects you to fight. The salvation of the country depends on your doing so."

Rusk loyally showed this insulting message to no one save the General. Houston replied bitterly to Burnet that the President and the cabinet, all able-bodied men, had retreated a good deal faster than the army. The General added that when the ad interim government moved to Harrisburg it caused more panic among the colonists than anything else except the fall of the Alamo.

When Rusk first arrived, some of the malcontent officers swarmed around him. Soon, in disgust, they were saying that the Secretary of War had "fallen under the God damned old Cherokee blackguard's spell," but in this they were mistaken. Tom Rusk had a mind and a strong will of his own, but he remained loyal to Houston because he realized that Houston was the only man in camp with the strength of character to mold this wild rabble into something that resembled an army. When Rusk let the army know he was backing the General he did much to strengthen Houston's position.

Not all the newcomers who arrived at Groce's and soon after were as helpful. In mid-April, for example, the army was joined by a private named Mirabeau Buonaparte Lamar, who saw himself as a candidate for Houston's job. Lamar was a thirty-eight-year-old Georgia poet and newspaper editor who had arrived on the Texas shore the previous April 6 and had walked to Houston's army. Lamar had been in Texas the year before on a visit, and had liked it so much that he'd gone home to Georgia to settle his affairs. When he landed at Harrisburg on April 6 he had $6,000 in his pocket to buy up Texas real estate for a Georgia syndicate. Lamar met the ad interim government leaders and apparently came under the influence of

Burnet. Certainly it was at Burnet's instigation that Lamar began undermining Houston's leadership as soon as he got to the army. Yet, when Lamar wanted a member of the cabinet to hold his $6,000 for safe-keeping while he went off to Houston's army, he decided that De Zavala was the most trustworthy. The Vice-president did prove a good guardian of the cash.

At Houston's camp, Private Lamar went about explaining a plan he had: he wanted three hundred volunteers under his leadership to take the *Yellowstone* and make raids on Mexicans along the stream. Lamar said something about attacking Gaona, although that phlegmatic Mexican General was leading his division many miles inboard from the Brazos in mid-April.

That evening Houston posted notices throughout the camp that anyone who "beat for volunteers"—that is tried to raise a personal force within the army—would be considered a mutineer and would be shot immediately. Tom Rusk supported this proclamation. Private Lamar thereupon lost interest in his plan. Somehow, he quietly acquired a horse and from then on he rode with the cavalry.

The two other principal candidates for Houston's job were the only high-ranking officers with full uniforms, Col. Sidney Sherman, the commander of the new Second Regiment, and the Adjutant General, Col. John Austin Wharton—the same Wharton who'd written to Houston urging him to come to Texas and lead rebel forces back in 1832.

Wharton wore a well-tailored blue woolen uniform with brass buttons and a pair of respectable boots. His one departure from normal soldierly garb was a most unmilitary Mexican sombrero. Like Houston, he carried a gourd canteen. He was a tall, wiry man of thirty. In the early part of the campaign,

Wharton had helped quiet mutinous attitudes toward Houston, but gradually, under the influence of Burnet's friends in the army, Wharton had cooled toward the General. To some extent Houston's uncommunicative attitude had estranged this old friend. Had he confided in the proud and sensitive Wharton, the younger man might have remained loyal to Houston.

Sidney Sherman was a tall, brown-bearded, thirty-year-old native of Massachusetts. He was new to Texas and new to war. Before the Revolution, he had lived in Newport, Kentucky, across the river from Cincinnati. There, he had been a prominent industrialist and an innovator in his field. He was said to be the first manufacturer to make cotton bagging by machine, and he was also the first maker of sheet lead west of the Alleghenies. When the Texas Revolution broke out, he sold his cotton-bagging factory and used the funds to outfit and finance a company of fifty-two volunteers for the Texas army. Then this resolute and intelligent businessman led his company to the embattled province.

The Kentucky company got to Nacogdoches while that city was electing delegates to the Washington-on-the-Brazos Convention. When Sherman's men demanded the right to vote in the election and the Nacogdoches citizens objected, the newly arrived defenders of Texan liberty pointed a small cannon at the door of the building where the voting was taking place. They were permitted to cast their ballots. Robert Potter's presence at the Washington Convention was in part the result of this incident.

The soldiers Sherman brought from Kentucky were the real problem children of this tough army. One observer said:

The company from Kentucky was composed of the most reckless, drunken and lawless men in the army. Often fist fights would start between two in the Kentucky company

ranks and soon bring about a general melee. They struck
at each other indiscriminately. Officers interfered and
soon mingled in the row, giving and receiving blows.

Only a few in the outfit were native Kentuckians. The others
came from Maine, Massachusetts, Illinois, Maryland, Mississippi, Ohio, and Tennessee. One, a sixty-year-old veteran
of the Napoleonic wars named Achelle Marre, said that he'd
been a pirate under Jean Lafitte years before.

When the Second Regiment was organized at Groce's,
Houston, recognizing Sherman's ability despite their differences, placed Sherman in command of the newly formed
force. Sherman left his troublesome Kentucky company in the
First Regiment under Colonel Burleson. Private Kuykendall,
an admirably impartial observer who had been under Ned
Burleson since the organization of the First Regiment, com-
pared the two colonels this way:

> I noticed the contrast in the appearances of Colonel Ned
> Burleson of the First Regiment and Colonel Sherman of
> the Second. Burleson wore faded blue homespun, had no
> arms except a pair of pistols. Sherman had a much more
> military appearance. He wore a blue cloth round jacket,
> trimmed with silver lace. A handsome dress sword was
> suspended at his side. Yet Burleson had much military
> service, both in Texas and in the United States, while
> Sherman was in his novitate.

Colonel Ned Burleson was one man who might well have
succeeded had he set himself up as Houston's rival, for Burleson was a patient and effective officer, a veteran at both fighting
and controlling an army, and immensely popular with the
men. He was already, at the time of the San Jacinto campaign,
a famous Indian fighter, and he had been commander of the

hastily assembled army that had driven General Cos from San Antonio the previous December.

Perhaps Burleson's experiences in the battle with Cos accounted to some degree for his satisfaction with his post as regimental commander under Houston, for in that campaign Burleson had faced problems similar to Houston's. While Burleson's force held Cos under siege in San Antonio, an impetuous fellow named Ben Milam decided that the commander was too slow about attacking. Milam went through Burleson's camp baying, "Who'll go to Bexar [San Antonio] with old Ben Milam?" and acquired four hundred followers. They stormed and took the town. Some of the sting was taken out of Milam's success by the fact that Milam himself was killed in the fighting and it was Burleson who negotiated the surrender of Cos and his men. But throughout the San Jacinto campaign, Burleson showed little disposition to take over the army.

Houston was not certain during the weeks at Groce's whether Santa Anna was still with the Mexican forces in Texas, and his spies hadn't been able to find out. One report was that the Mexican President had gone home after the battle of the Alamo. On April 12, for the first time, Houston obtained definite information on Santa Anna's whereabouts. This report came from Joseph Powell, a son of the innkeeper, Mrs. Elizabeth Powell, who had been forced to entertain Santa Anna on the night of April 10.

Powell told Houston and Rusk that Santa Anna was then at Fort Bend and reported that the Mexican President planned to make a quick drive to Harrisburg where he hoped to "disconcert the rebellion" by capturing and executing Burnet and the cabinet. Powell had heard that Santa Anna with a small force might go on occasional raids out ahead of his main armies and when he told Houston and Rusk about that possibility, he gave them fresh hope and something to build their plans around. They could look for a chance to isolate Santa Anna and his task force and whip *El Presidente* before Filisola and the other columns could come up to his relief. After talking with Powell the General and the Secretary of War determined to take the army across the Brazos and march it down the road the seventy miles from Groce's to Harrisburg. They said nothing about their plans to the other Texan officers. Several of Houston's aides were sending information to Burnet and Potter, and these reports could be intercepted by the enemy.

On April 11 the army got its first cannon, two mounted 6-pounders sent by some citizens of Cincinnati, Ohio. The Ohio city was one of the hatching places of the Texas Revolution, and many soldiers and real estate operators came from there to the colony. It was against the law in the United States to ship arms to Texas, so *The Twin Sisters,* as the cannon were called, were labeled "hollow ware" and smuggled to Texas by ship. The big guns were landed at Harrisburg and hauled to Groce's. Houston placed Lt. Col. James C. Neill in command of the brand new artillery corps.

On April 12 and 13 the army crossed the river, using the *Yellowstone* and a yawl. The march in the direction of Harrisburg began on April 14. As usual, it was raining. After Houston passed near what is now Hempstead, Waller County, an unusually forlorn-looking crowd of civilians fell in behind the army. These wretches begged Houston to furnish them armed escort to the United States border, for they had a wild story that the Indians ahead along the Trinity River were ready to go on the warpath. The Indians on that river, the Coushattas, had promised Houston some time before not only not to molest the rebels, but even to help them. The Indians had agreed to furnish ninety warriors for the Texan army, and Houston had lately sent a Capt. Jacob Sheppard to remind Kalita, principal chief of the Coushattas and a good friend of Houston's, about the warriors. So Houston assured the refugees that the Trinity Indians were friendly, but this reply didn't satisfy the civilians and they stubbornly decided to remain with Houston's army, at least until they came to the turnoff leading to the United States. At that point, Houston's army would have to take a different direction if the General was planning to seek out the Mexican army, but apparently the refugees secretly hoped that Houston would instead head for the United States.

Within days after the army left Groce's, Mosely Baker and Wily Martin, both of whom had criticized Houston bitterly since his retreat from San Felipe in late March, rejoined his army. Baker, who had finally fallen back from the Brazos crossing at San Felipe, met Houston's column on April 15. The minute he saw the General, Baker reproached him: "You said you didn't attack the Mexicans on the Colorado because you didn't have any artillery. Now you got two brand spanking new cannon and yet you didn't stand and fight on the Brazos. Are you going to Harrisburg or not?" Even though Houston refused to answer, Baker threw his company in with Burleson's regiment.

Old Wily Martin, worn out from the hopeless job of trying to guard the Fort Bend crossings, was convinced that Houston wasn't going to fight, and he didn't want to go on serving under the General. Houston and Martin had once been good friends, and the General didn't make an issue of Martin's insubordination. He "ordered" Wily's company to guard the crowd of refugees clinging to the army. The next day the civilians were to turn left at a fork in the road and take off for the United States border, while Houston, though he still didn't say so, intended to turn right and head for Harrisburg. Martin agreed to the assignment.

As the army neared the fork in the road Houston encountered a Negro on a mule who was bringing a message from Santa Anna in Almonte's now-familiar English handwriting: "Mr. Houston, I know you're up there hiding in the bushes. As soon as I catch the other land thieves [Burnet and the cabinet] I'm coming up to smoke you out." This tantalizing dispatch must have made Houston and Rusk more determined than ever to seek out Santa Anna in the Harrisburg neighborhood, but their plans remained secret.

There were many in the army who still thought that Houston would follow the civilians on the left-hand road to the United States, instead of taking the right-hand path to Harrisburg. The point of the army reached the fork on the morning of April 16. According to some witnesses, Houston ordered the line of march down the Harrisburg road. Others said there was no order, that the men in the van made the decision. Still others said that Rusk forced Houston to let the army take the right road. However it happened, the fork in the road was the turning point. When the men had passed it, they knew where they were going.

Shortly after the army turned right and headed for Harrisburg, Houston had a falling out with a woman named Mrs. Pamelia Mann. Mrs. Mann was a young, strong, resolute woman of property, and she had a personal caravan of two large freight wagons pulled by eight oxen. She had a spare yoke of oxen which she had loaned to Houston earlier in the march to pull the cannon through the mud. One of Houston's unfriendly aides, Robert Coleman, said that the General and Mrs. Mann had been on very cordial terms before the fork in the road. At Groce's, Coleman said, some survivors of Fannin's expedition had once entered Houston's crude tent suddenly without announcing themselves. They found Sam lying down with his head in Mrs. Mann's lap. She was combing the General's wavy, chestnut-colored hair. As Coleman told it, the startled Mrs. Mann had exclaimed: "Boys, you nearly made me drive the comb into the General's head." The trouble between Mrs. Mann and Houston that came up on the road to Harrisburg concerned her oxen, which Houston had not returned.

Private Hunter, the poor speller from Fort Bend County, told about the argument:

The road forked and the Harrisburg road turned to the right, almost rightangle. We got about 10 or 12 miles down the road and Mrs. Mann over took us out on the big prairie hog wallow & full of water & a very hot day. She rode up to the general & said, general you tole me a dam lie, you said you was going on the Nacogdoches road. Sir, I want my oxen. Well, Mrs. Mann, we can't spare them. We can't git our cannon a long without them [said Houston]. I don't care a dam for your cannon, I want my oxen. She had a pare of holster pistols on her saddle pummel & a very large knife on her saddle. She turned a round to the oxen & jumpt down with the knife & cut the raw hide tug that the chane was tide with. The log chane hook was brok & it was tide with raw hide. No body said a word. She jumpt on her horse with whipin' hand & away she went in a lope with her oxen.

Capt. Rover [Rohrer, Houston's wagon master] rode up to General Houston & said general we can't git along without them oxen. The cannon is don boged down. [Houston replied:] Well, we have got to git a long the best we can. The Capt said, well, general, I will go and bring them oxen back. The Capt got a hundred yeard or so.

The General rased in his stirrups and hollowed, Capt that woman will fite. The Capt said dam her fitcing. Houston jumpt down off his horse and said, come Boys, les git this cannon out of the mud. The mud was very near to his boot top. He put his shoulder to [the] wheel & 8 or 10 men more lade holt. Out she come & we went & got down a bout 6 mile & campt at a big mot of timber. About 9 or 10 oclock Capt Rover come in to camp. He did not bring no oxen. The boys hollowed out, hai Capt where is your oxen? [Rohrer said:] She would not let me hav them. How come your shirt tore so & some of the boys would say Mrs. Mann tore it off him. What was that for? She wanted that shirt for baby rags.

Private Hunter said that on April 18

we got to the river [Buffalo Bayou] opposit Harrisburg and campt. About an hour or so after camping Deaf Smith come in & brung word of Sant Anna. He [Santa Anna] was going down for New Washington on San Jacinto Bay. General Houston giv orders to move out at daylight.

On the eighteenth, Karnes and Deaf Smith swam their horses across the three-hundred-foot-wide Buffalo Bayou and ambushed and captured a Capt. Miguel Bachiller and two other Mexican couriers. Rusk said later that Bachiller was a *correo* (express-rider) who'd come all the way from the City of Mexico, but judging by the saddlebags he carried it seemed that Bachiller had been in on the assault of the Alamo and had picked up some spoils. The deerskin wallets were inscribed with the name *William Barret Travis*. An indication of Houston's control over his headstrong followers is the fact that Bachiller wasn't killed, for the sight of Travis's name on the saddlebags must have been like a red flag to the Texans.

But the rest of Bachiller's costume, thanks to Deaf Smith, was more comical than inflammatory. After he'd captured the Mexican officer, Smith made Bachiller swap trousers and headgear. Smith, the larger man, had trouble getting into Bachiller's new blue trousers, but these wool pants were a lot more comfortable than Smith's mud-stiffened buckskins. Deaf also preferred Bachiller's ornamented sombrero to his own old skin cap. Bachiller looked like a clown when he rode into the Texas camp, and the Texas soldiers bayed foxhound laughter at the sight of the Mexican officer, with his shoulderboards and bemedaled blouse above the stiff skin pants, and the whole outfit topped off with a limp, too-large coonskin cap.

Bachiller was carrying dispatches from the City of Mexico government, via General Filisola at Fort Bend, intended for Santa Anna at New Washington. The letters were translated for Houston by one of his aides, Maj. Lorenzo De Zavala, Jr., the Vice-president's son, who had recently joined the army. De Zavala was the neatest-looking of Houston's aides, for he was accompanied by a Parisian valet he'd acquired while his father was Mexican Ambassador to France.

One message was a letter from the Mexican Secretary of State congratulating Santa Anna on his Goliad and Alamo victories: "Providence is propitious to us and has destined Your Excellency to be the savior and preserver of the Republic. Your Excellency has garnished your temples with laurels of everlasting fame." More important were letters from Filisola which revealed that the Mexican President was even farther ahead of his three principal columns than they'd suspected. The letters told them that Santa Anna with about a thousand men was that day at New Washington. Also, Filisola acknowledged a request from Santa Anna for five hundred reinforcements and said that these were on the way. The capture of these dispatches at Harrisburg was one of the most important preliminary events to the battle of San Jacinto. After he'd "read old Santa Anna's mail," Houston definitely became the hunter and not the hunted.

Later, Santa Anna commented bitterly on the Texans' capture of Filisola's courier: "The enemy acquired positive information at a time when it was retreating, wondering what to do, astonished by our operations and triumphs. Thus the rebels first became aware I was at New Washington." Filisola also later analyzed the Texan strategy after the couriers were intercepted at Harrisburg:

> General Houston had it in his power to attack Gaona or my column at Fort Bend or the forces under President Santa Anna. Houston thought it better to attack the president because Santa Anna was on the east side of the Brazos and unconnected with his other forces. . . . Houston then sent the steamboat down the river to attract our attention and marched against His Excellency."

There's no record that Houston actually ordered the *Yellowstone* down the river, but the steamboat did run the gantlet of Mexican troops on the west shore of the Brazos, and didn't lose a man or sustain any serious damage. Those on board were protected from Mexican fire by cotton bales. A Mexican officer said that the Santanistas from "the inner provinces" were terrified at their first sight of a steamboat. Some of Filisola's cavalrymen who were less awed tried unsuccessfully to rope the *Yellowstone*'s smokestacks as she steamed by Fort Bend close to shore.

Before the army left Harrisburg, fresh cases of children's diseases broke out among the men. A snug camp was made in the woods near Harrisburg and about two hundred twenty-five men, either ailing or ordered to stay, were left there to guard the army's baggage and a few prisoners. The others, with light marching orders, set out on April 19 along Buffalo Bayou to find the narrowest possible crossing of the flooding stream. Before leaving Harrisburg, Houston wrote to his friend Henry Raguet of Nacogdoches: "This morning we are in preparation to meet Santa Anna."

Before the army crossed Buffalo Bayou, Houston made his first formal speech of the campaign. The soldiers were in a hollow square formation with Houston and Rusk in the center. Houston sat astride a big white stud named Saracen, which he had gotten at Groce's, and delivered his words in a booming voice. While he talked, the men could see behind him, across the flowering savanna, smoke rising from the tall timber around New Washington. Santa Anna was burning another Texas town. The General said:

"Victory is certain! Trust in God and fear not! The victims of the Alamo and the names of those who were murdered at Goliad cry out for cool, deliberate vengeance. Remember the Alamo! Remember Goliad!"

The ragged, muddy men took up the cry: "Remember the Alamo! Remember Goliad!" Instead of Goliad, some of the West Texans chose to cry, "Remember La Bahia!"

Among Houston's men were seven survivors of the Goliad massacre. Others had cause to shout with feeling. Even some of the newcomers had known men who died at Goliad. Trooper Mirabeau Lamar, for example, had been a close friend of James Fannin's back in Georgia. Lieutenant Colonel Alexander Somervell, second-in-command of the First Regiment, said when Houston had finished: "That speech made me damned sure of one thing: no man in this army will be taken prisoner."

Patrick Usher, a private in Moseley Baker's outfit, said he, like the rest of his company, had been close to mutiny many times until he heard the Houston speech. Usher, later a Republic of Texas judge and Congressman, wrote:

> I had been impatient, weary of wading through mud and water, often hungry and angry. Yet while General Houston spoke and towered with constantly ascending eloquence and earnestness, I was reminded of the halo encircling the brow of Our Savior. Had General Houston called upon me to jump into the whirlpool of the Niagara as the only means of saving Texas, I would have made the leap.

When the shouting had died down, Houston ended his speech, saying: "It is no use looking for aid. None is at hand. Colonel Rusk is with us. And I rejoice in this."

This was his introduction of the Secretary of War for a speech.

Only ten of the fifty-nine signers of the Declaration of Independence were with the army that day. The ten were Houston, Rusk, the Secretary of War's young aide, Dr. William Junious Mottley, James Collinsworth, Dr. Thomas J. Gazley, Robert Coleman, William Scates, E. O. Legrand, John W. Bunton, and Andrew Briscoe. Rusk referred in his speech to the missing delegates, many of whom, at Washington-on-the-Brazos, had promised to raise big forces of riflemen and yet, for various reasons, were not there. The Secretary of War said:

> Santa Anna himself is just below us, within the sound of a drum. A few hours more will decide the fate of the army. What an astonishing fact it is that when the fate of our wives, our children, our homes, and all we hold dear are suspended on the issue of one battle, not one fourth

of the men of Texas are here. I look around and see that many I thought would be first on the field are not here.

Some of the men found Rusk's speech as rousing as Houston's. The Secretary, growing increasingly moved himself, cried out suddenly: "May I not survive if we don't win this battle!" At this point he seemed to realize that these angry, lice-ridden men needed no more prodding to stir them against the Santanistas. So Rusk broke off abruptly, saying: "I have done."

And the hoarse cries soared again:

"Remember the Alamo! Remember Goliad! Remember La Bahia!"

Those of the Latins who knew no English shouted:

"Recuerden el Alamo!"

Karnes and Deaf Smith and the other scouts crossed Buffalo Bayou first, swimming their horses across the three hundred yards of water, and the rest of the cavalry followed. Houston rode over on a crude raft made of heavy timbers with an old cabin door fastened over them; on the way, he ripped the seat of his pants on a hinge. Most of the infantry and the artillery crossed on an old ferryboat which had been repaired but still leaked badly, especially under the iron burden of the cannon.

Once they were all across, the main body of troops marched down the right bank of Buffalo Bayou until midnight of the nineteenth. They rested for a few hours, and then in the early morning walked on to Lynch's Ferry. They seized the ferry Nathaniel Lynch had used so profitably during The Runaway Scrape.

Across the San Jacinto the men saw some Anglo-Americans watching them from the hill above the town of Lynchburg. At first they thought these Texans were reinforcements, but after a short while the men on the hill turned away and walked out of sight. Later Houston's men learned that they were Santa Anna sympathizers waiting to guide the Mexican President to the United States border. The Tories had, when they first saw them, mistaken the Texans for Santanistas.

When Houston learned that the Santanistas had not yet reached Lynch's Ferry, he drew the army back into a grove of live oaks along Buffalo Bayou. From the woods they could watch the wagon road leading to the ferry. The Texans were scattered out for about five hundred yards among the Spanish-moss-hung trees of the grove. A short distance to the southeast of their position, there was a broad, pretty, rising plain called the field of San Jacinto.

—◆◆ ⑆ 6 ⑇ ◆◆—

Cavalry and Cannonballs

Some of them [the Texas rebels of 1836] were for independence, some were for the Mexican Constitution of 1824, and some were for anything, just so it was a row.

—PRIVATE NOAH SMITHWICK OF THE TEXAS ARMY

OF THE ARMY of Texans strung out among the trees near Buffalo Bayou, only 171 men were landowners in Texas. Since real estate in Texas was practically free, the obvious implication is that some 80 per cent of the men who participated in this most crucial phase of the Texas Revolution were newcomers to the state.

Only one company in Houston's army was composed entirely of native Texans. All these men had Latin names, and many of them spoke no English. They were commanded by a resolute, thirty-year-old captain named Juan Nepomuceno Seguin. Don Juan was the son of one of the wealthiest and most respected patriarchs in Texas, Erasmo Seguin, and he had been the political chief of San Antonio. While General Cos had occupied San Antonio, the Santanistas had made the mistake of mistreating Erasmo Seguin, and as a result this influential clan which might have remained neutral became staunch Revolutionists. Don Erasmo turned over to the colonists the resources of his big ranchos around San Antonio, and

101

he made huge contributions of food, horses, and mules to the rebels.

When San Antonio was stormed and taken from Cos in December, 1835, Juan Seguin had led a company of Latins. Seven of this original Seguin company died in the Alamo. Seguin himself escaped the fate of the others only because, late in the Alamo siege, Travis had insisted on sending the Latin Captain through the Santanista lines as a messenger.

Unlike De Zavala's impeccable son, Seguin was dressed for the San Jacinto campaign like most of the other men, in rags and greasy buckskins. However, the burly Captain rode a handsome stallion from his rancho, Casa Blanca, near Floresville, Texas.

At Buffalo Bayou, Seguin had about thirty men, all from the San Antonio area. One of them, Sgt. Antonio Menchaca, both wrote and spoke English as well as Spanish. Menchaca, who was 6 foot 2 and had a hearty bass voice, acted as interpreter for Seguin and the others of the company who neither spoke nor understood English.

During most of Houston's retreat Seguin's company had been a rear guard, and they had had several bloody brushes with Santa Anna's advance men. When the army left Harrisburg, Houston had asked the Seguin company to stay and guard the sick and the baggage. Possibly the commander in chief was afraid some of his Latins might be shot by mistake in a general engagement. But Don Juan and his men were insulted by this suggestion. Menchaca, interpreting for Seguin, protested to the General: "If we'd wanted to be camp guards we would have stayed with our old people and our women and children, who are out there now driving their sheep and cattle toward the United States border. We certainly did not join your army, General, to ride herd on sick folks. We men from Bexar have more grievances to settle with the Santanistas

General Santa Anna

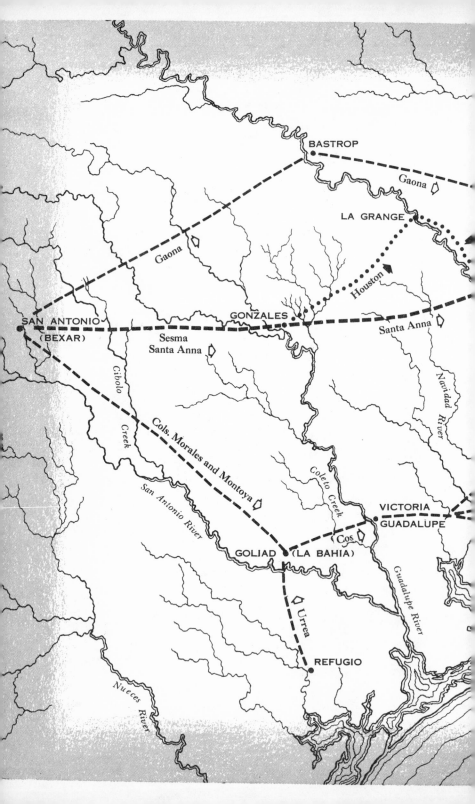

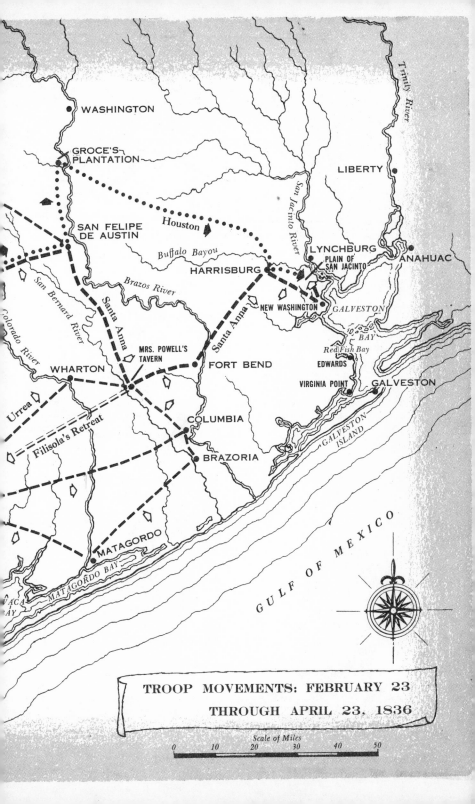

WASHINGTON

GROCE'S
PLANTATION

LIBERTY

SAN FELIPE
DE AUSTIN

Houston

Buffalo Bayou

San Jacinto River

LYNCHBURG

Trinity River

PLAIN OF
SAN JACINTO

HARRISBURG

ANAHUAC

Brazos River

Santa Anna

NEW WASHINGTON

GALVESTON

Santa Anna

San Bernard River

MRS. POWELL'S
TAVERN

FORT BEND

BAY

Red Fish Bay

EDWARDS

Colorado River

WHARTON

VIRGINIA POINT

GALVESTON

Urrea

COLUMBIA

*GALVESTON
ISLAND*

Filisola's Retreat

BRAZORIA

MATAGORDO

MATAGORDO BAY

GULF OF MEXICO

*ACA
AY*

TROOP MOVEMENTS: FEBRUARY 23
THROUGH APRIL 23, 1836

Scale of Miles

0   10   20   30   40   50

*The march to the Goliad massacre,
as painted by Sam Houston's son,
Andrew Jackson Houston*

Juan N. Almonte

General Cos

than anyone else. For we have suffered the most from them. We want to fight."

"Spoken like a man," said Houston. So Seguin's company was with the grimy, ill-clad men among the woods at Buffalo Bayou in the early hours of April 20.

Of the newcomers to the province and the army, even some of the most troublesome discharged duties of importance with enthusiasm, if not absolute loyalty to their commander. Sidney Sherman, for example, commanded not only the Second Regiment, but the sixty-one-man cavalry troop as well.

Among the most aggressive of his troopers was Pvt. Mirabeau Lamar, the young Georgian who had arrived at Groce's with an improbable plan for harassing Gaona. Whatever Lamar's other motives for joining the Texas Revolution, it is certain that grief had played a part in his decision to come to the embattled colony. At the time of the San Jacinto campaign, Mirabeau was still in mourning for a wife who had died at the age of twenty-one some years before. He had left Georgia to get away from reminders of his gentle Tabitha. He'd written a poem about her:

> When she died and left me here
> My soul in desolation—
> I broke the shell she loved so well
> Destroyed the songs I wrought her.

Mirabeau's favorite weapon was a long, curved saber, with which he was so adept that in Georgia his swordsmanship had won him some medals.

Sherman and his followers had had little patience with Houston's leadership throughout the campaign, and their loyalty to the General was always precarious. By contrast, the men in the scout company, commanded by Captain Karnes, were staunchly reliable. Karnes, "whose robust frame, red hair, and bold Scottish cast of features offered a good personification of Rob Roy," was a twenty-three-year-old Tennessee native who'd spent most of his life on the frontier. One story said that once, when he had been captured by the Comanches, the color of his hair had saved his life. The Indians thought his flaming locks were painted, so they had some of their women give him a rough shampoo to wash out the paint before they executed him. The hair stayed red under the water test, and Karnes remained scornfully defiant. The Comanches were so impressed with his bright hair and cool nerve that they turned him loose. One of Karnes's acquaintances described him as a man of the kind Napoleon liked to use as field marshals. His only disadvantage as an officer was a piping, almost effeminate voice said to have been caused by an injury to his throat muscles.

Karnes was on very cordial terms with Houston. Some weeks before, when El Colorado, as the Captain was called, had been out on a scout, the General had sent him a message in which he drily remarked: "The Army is in good spirits and the General is sober." The good-natured Captain wasn't in the least jealous that his outfit was often called "Deaf Smith's Spy Company." Smith was such a lone wolf that he could never have been pinned down to an officer's duties, and yet, as Karnes knew, old Deaf was the most valuable man in his company. There was only friendliness and understanding between the Captain and the private.

In a sense, those of Houston's soldiers who, like Lamar, had joined the Revolution to forget their grief over lost wives or sweethearts were well off. They, at least, had nothing but themselves to worry about while they were fighting. Many of the soldiers who had womenfolk to think about had good reason to be concerned. Deaf Smith, for example, like many other members of the spy company, had married a lady of Latin family, and Santa Anna had made it clear that Latins who sided with the rebels were traitors and could expect no mercy.

Guadalupe Ruiz Duran Smith was a descendant of Canary Island folk who'd come to San Antonio in the eighteenth century. To spare his beloved Guadalupe trouble, Deaf Smith had actually intended to remain neutral during the Revolution until, in December of 1835, he had tried to ride into San Antonio to see Guadalupe and the children, who were behind Cos's lines. The Cos sentries, mistaking him for a rebel, shot his sombrero off and chased him in the direction of the colonists' military camp outside the city.

Smith thereupon joined the rebels. He was one of three guides when the Texas volunteers took San Antonio and captured Cos. His services in this assault must have been remarkable, for when Cos got back to Mexico on parole he offered a $1,000 reward for Deaf's head.

On Wednesday, April 20, Smith knew that his wife and children were somewhere in The Runaway Scrape, but he didn't know exactly where they were or how they had fared. Actually, on that day poor Mrs. Smith was nearing the United States border after a terrible, month-long flight from San Antonio. Mrs. Rosa Kleberg, grand old lady of the clan that was to operate the great King Ranch, was among the fugitives, and she had seen Guadalupe Smith on the Brazos. She later wrote:

Deaf Smith's wife had a truck-wheel cart [a cart with two wooden wheels made from cross sections of a thick tree] and her two pairs of twins but no team to pull the cart. My brother, Albrecht [von Roeder], carried her with his team of oxen for a distance and then returned for us.

Several other people with teams showed Mrs. Smith the same consideration. And thus she managed to proceed on her journey.

Also lined up with the scout company that morning was Pvt. Horatio Alex Alsbury, a medical practitioner and lawyer, who, like Smith, was married to a Latin lady. Alsbury had more cause than anyone else to worry about his wife while he was with the army. Alex was one of the original settlers, called "The Old 300," of Stephen Austin's colony. His wife was a San Antonio girl of Corsican blood, the former Juana Navarro. She was a relative of Ursula de Veramendi, Jim Bowie's wife, who had died very young a few years before the Revolution. Juana was nursing the ailing Bowie when Santa Anna's army reached San Antonio, and she and her eight-year-old son by another marriage were in the Alamo during the siege.

Alex Alsbury knew that his wife and the boy hadn't been slain in the Alamo because Mrs. Dickenson, the Alamo veteran Almonte had used as a messenger, had told him at Gonzales that Juana, too, had survived. But unlike Suzanna Dickenson, Mrs. Alsbury wasn't permitted to leave San Antonio. Alex had had no news of his family since he'd talked with Mrs. Dickenson in Gonzales, and he knew Juana's position must be especially dangerous. She had been captured while taking care of one Revolutionist, she was married to another, and her brother, Antonio Navarro, was also a notorious rebel and had been one of the signers of the Texas Declaration of Independence.

Pvt. Hendrick Arnold, a close friend of Deaf Smith's and the only Negro in the spy company, was also married to a San Antonio girl, and on April 20 he had no idea of her fate.

Moses Lapham, a private in the infantry, was probably worrying about a married woman, Mrs. Tom Borden. Before the Revolution, Moses, a bachelor, had lived with various members of the Gail Borden clan while he worked as a frontier surveyor—a dangerous job in those days. He lived with Tom Borden more than with any of the others, and judging by his letters, he had fallen in love with Tom's cultured young wife, Demis. Apparently the stuttering Lapham never made advances to Demis, for he was able to remain on good terms with the lady's husband. Once when Lapham went home to Ohio on a visit, Tom Borden wrote to him suggesting that he get married before he returned to the Mexican subprovince: "The chance for a wife is pretty good in Texas now since the new crop [of emigrants] come in. But if you can get married as handy as not [in Ohio] do so."

Two of Tom's brothers, Lt. John Pettit Borden and Pvt. Paschal Pavolo Borden, were also in the Texan army, and they, like Tom, were Lapham's fast friends.

Among Houston's men were two companies of regular infantry. In the Texan army, regulars got more land for their services than reservists (eight hundred acres as against six hundred forty in some cases), but didn't have the right to elect their own company officers as the reservists did. A number of the regulars wore parts of United States Army uniforms disguised with buckskin accessories. They were garrison troops from Louisiana who'd been allowed to "desert" for a short, fighting vacation with the Texas rebels. The two regular companies were the most disciplined men in Houston's army of stubborn individualists.

The regular companies were commanded by an athletic, twenty-nine-year-old lieutenant colonel from Mississippi named

Henry Millard. Like Lamar, Millard had come to Texas out of sorrow. His aristocratic young wife, the former Mary Beaumont, had died not long before. Later, Millard was to name a Texas city in her honor. Another motive Millard had in common with other Revolutionists, including Lamar, was the hope of becoming a big real estate operator. During The Runaway Scrape he had sent messages to his land agent in Nacogdoches to buy the land of refugees fleeing from Santa Anna's army. Millard's military past was vague, but he handled his regulars in a firm and professional manner.

His second-in-command was Capt. John M. Allen, a tough idealist of a soldier of fortune who'd been a close friend of Lord Byron. Allen had been by Byron's side at Missolonghi, Greece, when, on April 12, 1823, the British poet had died.

The Texas army's band, three fifes and a drum, marched with the regulars. The musicians were Dick, a Negro from New Orleans who was destined to beat the big drum in Texas battles for years to come, and Fifers John Beebe, Luke Bust, and a mischievous, well-educated young German named Frederick Lemsky.

The proudest bunch in the Texas army was the newly formed artillery corps consisting of about thirty men under Col. James Neill. Because of a shortage of ammunition, these enthusiastic cannoneers had not fired so much as one practice shot since *The Twin Sisters* had arrived.

The real foundation of the army was Burleson's First Regiment, which included about two hundred men who'd walked all of the retreat from Gonzales. Ned Burleson called himself a "man of blood." As he explained: "I killed my first Indian at fourteen—he was about to slay my father. And I have been fighting ever since. Yet I've never shed blood for fame or for money or for revenge." It is easy to believe that the modest

Burleson never fought for fame or money, but the revenge part of his statement might be suspect, for few men in Houston's army were more bitter over the fate of the Texans in the Alamo and at Goliad than Burleson.

The quarrelsome Kentucky company was still in Burleson's regiment, commanded by a rugged officer named Capt. William Wood. This company had the only flag in the whole Texas army, a 6- by 3-foot silk banner made back in Kentucky by Mrs. Sidney Sherman and other Newport ladies. On the flag's field was the rather well-painted figure of a nearly nude Miss Liberty, a full-figured girl with a Grecian profile. Miss Liberty carried a sword in one hand, and from the sword flew a streamer bearing the inscription: "Liberty or Death." This flag was carried by James Austin Sylvester, a tall, twenty-nine-year-old printer who was the company's sergeant–color-bearer. On the top of the flagstaff, Sylvester had fixed a white dress glove given him, according to his own statement in an interview for the Galveston *News* years later, by a Newport girl before the Kentucky company left for Texas.

Another outfit in the First Regiment that had caused Houston some trouble was Moseley Baker's Company D. Though Baker had rejoined Houston's command after falling back from the Brazos crossing at San Felipe, the Captain was still dissatisfied with his General's conduct of the campaign. As Baker's third corporal and scribe, Isaac Hill, said of the company commander:

> Captain Baker knew very little about military matters and did not appreciate the importance of written orders —a great error considering his relationship with the commander-in-chief. During the whole campaign Baker denounced Houston in unmeasured terms because of the

general's Fabian policy. Baker thought Houston deserved
impeachment.

Despite Baker's reluctance to serve under Houston, Company
D was with the rest of the First Division at Buffalo Bayou on
the twentieth.

Even if he didn't always appreciate the written word himself, Baker had one of the most literate groups in the army.
Moses Lapham's friends, John and Paschal Borden, were in
Company D, John as a first lieutenant and Paschal as a private. Third Sergeant Moses Austin Bryan, also one of Baker's
men, was a good-looking, eighteen-year-old nephew of Stephen
F. Austin. Moses had traveled in Mexico with his famous
uncle and spoke excellent Spanish. On April 20 he was thin
and weak, for he, like many of the other men, was convalescing
from measles. Robert Kleberg, the husband of the Rosa Kleberg who saw Mrs. Deaf Smith in The Runaway Scrape, was
another of Baker's well-schooled soldiers. Kleberg held a
doctor of laws degree from a German university.

Company D could even boast a newspaper editor, a really
rare phenomenon in the Texas of 1836. He was 1st Sgt. Joseph
(Don Jose) Baker. Don Jose was not related to his company
commander; he was from Maine, while Moseley Baker was a
native of Virginia. Don Jose, in collaboration with Gail Borden, Jr., put out the Republic's only newspaper during the
war. In a desperate effort to keep the paper alive despite the
Revolution, Baker had some weeks earlier taken a furlough
from the army just long enough to help rescue the presses
from San Felipe before the Mexicans reached that town. The
presses were removed by wagon to Harrisburg, where the last
issue of the paper appeared on April 14, the day before Santa
Anna captured its three printers and destroyed the presses. In
that April 14 issue were an account of the fall of the Alamo

and, ironically, an editorial that began: "We promise the public of our beloved country that our press will never cease its operations until our silence shall announce to them that there is no more in Texas a resting place for a free press."

Perhaps the toughest soldiers in the First Regiment were the frontiersmen who made up Capt. Jesse Billingsley's company. Billingsley claimed that once while he was commanding eighty rangers, he'd kept them out on a scout for months and had fed and clothed them by killing wild beasts, charging the government only for coffee and salt.

One member of the Billingsley company was Pvt. James Curtis, universally known as Uncle Jimmy. He was said to be sixty-four years old, and he was certainly the oldest man in the army. He was also one of the noisiest. Curtis had his own battle cry: "Remember Wash Cottle! I'm going to skin them Meskins for Wash!" Washington Cottle, Curtis's son-in-law, had been one of the martyrs of the Alamo. While Cottle had lived, he had often had trouble with his father-in-law, for both had strong and belligerent personalities. But Curtis had had a sneaking affection for his burly son-in-law.

Uncle Jimmy, who could march as briskly as a boy, carried three bottle-gourds. One contained water, the second whiskey, and the third a mysterious liquid which the senior Texas private identified as "my rheumatism medicine." One ingredient in this concoction, he said, was boiled red ants.

Once during the retreat, Curtis had been one of a group of scouts who were watching for Gaona's division on the Colorado. One morning, while Uncle Jimmy was upstream alone guarding a ford, about six hundred Mexicans appeared with bugles blaring. As the Texas scouts started to pull out, gunsmith Noah Smithwick, who was a close friend of Curtis's, went to fetch the older man. During most of the campaign

Smithwick and Curtis were footsoldiers, but for this scouting mission they had been mounted. As Smithwick later described the incident:

> I galloped back and found Uncle Jimmy leaning against a tree with a bottle of whiskey beside him, as happy and unconscious of danger as a turtle on a log. "Mount and ride for your life!" I cried. "The Mexicans are on the other side of the river and our men are gone." The old man said: "The hell they are! Light and take a drink." I replied: "This is no time for drinking, Uncle Jimmy. The Mexicans may swim the river and be after us any moment." Curtis persisted: "Then let's drink to their confusion." Thinking it the quickest way to start him, I got off and took a drink and then we struck out.

There was one thing, and perhaps only one, that all the men with Houston on April 20 had in common. They were all tired of retreats and safe camps among the bogs. Whatever their attitudes toward their commander in chief, or their motives for joining the Texas Revolution, or their personal worries at the time, they were all ready and eager to fight the Santanistas. Not long after they took up their position in the woods near Peggy McCormick's ranch, they were to have their chance.

Wednesday, April 20, a chill, partly cloudy day, was one of great activity for the cannoneers and the cavalrymen. Early in the morning, Colonel Sherman of the Second Regiment was sent out at the head of forty horsemen to scout around New Washington. Near the headquarters of the James Routh plantation and about two miles from New Washington, they encountered Marcos Barragan and the other mounted Santanista scouts. When Barragan turned and rode to warn Santa Anna, the Mexican Captain thought he'd stumbled on the whole

Texas army. As Barragan's men fled, four of the stragglers were slain by Sherman's scouts.

Somewhere near New Washington Sherman's men broke off the pursuit of the Mexican dragoons and instead reined into a woods from which they could observe the Santa Anna force. They watched the Santanistas leave New Washington. According to the account of Dr. Nicholas Labadie, a surgeon with the Second Regiment, it was about 1 P.M. on the twentieth when Sherman's scouting patrol came riding into the Texas camp in the San Jacinto live oak grove:

> Sherman informed General Houston that the enemy was close by. Directly afterwards, the Mexican cavalry was observed in motion, passing through the prairie about a mile away and then, when striking our trail, advanced toward us in fine order and with trumpets sounding.

Only the two rebel cannon and about thirty artillerymen were in view. The cannoneers were about ten paces out on the prairie in front of the moss-hung trees. Behind them at the edge of the timber were the two elite companies of regular infantry. The cavalry was in the woods behind the regulars. Sherman's regiment protected the left side of the camp, and Burleson's riflemen were on the right wing.

When Santa Anna studied the woods by Buffalo Bayou, he saw only a few men and two small cannon. The sight of such a puny force, together with a fresh dose of opium, made the President eager for battle. Delgado believes that Santa Anna was trying to bring on a general engagement when he ordered a company of skirmishers out to a cluster of trees halfway between the two armies and had them fire on the rebels. While this order was executed, Santa Anna had his musicians play the sweetly sinister *Deguello* or "beheading song," the signal of no quarter which he'd played during the Alamo siege.

"The music of the Mexican trumpeters became louder and more piercing as it came closer," said Dr. Labadie. "Houston showed himself restless and uneasy, casting his eyes to our cannon out there in the open and then to the advancing enemy."

Under the protection of cavalry, Santa Anna advanced his 12-pounder about fifty yards and fired one shot. It cut through the trees over the Texas camp and lobbed into the bayou.

The Twin Sisters, which the rebels had never fired before, answered with a blast of broken horseshoes. The shots landed a little to the right of the Mexicans' advance position.

For the first time in the campaign, Colonel Delgado was in charge of the cannon. The whimsical Santa Anna had given his aide this job only that morning at the start of the march from New Washington. Delgado had been flattered and pleased at first, but he wasn't so happy about it when Santa Anna ordered him to wheel *The Golden Standard* out to the island of timber between the armies, to join the Mexican skirmishers who had been firing with no effect at the Texans' position. These skirmishers, militiamen from Toluca, were Delgado's only guards.

Delgado was even more nervous when the President, wearing his medal-laden uniform and Napoleon-style hat and mounted on a big bay, rode out and joined Delgado's group. The President certainly made a splendid target, and the fact that the Texas riflemen failed to pick him off is surprising. Castrillon came out at a gallop and protested: "Your Excellency, this is a good way to lose a war that we've already won." Santa Anna ignored the Major General. He ordered Delgado to fire on the Texas artillery.

The Santanista cannoneers did themselves proud. Their first shot fell directly into the Texas position and hit the artillery commander, Lieutenant Colonel Neill, on the rump. Houston was sitting on his horse near the Texan artillery when a bullet fired by one of the Toluca company marksmen clipped one of his bridle reins, but it struck neither man nor horse.

The Twin Sisters roared back with even better effect at the three-hundred-yard range. Near Santa Anna, a young Mexican captain named Fernando Urriza, who was about to mount his horse, was shot, like Colonel Neill, in the rump. Santa Anna remained cool, but he gave Delgado an order which confirmed the young Lieutenant Colonel's opinion that the President was crazy. Said Delgado:

> His Excellency told me to unload the powder and ammunition for the cannon right there in the island of timber and to turn over our twenty mules, on which the ordnance stores were packed, to Captain Barragan, who was instructed to bring in the knapsacks that had been dropped on the road from New Washington.

Then in fair view of the Texans in the woods, The Napoleon of the West rode back to his main column. "The enthusiam of my troops was high," said Santa Anna later. He also said that, as Delgado thought, he had tried his best to draw the rebels into a general engagement on the twentieth:

> Although our fire was returned I could not get the land thieves out of the woods. I retired about 1,000 varas and camped on a hill that gave me an advantageous position with water on the rear, heavy woods to my right as far as the banks of the San Jacinto, open plains to the left and a clear front.

Delgado stayed in the island of timber and, at long intervals, fired into the Texas position. Occasionally *The Twin*

Sisters answered his fire, but nothing further happened until one of Santa Anna's aides, Col. Juan Bringas, rode out to the artillery position. Bringas was the officer who had taken Old Whip from Jimmy Brown, and he was riding the big black stud on the afternoon of the twentieth. Bringas said that Santa Anna had ordered the company of Toluca sharpshooters to return to camp immediately. Delgado and the artillery were to follow as soon as they could gather up the ammunition for the cannon.

Although Santa Anna had ordered Delgado to give his twenty mules to Barragan, the aide had prudently given Barragan only fourteen of the animals. The other six he kept with the cannon. Delgado protested to Bringas that it would take a lot of trips for his six mules to carry back ordnance supplies that were usually carried by twenty animals.

"If Toluca leaves us, the enemy may pounce on our fieldpiece and ammunition," said Delgado.

"Do the best you can," said Bringas. "I gave you His Excellency's orders and I'm not going to argue with him in his present raving state of mind." Apparently, while the Santanistas set up a camp on the upper part of the field of San Jacinto, their leader was behaving irrationally.

"Bringas went back to camp followed by the Company of Toluca," said Delgado. "As soon as the enemy saw our artillery and stores unprotected the Texas cannon paid us special attention." One Texan cannon shot hit the 12-pounder's limber (the detachable fore part of the gun carriage), and another scattered ordnance boxes and killed two pack mules. Then the firing ceased for a little while. Delgado's men worked frantically, loading the remaining mules and sending them back with ammunition. The little beasts had to make several trips to and from the island of timber to carry back the forty heavy cases of ordnance supplies.

Texans in the treetops reported this activity of the Mexican artillerists. Sidney Sherman claimed that late in the afternoon he went to Houston and asked permission to take the cavalry and try to capture the Mexican cannon. Houston maintained that, on the contrary, he had told Sherman to reconnoiter with the cavalry but not to provoke a general action. In any case, Sherman, followed by sixty-one mounted men including Secretary of War Rusk, sallied out of the woods, too late to get the 12-pounder. Delgado's men were just dragging *The Golden Standard* over the brow of the hill just in front of the Mexican camp.

At this stage, Santa Anna was very much the cool, efficient commander. He sent fifty dragoons under Captain Miguel Aguirre out to the island of timber where the cannon had been. While the Mexicans, who got to the thicket before Sherman's party, sat calmly in their saddles, Captain Aguirre called out: *"Soldados God Dammes, vere usted."* ("God Damn Soldiers, come here.") The Texans took this invitation literally. Santa Anna described the skirmish like this:

> Daringly the rebels threw themselves on my cavalry. For a moment they succeeded in throwing us into confusion, seriously wounding one of our dragoons. I ordered two companies of riflemen to attack them and these were sufficient to rout the Texans.

As Dr. Labadie, watching from the Texas camp, saw it:

> Sherman drove the cavalry back under the guns of their main force. Then the Texans, being mostly mounted riflemen, had to dismount and unload. The enemy, perceiving their condition, at least half of the Texans on the ground, rushed down on Sherman's men, forcing them to defend themselves as best they could. They reloaded, got back in the saddle and forced the Mexicans back a second time.

Tom Rusk, in the front of this second cavalry charge, was hemmed in by several Mexican dragoons and might have been killed or captured if Pvt. Mirabeau Lamar hadn't come to his rescue. Lamar, with his big stallion, charged a Mexican horseman, knocking over the horse and thereby blocking out an opening through which both he and the Secretary of War escaped.

As the Texas cavalry retreated to the woods, Lamar saved another comrade's life. Walter Lane, a nineteen-year-old boy born in Ireland and raised in Baltimore, had been brushed off his horse when a Mexican lance touched him on the shoulder. His wound was slight, but he was on the ground and unable to defend himself when another Mexican lancer rushed to attack him. Lamar rode up in time to shoot the Mexican lancer with his pistol. Lane jumped behind another Texas cavalryman on a rawboned sorrel mare and made it back to the Texas camp. This boy, who owed his life to Lamar's daring intervention, later became a Confederate general. The dragoon Lamar shot to save Lane was the one Santa Anna referred to as seriously wounded. It was said that the Mexican cavalrymen paused to applaud Lamar's brave feats, and that Mirabeau reined in his horse and acknowledged this tribute with a bow.

While Santa Anna watched this fight, he had his orderly bugler sounding the *Deguello*. Had Houston brought his main force out of the woods there would most certainly have been a pitched battle there on the evening of April 20. According to Sherman, during the cavalry skirmish he sent his second-in-command on the sortie, Maj. Lysander Wells, back to Houston to ask for infantry support, and the General refused to send footsoldiers. Walter Lane said that Houston did send out two companies of infantry to help the cavalry get out of "that hornet's nest." Houston said that Sherman "tried to bring on a general action in violation of my orders. Confusion was the

Sam Houston,
from a painting by S. Seymour Thomas

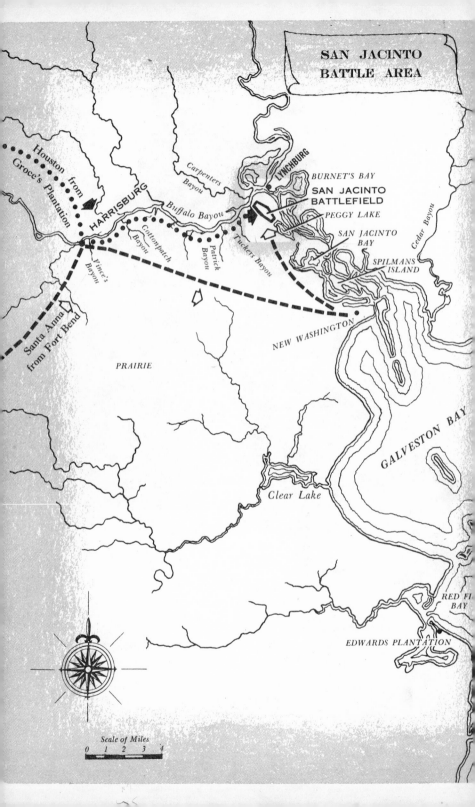

SAN JACINTO
BATTLE AREA

Houston from
Groce's Plantation

HARRISBURG

Carpenters
Bayou

LYNCHBURG

BURNET'S BAY

SAN JACINTO
BATTLEFIELD

Buffalo Bayou

PEGGY LAKE

Cottonpatch
Bayou

Vince's
Bayou

Patrick
Bayou

Truckers Bayou

SAN JACINTO
BAY

Cedar Bayou

SPILMANS
ISLAND

Santa Anna
from Fort Bend

NEW WASHINGTON

PRAIRIE

GALVESTON BAY

Clear Lake

RED FI
BAY

EDWARDS PLANTATION

Scale of Miles

0   1   2   3   4

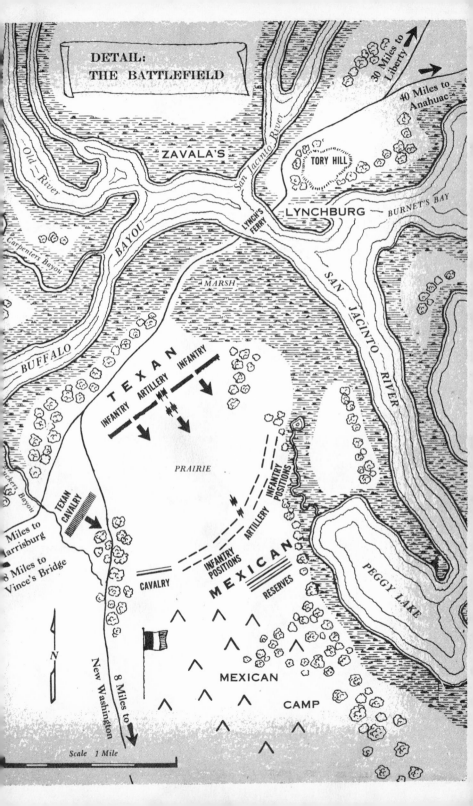

DETAIL:
THE BATTLEFIELD

30 Miles to Liberty

40 Miles to Anahuac

Old River

ZAVALA'S

San Jacinto River

TORY HILL

LYNCHBURG

BURNET'S BAY

Lynch's Ferry

Carpenters Bayou

BAYOU

MARSH

BUFFALO

SAN JACINTO RIVER

T E X A N

INFANTRY   ARTILLERY   INFANTRY

PRAIRIE

INFANTRY POSITIONS

ARTILLERY

TEXAN CAVALRY

INFANTRY POSITIONS

ARTILLERY

M E X I C A N

Miles to Harrisburg

CAVALRY

RESERVES

Miles to Vince's Bridge

cker's Bayou

PEGGY LAKE

N

MEXICAN   CAMP

New Washington

8 Miles to

Scale 1 Mile

Deaf Smith

Mirabeau Lamar

Sidney Sherman

Stephen F. Austin

result of it. Two men were wounded. A confused retreat took place."

One of the wounded was Owlyn J. Trask, a young United States Regular Army officer who had taken a furlough to serve as a private for Texas. Houston's corps of physicians, some of them medical college graduates and some of them quacks, argued learnedly over the proper treatment for Trask's hip wound, some, in the course of the discussion, poking dirty fingers into the wound. Perhaps Trask's subsequent death was the result of this excessive medical solicitude.

When Sherman returned from the cavalry skirmish, Houston had heated words with the Colonel, but Sherman, by the night of the twentieth, had become the hero of the camp. Not only had he led his men in two brushes with the enemy during the day, but at about 10 A.M. a group under his command captured a flatboat full of supplies that Santa Anna had dispatched the day before from New Washington for the use of his army.

"A sail was seen coming up the bayou," said Dr. Labadie. When the Texans saw that it was a large flatboat, a group of men led by Sherman hid themselves on the bank. They hailed the boat as it neared the shore, and at that, the Mexican boatmen jumped over the side. Amazingly, all the Mexicans seem to have made it to the opposite shore of the broad bayou even though shots were fired after them.

Labadie's narrative says:

One man lay flat in the boat. Finally, he put his head up and exclaimed in English: "Don't shoot! Don't shoot! I'm an American." He was told to show himself, when it was discovered that he was one of Gail Borden's printers who'd been captured by Santa Anna at Harrisburg.

When the boat was brought in to shore the Texans were delighted to find that its supplies included flour and coffee. That night for the first time in three days the army had bread and coffee to go with the usual boiled beef.

While the Texans cooked their bread on sticks, they discussed Sherman's daring cavalry actions of the day. Those who opposed Houston all agreed that Sherman was the man to succeed their cautious General. Later, Houston's severe critic Moseley Baker described the mood of the Texan camp on the night of April 20 as

> one of uproar and confusion. Colonel Sherman had demonstrated that the men before whom we had so long retreated were the same pusilanimous foe that we had ever whipped [in 1835]. . . . Various members of the army were seen publicly and fearlessly going from company to company, soliciting volunteers to fight the enemy without your [Houston's] consent.

The General remained aloof from all this. As was his custom, he beat tattoo on a big drum and then, after the men were in their blankets, he sat up for several hours.

Over across the savanna on the night of April 20, Santa Anna was in one of his efficient moods. His men slept on their arms in battle formation, and a good watch was kept.

7

A Bridge Is Burned

*When a man meets two Mexicans [couriers] and is
not allowed to kill either of them, by the time he
takes one and ties him, the other gets off so far it
tires out a horse to catch him. I wish you would let
me manage things in my own way, Boss.*

—PRIVATE DEAF SMITH SPEAKING TO GENERAL HOUSTON

ON APRIL 21, 1836, near the broad, muddy Trinity
River about twenty-five miles northeast of San Jacinto, Dr. Pleasant Rose and his family were grieving over the death of a child.

"Measles, sore eyes, whooping cough and every other
disease that man, woman or child is heir to had broken out
among us," said Miss Dilue Rose. She does not say what her
baby sister died of. The whole train of fugitives stopped for
the baby's funeral by the Trinity, and the mourners included
fierce-looking but well-behaved slaves fresh from Africa.

On the same day, the elderly but lively Cherokee chief,
The Bowl, at his camp in a tall pine woods about a hundred
miles north of San Jacinto, put on the cocked military hat that
his friend Andrew Jackson had given him and greeted two
courtly officers from Filisola's division. Like many other partic-
ipants in the 1836 war, Vicente Filisola hoped to become

121

a big Texas real estate man. He had a contract with the Mexican government to settle thousands of acres of East Texas land, some of which the Cherokees, with the permission of the City of Mexico but without secure land titles, were then occupying. The previous February when Houston had called on the Cherokees to invite their cooperation with the Texans, he had taken not only gifts of knives and tomahawks but also the much more important gift of his promise that the Texas government would confirm the Indians' ownership of their lands.

Filisola's two emissaries suggested politely but firmly to the Cherokee chief that, since the Mexican armies would soon be swarming all over East Texas, he'd better get his warriors on the winning side. "The Mexican eagle is even now closing in on Houston's scarecrows," said one of the officers. The Bowl, equally polite and firm, said the Cherokees would remain neutral.

A day or so before the Cherokee leader had received a letter which began:

MY FRIEND, COL. BOWL: I am busy and will only say *How Da Do* to you. You will get your lands as it was promised in our treaty. You may rest satisfied that I will always hold you by the hand and look to you as a brother and treat you as such. You may give my best compliments to my sister [Mary Bowles, The Bowl's attractive granddaughter] and tell her I have not wore out the mockassins she made me; and I hope to see you and her and all my relations before they are wore out.

The letter was signed by Sam Houston.

Also on April 21, Jose Urrea, the valorous Mexican Brigadier who had defeated Fannin, entered the town of Columbia on the Brazos, about fifty miles from San Jacinto. Not only was there no opposition, but the Santanistas got a kind of chamber of commerce reception.

Early in the Texas campaign Urrea had captured an American who styled himself "Dr. Harrison" and claimed to be a son of the Gen. William Henry Harrison who was to become the ninth President of the United States. This young American told Urrea: "If you will turn me loose I'll ride ahead of your division and tell the colonists that you'll not harm them if they lay down their arms."

Urrea had none of Santa Anna's ruthlessness. Although Fannin's helpless men had been executed on the President's orders and in violation of Urrea's own explicit command, the slaughter may have haunted him. Possibly it was a troubled conscience that prompted him to accept the American's proposal and send him eastward on a good horse. Harrison must have been quite persuasive, for in most towns along the Gulf delegations of colonists greeted Urrea and declared that they were not sympathetic with the rebels. While Santa Anna's main column marching through the heart of settled Texas usually came into burned-out settlements, Urrea said that in his drive along the coast he found "goods, food supplies and liquors in abundance."

Urrea said that when he reached the Brazos on the twenty-first

many English, American and German colonists awaited me with their families as the result of the commission I had given Dr. Harrison to allay their fears. . . . Men were not lacking, of those who had served under him, who now offered to lead me to that formidable Houston. They desired his defeat because the greater part of the men under his command were adventurers who were worse enemies of the colonists than ourselves. . . . I was assured that Houston did not have more than seven or eight hundred men.

According to Urrea, one group of the Columbia colonists went so far as to promise that they would help him capture Galveston Island, asking only that he spare the thousand or so refugees there.

For Houston's army, April 21—the day of San Jacinto— began at 4:00 A.M. when Dick, the big Negro freedman, beat reveille. To the disgust of many of his eager men, Houston himself, lying on his saddle blanket with his head on a coil of rope and getting his first unbroken sleep in over a week, slept on despite the drum rolls. At four, a 38-degree blue norther was sweeping off the water over the plain of San Jacinto, but by big sunup the skies were clearing and the north wind died.

In the early morning, reinforcements arrived at the Texas camp: nine young recruits from the United States. They'd sailed and rowed from Galveston in an eight-oar cutter. The nine men knew that a Mexican army was in the neighborhood, but they didn't know what waited for them as they came to a landing on "the San Jacinto peninsula in a spacious wood where giant live oaks, pecans and magnolias crowded to the water's edge."

As one of the recruits later wrote of their arrival:

Here to our inexpressible joy we found the Texian force under Gen'l. S. Houston encamped in the timber near Lynch's ferry over the San Jacinto River. A scene singularly wild and picturesque presented itself to our view. Around 20 or 30 campfires stood as many groups of men: English, Irish, Scots, Mexicans, French, Germans, Italians, Poles, Yankees, all unwashed and unshaved, their long hair and beards and mustaches matted, their clothes in tatters and plastered with mud. A more savage looking band could scarcely have been assembled. Yet many were gentlemen, owners of large estates. Some were distinguished for oratory, some in science, some in medicine. Many had graced famous drawing rooms. Their guns were of every size and shape. They numbered less than 800.

Beyond the sheltering timber, the new men saw

a pretty prairie with islands of big trees in it, and here and there a gentle eminence. About a mile across the rising ground of the prairie and in another dense and moss-bearded wood along the San Jacinto was the camp of the President of Mexico, Gen'l. Santanna.

In the Mexican camp, too, the day had begun early. Unlike the weary Texan General, Santa Anna was up before sunup, watching his enemy's position through a spyglass. Smoke rose from the woods by Buffalo Bayou, and a few rebels were out on the edge of the timber in the prairie grazing horses.

Santa Anna was well satisfied with his position as he sat his horse on high ground and looked down toward the Texas camp by the bayou. As he later said: "I could choose the location for battle. I had the enemy shut up in the low, marshy angle of the country where retreat was cut off by Buffalo Bayou and by the San Jacinto River. Everything was favorable for our army and the cause we were defending." After making these observations, Santa Anna fussed around his camp, supervising the building of breastworks and cursing his officers.

Neither Castrillon nor Delgado agreed with the President that the camp was a good one. Delgado said that on the same day he and Castrillon stood outside of Santa Anna's tent and engaged in the following dialogue.

Delgado remarked: "This camping ground of His Excellency's is, in all respects, against military rules. Any youngster could have picked a better one. We have the enemy on our right, within a wood, at long musket range. Our front, although level, is exposed to the fire of the enemy, who could keep it up with impunity from his sheltered position. Retreat is easy for him on his right while our troops have no space for maneuvering."

"What can I do, my friend?" replied General Castrillon. "I know it well that we are in a dangerous position, but I can not help it. You know that nothing avails here against the caprice, arbitrary will and ignorance of THAT MAN!"

Delgado said that Castrillon cried this "in an impassioned voice and in close proximity to His Excellency's tent." It seems safe to assume that the President didn't hear this dialogue.

Early on the twenty-first, the Mexican army, like the Texan, was joined by reinforcements, but there was some contrast between the strength of the two new forces. As Delgado later wrote:

> At 9 o'clock on the 21st General Cos came in with a reinforcement of about five hundred men. His arrival was greeted with a roll of drums and with joyful shouts. As it was represented to His Excellency that these men had not slept the night before he instructed them to stack their arms, remove their accoutrements and to go to sleep quietly in an adjoining grove.

The approach of Santa Anna's brother-in-law with most of his command was observed by Texan scouts around 8 A.M. One of Karnes's men, probably Deaf Smith, awakened Houston and whispered to the general that the Mexicans were getting what looked like around five hundred reinforcements from the direction of Vince's Bridge. When he arose from his saddle-blanket and rope-coil couch, Houston is said to have exclaimed: "The sun of Austerlitz has risen!" Another story is that he looked at the warm sun, tested the light breeze, and declared: "This is going to be a damned good day to fight a battle." Fair weather was important to Houston, for the old, muzzle-loading rifles with flintlocks carried by most of his men were very unreliable weapons in rain and wind, and so were *The Twin Sisters,* which had to be ignited by flares.

The arrival of the Cos column couldn't have been a complete surprise to Houston, for Cos's men were actually joining Santa Anna in belated response to *El Presidente's* message to Filisola, dispatched about a week earlier, requesting reinforcements. Since Houston had seen Filisola's acknowledgment of this request on April 18, when Deaf Smith had captured Filisola's courier, Bachiller, the Texan General must have been aware that Cos was on the way. Even so he was not indifferent, and by nine o'clock, when the point of the Cos column arrived at the Santanista camp, Houston was out on the prairie about fifty yards from the edge of the timber. The condition of the ground had forced Cos's men to move slowly, as had Santa Anna's own troops, and even after the bulk of his force was established at San Jacinto, his rear guard, commanded by a Col. Mariano Garcia, lagged far behind.

Except for observers out on the prairie or in tree tops, few of the Texans could see Cos's column. Private George Erath of Billingsley's company said that "an effort was made to keep knowledge from us [the rank and file of the army] that Cos' division had arrived for fear it might intimidate us. But we knew very well of the reinforcement. It had the effect of making us calm and determined and of reinstating order."

Colonel Alexander Horton, an aide who was with Houston out on the prairie, later said: "After he saw Cos' troops coming up, General Houston said, at once, that he was going to have Vince's Bridge destroyed and that we would fight that afternoon before Santa Anna got any more reinforcements."

As Castrillon had proved when he took the Mexicans' cannon around the head of Vince's Bayou, the trip was not impossible. But it took several hours and not only Santa Anna's army, but also Houston's own men and the Mexican reinforcements had taken instead the direct wagon road and had crossed the bridge near Allen Vince's ranch, about eight or nine miles southwest of Lynch's Ferry. For Houston's men to destroy Vince's bridge would effectively hamper any more reinforcements heading for Santa Anna's camp.

Just behind Houston and Horton was Captain Karnes's scouting company, mounted and drawn up in a line at the edge of the timber. As Perry Alsbury, whose brother's wife had nursed Jim Bowie in the Alamo, described the scene:

> On the morning of The Day of San Jacinto, the spy company was assembled on the edge of General Houston's position. We were between 30 and 40 horsemen. The Mexican cavalry, whom we had fought the evening before, was drawn up that morning in a line on the south of our position, about 600 yards distance. They seemed to invite us again to combat. Prudence, in my humble opinion, dictated to our leaders a different course than to engage them at that moment.

Captain Karnes and Deaf Smith rode out on the prairie and joined the general. There is some controversy as to whether the plan to destroy the bridge really originated with Houston. A company commander named William Jones Elliot

Heard claimed that after the Cos reinforcement had passed, he heard Deaf Smith say to Houston: "General, they're following in our tracks. Let me go cut down Vince's Bridge so they can't get any more help that way from the other Mexican armies."

Perry Alsbury's impression was that the idea was Houston's, and that the General asked if Smith could destroy the bridge "without being cut to pieces by the Mexican cavalry?" In the light of Houston's fondness for the tough, loyal Smith, Alsbury's description of this conversation sounds thoroughly plausible.

But there is one other story on the subject that also sounds plausible, and that is that Moses Lapham, the young man who admired Tom Borden's wife, originated the plan. From the time he joined the army, Lapham, a puritanical young man and a former schoolteacher, had been a footsoldier. But on the day of San Jacinto, he suddenly became a mounted scout. It is certain that Lapham would have preferred the comparatively elite spy company to his place in the infantry, for judging by his frequent letters to his papa back in Ohio, Moses wasn't happy in the company of rough Texas frontiersmen. He once said: "Although I make myself as much at ease as possible in this society I am compelled to associate with, yet their principles and morals are most disgusting."

Lapham thought that most of the Texas leaders, Stephen F. Austin and Houston included, "were great scoundrels." And he once accused Padre Muldoon, the chaplain of Austin's colony, of fornicating "with blackamoors." In support of Lapham's later claim that he suggested destroying Vince's Bridge is the fact that his abrupt transfer to the scout company took place on the very morning that the bridge was destroyed, and that, since the army had lost several horses in the cavalry action the day before, they must have been suffering a more serious shortage of horses than of men able and eager to ride them.

In his official report of the battle of San Jacinto, Houston said that he ordered Smith "to destroy the only bridge on the road to the Brazos, distance eight miles [from the Texas camp]." If Lapham, Smith, or anyone else suggested such a move to the General, his report makes no mention of that fact. Old Deaf, a man of very few words, never commented about it at all.

Once it was decided that Smith, with six volunteers from the Karnes company, would undertake to destroy Vince's Bridge, Houston gave his favorite spy another small chore to perform before he left. Deaf was asked to ride out toward the San Jacinto River to a rise between Houston's camp and Santa Anna's. He was to climb the rise far enough so he could see the tops of the Mexican tents. The idea was that if Smith could count the tent tops, he would be able to estimate Santa Anna's troop strength.

Deaf picked Walter Lane, the young cavalryman whose life Lamar had saved the day before, for a helper on this little expedition. At about 10 A.M. the two men rode out about two hundred fifty yards from the Texas camp and dismounted on the rise, which gave them a fair view of at least part of the Mexican camp. Lane later reported that he held the horses while Smith studied the Mexican position through a spyglass.

When Mexican infantry appeared from the timber about three hundred yards away and began firing, Lane said: "The balls whistled over our heads—greatly to my demoralization, but Smith did not appear to notice and went on counting tent tops through the spyglass." Presently, though, some Mexican horsemen came from under the trees at a lope, and Smith said to Lane: "Let's git!" Lane wrote later: "I never obeyed an order more cheerfully in my life. We'd been out there for about 20 minutes under fire and I expected to be murdered at each round. We got to camp and Deaf reported to General Houston." Smith said he estimated the enemy numbers at "upwards of 1,500 men," which wasn't too far from Santa Anna's true strength.

Whoever had originated the idea to destroy Vince's Bridge, it is possible that the plan had existed before April 21, for when Smith had finished counting tent tops, Houston told him to pick up two axes Commissary General John Forbes had left under an oak near the bayou, perhaps for just this purpose. Smith was then to head for the bridge. The general also told Deaf: "Be speedy on your return for there are scenes to be enacted here."

Smith rode back to the spy company and got his six volunteers. Perry Alsbury said that he was one of the six, and the others were Moses Lapham, Denmore Rives (or Reaves), John Coker, E. R. Rainwater, and John Garner. The last two men had been in infantry companies up to that day.

Smith and his six volunteers got a good break just before they set out for Vince's Bridge, for after the Mexican cavalry had investigated Smith and Lane out on the prairie, Santa Anna had told them to take time out to eat and to feed and water their horses. According to Santa Anna, Miguel Aguirre, the commanding officer of the dragoons, was told "to again take up his position watching the Texans as soon as the men and horses were through eating."

Perry Alsbury described the seven Texans' trip to the bridge:

We moved rapidly some eight miles on the road leading to the Brazos until, reaching the mouth of the lane on the

north side of which was situated the double log house
belonging to Mr. William Vince, we filed off to the left
so as to avoid ambuscade should the enemy be concealed
in the dwelling. We threw down a fence where it joined
Vince's Bayou. One hundred and fifty yards from the
fence we came to Vince's Bridge, over which Deaf Smith
and myself passed with a view of reconnoitering. We left
the remainder of the party to "strike fire" and make
preparations for burning the bridge on our return.

Alsbury does not say whether the axes Smith had been told
to pick up on the way were ever used.

Apparently, the Texans believed that Santa Anna was still
traveling through Texas in his coach, for Alsbury said that
when they saw what they thought were carriage tracks in the
road, Smith thought that Santa Anna had just passed on his
way back to the Brazos. Alsbury suggested that they gallop
on two more miles to Sims Bayou where the Brazos road went
through a rather difficult ford, and there they might intercept
Santa Anna or whoever was leaving the tracks in the sand.

"No," replied Smith, "my orders from General Houston are
to burn the bridge and get back as quick as possible." By the
time Smith and Alsbury got back to the bridge, their comrades were ready with "fire and plenty of dry rails. And in a
few minutes the bridge was in flames."

On the way back, Perry Alsbury said, nothing happened until "we reached the first deep, dry hollow, a half or three-
quarters of a mile from our camp." Here Smith told the volunteers to rest: "I'll ride up to high ground and see whether any
of the Mexican horsemen are near." When Smith got up on the
rise he dropped his head down around his horse's mane and
hurried back. He shouted to his comrades: "The prairie is full

of Mexican horses! What will we do now?" The men answered that they'd follow wherever Smith led.

"Get your guns ready," said Smith. "Follow me Indian file to where this hollow joins Buffalo Bayou. Then turn right and run for the level above. If the Mexicans see us, raise the Texan yell and run through them. General Houston's orders are for us to get back to camp, dead or alive."

Alsbury's account goes on:

When fairly on the level, which commanded a partial view of both armies, we saw no Mexican cavalry. We knew from Deaf's hearty laughter that he'd just been putting our fidelity to a test.

Smith told his men to tell no one outside of the secretive spy company about burning the bridge. Houston planned to have Deaf announce what had happened to the only bridge on the road to the Brazos—later.

When Smith and the six other horsemen returned to camp they found they had a full colonel commanding them. He was Mirabeau Lamar, advanced that morning by Houston all the way from private for his heroic actions the day before. Rusk, who owed his life to Lamar, endorsed the promotion.

When, on the morning of April 21, Houston had first approached Lamar on the subject of promotion, the General had suggested that Lamar take command of the artillery in place of the sore-bottomed Colonel Neill, who'd been taken in a boat to Lorenzo De Zavala's house across Buffalo Bayou. Lamar had answered that the Texas artillery had performed so brilliantly the day before that he didn't want to horn in on their glory, and that, for himself, he was content to stay a cavalry private. This reply brought cheers, especially from the artillerymen and the cavalry. The mounted men, including the generous Karnes, asked the new Colonel to become their commander. After some pleading, Lamar agreed.

When Smith returned from the bridge, Houston was just winding up the first and only council of war he held during the whole campaign. "I attended the war council between 12 noon and 2 P.M. on April 21 with seven other field officers," said Lt. Col. Joseph Bennett, second-in-command of the Second Regiment. The leaders present besides Houston, Rusk, and Bennett were Sherman, Burleson, Wharton, Lamar, Somervell, Lt. Col. Henry Millard, and Lysander Wells.

Houston asked the council whether they thought the Texans should attack that afternoon or remain in their position and let the enemy attack them. Secretary Rusk made a short speech in which he advised against sending raw troops with few bayonets across a mile-long prairie in the daylight against veteran Mexican troops behind fortifications. Strangely, Sherman, Wharton, and Lamar, who had been deploring Houston's caution all during the campaign, also voted against immediate attack.

"They said that we had not the bayonets to charge with through an open prairie," said Bennett. "They said that our position was strong and in it we could whip all of Mexico." Of all the eight field officers only the juniors, Millard and Wells, voted to assault Santa Anna's position that afternoon.

Colonel Bennett reports:

When General Houston had received the sense of the council, he gave no opinion, himself, but dismissed the members. Soon after I was riding out to graze my horse on the prairie and take a look at the enemy. Houston spoke to me: "Don't be gone more than 30 minutes, colonel, as I'll want you." I came back in less than a half hour and Houston sent me through the camp to see the captains and men and ascertain their feelings about fighting that afternoon. I reported back to him and said the men were ready to fight. Houston then ordered the troops to be paraded.

Between 3 and 4 P.M. the army arranged itself into an awkward pattern for attack. There was many an oath as the men paraded into a long, narrow, treeless hollow in front of the dark, moss-hung grove in which they'd spent the night.

Houston and several others who were there said there were 783 effectives in the Texan battle line. Tom Rusk said "about 750." Later, more than 900 men claimed to have been there. "I was on the extreme left when the battle line formed," said Sgt. Robert Kemp Goodloe, who was later a medical doctor. "The whole line counter-marched in front of me and I tried to count the men." The Sergeant thought he counted "760-odd" warriors.

Anyway, *Soldados God Dammes* were strung out for almost nine hundred yards in that hollow, usually two men deep. Cities, counties, towns, streams, mountains, hospitals, libraries, all kinds of ships, all kinds of schools, highways, aircraft, and a national forest were to be named in honor of these fighting men. Yet between 3 and 4 P.M. on that Thursday they were just a line of dirty, unshaven, confused human beings, bedeviled by everything from doubt to lice.

Beyond the hollow and across the rising prairie the Mexican camp was quiet—too quiet, it must have seemed to the anxious Texans. Observers with spyglasses in the mastlike magnolia trees and in the lofty pecans reported to Houston that the Mexican dragoons, who'd watched the Texans all morning from the edge of the President's camp, had not reappeared. There wasn't a single Mexican sentry in sight.

When the men were all in position for the attack, Houston
began his final inspection. The first group the General encountered, on the extreme right wing, was his sixty-one-man
cavalry troop, now led by Mirabeau Lamar, mounted on a
big-chested roan. Next to them were the two well-disciplined
companies of regular infantry under Henry Millard.

The musicians, Dick the drummer and the three fifers, were
with the regular infantry. Possibly it was Lemsky, the whimsical fifer from Germany, who selected the song to which the
Texans marched into battle that day. Trooper Walter Lane
always claimed that the tune was "The Girl I Left Behind,"
but almost every other source says it was "Will You Come to
the Bower." Francis Cynric Sheridan, a flippant young British
diplomat who came to Texas soon after the battle of San
Jacinto, wrote:

> The devoted army of the young republic went into action
> at San Jacinto to the strains of "Dilly Dilly Duckling,
> and Be Killed" or better known probably as "Will You
> Come to the Bower I Have Shaded for You," that ex-
> quisite production of Mr. Thomas Moore, the author of
> "Lalla Rookh.'"

Sheridan, a grandson of dramatist Richard Brinsley Sheridan,
said that the song, with its rather suggestive lyrics, became the
"Texas national anthem." It is possible that Mirabeau Lamar
and not Lemsky might have selected "Come to the Bower,"
for the cavalry Colonel was a great admirer of Thomas
Moore's verse. In Lamar's own poetry there are quotations
from the Irish writer. Still, the song may have been selected
just because it was very popular and all four musicians knew
the tune and even the lyrics, which went like this:

> Will you come to the bow'r I have shaded for you?
> Our bed shall be roses all spangled with dew.

Will you come to the bow'r I have shaded for you?
Our bed shall be roses all spangled with dew.
There under the bow'r on roses you'll lie
With a blush on your cheek but a smile in your eye.

To the left of the regulars and a few paces ahead of them were the thirty men in the artillery corps. George Hockley, a close friend of Houston's, had assumed the post of artillery commander, left vacant when Neill was wounded, that Houston had earlier offered to Lamar.

Next to the cannoneers was Burleson's First Regiment, the foundation of the army. While inspecting the First, Houston stopped the longest near Moseley Baker's Company D. The antagonistic company commander was making a violent speech when Houston rode up, and the General took a fresh chew of tobacco and listened grimly. For once, the bold Baker, who was a good talker, wasn't cussing his General. Captain Robert Calder, a twenty-six-year-old Maryland native who had an adjoining company in the battle line, reported that "Baker made a stirring appeal to the patriotism of his men. Not being an orator, myself, I told my company to avail themselves of Captain Baker's sentiments." Said Corporal Hill:

> Captain Baker harangued the company, saying he wished his men to neither ask or give quarter. As a token he proposed the company carry a small red flag. A vote was taken. Only one man, Pvt. John Money, voted against the red flag. So a red handkerchief was hoisted on a stick, but it was lost before we got to the Mexican breastworks.

After listening to Baker, Houston rode on to Company F of the First Regiment, commanded by Captain Heard, the officer who claimed that within his hearing Deaf Smith had suggested destroying Vince's Bridge. Heard was an intelligent fellow from Egypt on the Colorado River. Before leaving the

fertile land of Egypt, Heard had buried his most valuable possessions and set up wooden crosses as if for a fresh graveyard.
The invading Mexicans were fooled by this camouflage.

In eastern Tennessee years before Houston had been Heard's
schoolteacher for a term. Heard wasn't enthusiastic about his
former master's way of running the San Jacinto campaign.
Like most of the West Texas officers, he thought Houston
should have made a stand on the Colorado.

Heard raised unusually good saddle horses. He was sitting
on a bay half-thoroughbred when Houston approached on his
inspection of the line. Despite the democratic atmosphere in
this volunteer army and their long acquaintance, Houston
and Heard were not on a first-name basis. There is a story
that a few minutes before the Texans charged the Mexican
camp, Houston tried to swap his white stallion for Heard's bay
gelding. Heard maintained that his former teacher wanted to
trade horses because, while Houston's vanity had prompted
him to choose a spectacular light-colored steed to ride before
the battle, at the last minute he realized that the big, bright
animal would make a pretty target for Mexican fire.

"This old bay is a pet, General," said Heard. "I couldn't
any more trade him off than I could a child."

The General nodded and rode on.

To the left of Heard's men was Captain Jesse Billingsley's
company, and Houston stopped before them just long enough
to speak a few words of encouragement to these tough frontiersmen.

The General's inspection ended with the Second Regiment,
under Sidney Sherman's command, on the extreme left wing
of the line. In front of the Second Regiment Houston had a
conference with Tom Rusk, and they decided that Rusk should
stay with Sherman's regiment at the start of the attack. The
reason for this decision was not, as some thought, that Houston

mistrusted Sherman. Rusk was to ride with the Second Regiment only until it had made contact with the enemy, and then he was to gallop over to the center of the line and let Houston know how the Second was doing. Since the plan called for an attack by Sherman's regiment on the right side of the Mexican camp, which was in a grove of live oaks, the Second's movements would be screened from Houston and most of the rest of the army.

At around 4 P.M. Houston trotted Saracen in front of the First Regiment and pulled rein at the eastern rising of the hollow. For a moment he was still, silhouetted there in the bright sunshine. Then Houston's rich baritone rang out:

"Trail arms! Forward!"

As the command was echoed down the hollow by regimental and then by company officers, the men began to move out toward the silent camp of the President of Mexico.

8

Recuerden el Alamo!

They poured upon us a volley of God dammes *and other abusive expressions.*

—PEDRO DELGADO IN DESCRIBING TEXAS ARMY SPEECH HABITS

WITH much quiet blasphemy, the Texas artillery-men hauled *The Twin Sisters* by rawhide ropes up the slope toward the Santanista camp. The job was exasperating, for despite the warm sun and the carpet of tall grasses and flowers, the prairie was soft. Officers got on the ropes and heaved along with the men.

The infantry moved most of this mile of meadows and timber islands in a two-man-deep formation. Except for its cursing, tobacco-chewing General, riding from five to thirty yards ahead of the battle line, this army had no skirmishers. Houston cantered laterally, shouting in his booming way: "Hold your fire until we crest the hill! Hold your fire, God damn it!"

Both Walter Lane and Captain Heard said that the Mexi-cans began to fire when the rebels were about three hundred yards away. "Their artillery and infantry opened on us, but as we were going up a slight ascent, they overshot us," said Walter Lane. "Our company never fired a shot until we got within 40 yards. The command all along the battle line was 'Halt, fire and then charge!'"

"General Houston was a few paces in front of my company when we arose the hill in fair view of the enemy," said Captain Heard. Houston's former first-grade scholar said the General yelled: "Halt! Halt! Now is the critical time! Fire away! God damn you, fire! Aren't you going to fire at all!"

John Pettit Borden said the canny Texas riflemen made their own decisions about when to fire: "Our company was told to fire at 200 yards. Some, thinking the distance too great, reserved their fire."

Some accounts, not from men who were there, have the Texas field musicians playing all across the plain between the two camps, but all the eye witnesses said there was no music until the first shot was fired. Private John S. Menifee said: "We marched upon the enemy with the stillness of death. No fife, no drum, no voice was heard until, at 200 yards, the Mexicans started shooting at us." Menifee's testimony is questionable when he says "no voice was heard," for the overwhelming evidence is that Houston shouted orders all across the prairie. Menifee claimed that the General controlled the evolutions of his men across the plain with hand signals.

The artillery pieces kept about ten yards ahead of the line of infantry, said gunner Ben McCulloch, a future Confederate general. Both McCulloch and Houston said that *The Twin Sisters* were fired first at about two hundred yards, and the General also reported that "no infantryman fired until we had advanced within point blank range."

At one point Houston narrowly escaped being blown up by his own artillery. Just as McCulloch started to touch taper to his cannon for either a second or third shot, he jerked back the flare, for at that moment: "General Houston passed some thirty yards in front of the gun," said McCulloch, "and about that distance in advance of every man in that part of the field."

According to Houston and some of the other men, when the center of the Texans was about sixty yards from the enemy, Deaf Smith came galloping along the battle line, shouting: "Vince's Bridge is down! Fight for your lives! Vince's Bridge is down!"

If this incident really did take place, it must have been a little psychological drama "preconcerted" (to use Houston's phrase) by the General and the scout, for the taciturn Smith would hardly have done such a thing on his own initiative. Moreover, Deaf tended to be a mumbler, so probably few men could understand him in all the excitement.

Both Smith and Houston, riding between the Texan and Mexican battle lines, were exposing themselves to a dangerous cross fire, for Sherman's eager men had hit the Mexican right wing with hornet hate, and all along the battle line hot fighting raged. John Borden said that "soon the smoke from the cannon and the small arms" made it hard to see anything.

In his official report, Houston seems to give Sidney Sherman credit for being first to shout the terrible war cry: "Remember the Alamo! Remember Goliad!" The *grito* went like a fuse all down the battle line. Tony Menchaca, the bass-voiced interpreter in Seguin's company, took up the cry in Spanish, shouting louder even than the impassioned men around him. Probably it was Menchaca's savage roar that struck the greatest terror into Santanista hearts. Dick, the Negro drummer, made the words a kind of African chant. Robert Calder said he believed the sudden, thunderous war cry, "coming after perfect silence," had a more demoralizing effect on the Santanistas than did the gunfire.

As he had agreed beforehand, when the battle was under way, Rusk left Sherman's regiment and rode out in front of the battle line to report to Houston. Rusk was followed closely by his twenty-four-year-old aide, Dr. Junius William Mottley.

As they neared the General, Mottley, who had been like an affectionate son to Rusk, was shot from his horse. He took a copper ball in the abdomen. Rusk stopped momentarily. His wounded aide, still conscious, urged Rusk to go on. Rusk galloped to Houston and reported to the General that the Second Regiment had made contact with the enemy in "gallant style."

When Houston, with Rusk nearby, was about forty yards from the Mexican lines and almost directly in front of *The Golden Standard,* a sudden volley of shots caught the General's horse. Five bullets hit Saracen in the barrel and in the chest, and the big stallion sank to the ground, slowly, without any screaming. Houston landed on his feet.

Private Achelle Marre of the Kentucky company caught a riderless horse for the General, and Houston got into a saddle with stirrups so short he couldn't use them and went away with his long legs dangling. Those legs offered a good target to someone. When Houston was near the breastworks he was hit just above the right ankle by a 3-ounce copper ball. At the same time, his second horse in the battle was blasted from under him. Aide Alex Horton dismounted and gave the wounded General his horse. Then, Gunner Ben McCulloch said, Houston charged among the tents.

The Texas cavalry, while advancing on the right wing, had tried to block the Mexicans' only exit from the battlefield, but Mirabeau Lamar didn't have nearly enough men in his command to do this chore thoroughly. Even so, the horsemen did manage to empty a lot of Santanista saddles, and riderless horses added to the confusion in the Mexican camp.

When the Texans made first contact with the enemy, the infantrymen were no longer in their original two-man-deep formation. They'd covered the last hundred yards at a trot, and in the process they'd thinned out into a line at least fifteen hundred yards across. Delgado, who was on duty at the time and later implied that he was the only officer in the camp who wasn't either asleep or having a party, was watching the artillerymen repair *The Golden Standard*'s limber when the Texans charged over the rise on the plain. The Mexican Colonel jumped onto an ammunition box so he could see better. What he saw was "a mere line of one rank and very extended" that "advanced resolutely upon our camp with a brisk fire of grape, muskets and rifles." And, Delgado added, they were "yelling furiously."

Earlier that afternoon—the exact time is not known—Santa Anna had gone to his marquee for what he called a siesta. According to evidence unearthed by the famous British ethnologist William Bollaert when he visited the Republic of Texas in 1838, His Excellency must have had a diverting nap, for Morgan's slave girl, Emily, was in the Presidential quarters at four-thirty on the twenty-first when the battle of San Jacinto began.

General Castrillon and Lt. Manuel Arenal were in a tent about twenty yards back of the cannon drinking champagne at 4:30 P.M., "the fatal moment when the bugler on our right signalled the advance of the enemy on that wing."

The bugler who gave the first warning to the Mexicans didn't live to play very long. Sherman's regiment had sneaked up through the timber, just inboard from marshes and the San Jacinto River, and they were a complete surprise when they fell upon the relaxed Santanista battalions in the groves. Sherman's footmen, "thirsting for gore," as Noah Smithwick put it, slaughtered men who had been playing monte, men who had been sleeping, men who had been eating. Here most Mexican arms were stacked and there was no cannon, so casualties were lighter in the Second Regiment than among those in the center of the Texan line.

Private Alphonso Steele, of Captain James Gillaspie's company, Second Regiment, said:

> When within 60 or 70 yards we were ordered to fire. Then all discipline, as far as Sherman's regiment was concerned, was at an end. We fired as rapidly as we could. As soon as we had fired, each man reloaded and he who got his gun ready first moved on without waiting for orders.

When Moseley Baker fell, slightly wounded, John Borden tried to take command of Company D. Borden said he attempted to form the company into a line, but "this was impossible, for each man appeared to be fighting and charging the Mexicans on his own. During this helter-skelter, every-fellow-for-himself fight, it was hard to tell friend from foe."

When General Castrillon and Lieutenant Arenal heard the bugle and the sounds of fighting, they dropped their champagne glasses, ran out of the tent, and took charge of the cannon. At the same time Delgado dashed about spanking scared infantrymen on the backsides with his saber in an endeavor "to force some of them to fight, but all efforts were in vain; they were a bewildered and panic-stricken herd."

The Mexican resistance was stoutest under Castrillon around the 12-pounder. Consensus of Texas and Mexican reports is that *The Golden Standard* was discharged three times and was loaded for a fourth shot when the Texas fieldpiece fired by McCulloch hit the Mexican cannon's water bucket. The same shot stunned some of the gunners and put the others in flight. Rusk wrote:

General Castrillon was standing on an ammunition box behind the 12-pounder. He used every effort to keep his men at the gun. When he found that to be impossible, he folded his arms, stood and looked sullenly, without moving upon our troops.

Walter Lane said:

As we charged into them, the general commanding the Tampico Battalion, their best troops, tried to rally his men but could not. He drew himself up, faced us, and cried out in Spanish: "I've been in 40 battles and never showed my back. I'm too old to do it now." Colonel Rusk hallooed to his men: "Don't shoot him!" And Rusk knocked up some of the Texans' guns but others ran around and riddled the Mexican general with balls. I was sorry for him. He was a Castillian gentlemen, General Castrillo.

The companies commanded by Turner, Heard, Wood, Billingsley, and Baker swarmed over the area around the 12-pounder. Captain Heard said his men would fall to the earth when they thought *The Golden Standard* was about to be fired, then raise up and "sprint like bucks" directly after the artillery had boomed. Two men later claimed that together they had captured the Mexican cannon. They were Marre, the mysterious Frenchman who said he'd once been a buccaneer under Lafitte, and Pvt. John Wheeler Bunton, a signer of the Texas Declaration of Independence. Bunton used his clubbed rifle to brain an already-groggy corporal at the cannon. With Castrillon's saber, Marre slew two more dazed gunners.

Ramon Caro said:

Engraved in my mind is the sight of General Castrillon where he fell, already stripped of some of his clothes. A short distance from him and in the same condition, I saw the bodies of Colonels Peralta, Trevino, Luelmo and other officers I did not know and about 50 soldiers.

What of Santa Anna during all this? There are contradictory stories. Private Erath said that he and other members of Billingsley's company thought they saw the dictator ride off at a gallop just before they reached the Mexican barricades. Another good witness, Captain Calder, said:

> Santa Anna and a good portion of his staff broke from the field at the first discharge, escaping around our right wing. A ridge was between my position and the ground that Santa Anna and his staff passed over, yet I saw their heads and portions of their persons as they rode from the camp.

Bollaert, the British ethnologist who said that Emily was with Santa Anna at the start of the battle, got his story during a visit he paid to Emily's master, James Morgan, at New Washington. Bollaert's information indicated that the

> Battle of San Jacinto was probably lost by the Mexicans owing to the influence of a mulatto girl, Emily, belonging to Colonel James Morgan. She was closeted in the tent with General Santanna at the time the cry was made: "The enemy! They come! They come!" She detained Santanna so long that order could not be restored readily again.

Apparently, witnesses at San Jacinto would not have argued with Bollaert. One of them, Private Erath, said: "Much of our success was due to Santa Anna's voluptuousness."

Santa Anna claimed he was asleep at 4:30 P.M. "from fatigue and long vigils" when the "din and fire of battle awoke me. I immediately became aware that we were being attacked and that great disorder prevailed. The enemy had surprised our advance posts."

Secretary Caro wrote cynically of this statement by his boss:

Imagine our being surprised at 4:30 in the afternoon, in the middle of an open plain, with nothing to obstruct the view of the enemy from our front! They succeeded in advancing to within 200 yards of us without being discovered. And from there spread terror and death among our ranks. The shadows of those who fell, so cowardly murdered at Goliad and the Alamo, had called for vengeance for some time.

Santa Anna implied that if he'd had a few minutes of warning he might have rallied his startled troops. He said:

Although the evil was done, I thought for a moment that it might be repaired. I ordered the permanent battalion of Aldama to reinforce that of Matamoros, which was sustaining the line of battle; and hurriedly organized an attack column under orders of Col. Manuel Cespedes, composed of the permanent battalion of Guerrero and detachments from Toluca and Guadalajara which, simultaneously with the column of Colonel Luelmo, marched forward to check the principal advance of the enemy.

Caro again disagrees.

The principal movement of the enemy was the complete surprise. The rest of the engagement developed with lightning rapidity. So that by the time he [Santa Anna] reached our front line it had already been completely routed. When did he organize the two columns, then? Colonel Cespedes is here now and can testify to the truth.

Delgado said that when the

unpleasant clamors [of the Texans] were in close proximity I saw His Excellency running around in the utmost excitement, wringing his hands, and unable to give an order. Some cried out to commence firing; others to lie down to avoid grape shots. Among the latter was His Excellency.

Santa Anna said that the two columns, which he claimed to have organized, were dispersed. He saw General Castrillon killed. And the Texans, "shouting madly," were almost upon him when

a servant of Juan Bringas with noble kindness offered me the horse of his master and earnestly pleaded that I save myself. I remembered that General Filisola was sixteen leagues distant on the Brazos. And, without hesitation, I tried to make my way to that place through the enemy ranks.

The usual Santa Anna luck and the half-thoroughbred Old Whip carried the dictator from the battleground.

Third Sergeant Moses Bryan of Baker's company said the Mexican small-arms fire from behind the breastworks was pretty hot when the Texan line first came over the hill. Like the other Texans, Bryan was wearing an incongruous ensemble as he rode into battle that day. It consisted of the usual buckskin britches, moccasins, a big sombrero, and an old clawhammer-tailed frock coat that had belonged to his distinguished uncle, Stephen F. Austin. As Bryan described his part in the fighting:

Burleson's regiment, to which I belonged, was in the center and marched straight to the Mexican works, where we could see only heads of men behind them. In the advance I had three holes shot in the skirts of my frock coat

—the coat flew out as we advanced in a trot. And I heard bullets whistling as they overshot us.

The Second Regiment [Sherman's] was on our left and a little in advance of Burleson's. The Second routed the Mexican reinforcements under Cos, who had joined Santa Anna that morning and who were lying down asleep. When we made the attack, they [Cos's men] rushed down, many of them leaving their guns (so I was told later by Mexicans we captured) and mixed with the veteran troops behind the breastworks and threw them in confusion.

Burleson's regiment went right over the breastworks and the Mexicans who were not killed retreated. The most awful slaughter I ever saw was when the Texans pursued the retreating Mexicans, killing on all sides, even the wounded.

I had a double-barrel shotgun and had shot only four times when we crossed the breastworks. After that I shot no more at the poor devils who were running. I came upon a young Mexican boy (a drummer, I suppose) lying on his face. One of the volunteers brought to Texas by Colonel Sherman pricked the boy with his bayonet. The boy grasped the man around the legs and called in Spanish: *"Ave Maria prissima per Dios salva me vida!"* I begged the man to spare him, both of his legs being broken already. The man looked at me and put his hand on his pistol, so I passed on. Just as I did so, he blew out the boy's brains.

It was almost as dangerous to be a wounded Texan, according to Alphonso Steele. This nineteen-year-old, who was destined to outlive everyone else in the Texan army at San

Jacinto, was shot down early in the action. His friend David Rusk, the brother of the Secretary of War, asked someone to stay with the wounded man. Steele told him: "Take off. I'll tend to myself."

While Steele, bleeding at the nose and mouth, was dazed and helpless, one of his fellow soldiers stole his pistol and ran on into the Mexican camp. Another Texan fetched the wounded man a gourd canteen full of water. Said Steele:

> Just as he went to hand me the water, a couple of Mexicans came running toward us. I suppose they had hid in the grass until our men had passed, and were now running back to get out of the way. When they got in about 20 steps of us, they saw us and threw up their hands and began to jabber something.

The unnamed Texan who'd brought Steele the water refused to shoot at the helpless fugitives. Steele picked up his rifle and killed one of the Mexicans, and the other ran off into the timber. By this time Steele was going blind from his head wounds.

> I could hardly see anything and I sat down on a dead Mexican. While I was sitting there some of Millard's regulars, who'd stayed at the breastworks and were busy sticking their bayonets through wounded Mexicans, came along. And one of them had his bayonet drawed back to stick through me when Tom Green of our artillery corps [Pvt. Thomas N. B. Green] stopped the regular from killing me.

Green, who, like Lane and McCulloch, was to become a Confederate general, put his wounded friend on a Mexican horse and started Steele back to the Texan camp. .

About fifty yards behind the Mexican camp and toward San Jacinto Bay there was a tidewater bayou and a lake or small bay, named Lake Anna Maria Francisco, sometimes called Peggy Lake in honor of Mrs. McCormick. Here, according to Pvt. Washington Winters, "occurred the greatest slaughter. The Mexicans and horses killed made a bridge across the bayou."

And here the gallant Col. John Wharton, who'd recently been so critical of his friend, Houston, found out how tough it was to discipline this army of frontiersmen. Wharton saw old Jimmy Curtis about to cut the throat of a Mexican colonel with a 5-pound Bowie knife. Curtis was shouting at the Mexican: "You killed Wash Cottle. Now I'm going to kill you and make a razor strop from your hide."

"Wharton tried to stop the slaughter and he grabbed this Mexican officer and pulled him up behind him on his horse," said Washington Winters. "Wharton said: 'Men, this Mexican is mine.' But Jim Curtis shot the Mexican right off Wharton's horse." Curtis ignored the raging Wharton. The old man took a drink of whiskey from his gourd and bawled: "Remember Wash Cottle!"

Wharton had more trouble just ahead. As Moses Austin Bryan described it:

There was an island in this lake or bay, and two or three hundred Mexicans had jumped into the water to reach it. Some 15 or 20 of our riflemen were shooting at the Mexicans every time they raised their heads out of the water to get breath.

Adjutant General Wharton rode up and ordered the riflemen to stop firing. One of Sherman's men, Joe Dickson, who was engaged in shooting the Mexicans, said: "Colonel Wharton, if Jesus Christ were to come down from Heaven and order me to quit shooting Santanistas I wouldn't do it, sir!" Colonel Wharton put his hand on his sword. Joe Dickson took a few steps back and cocked his rifle. Wharton, very discreetly (I always thought) turned his horse and left.

The San Jacinto battle rolls mention no Joe Dickson, so it is probable that the obstinate private who defied Colonel Wharton was one J. H. T. Dixon, who served in the company commanded by his uncle, Capt. Richard Roman.

When Colonel Sherman of the Second Regiment undertook a similar humane effort, he was more successful than Wharton had been. Sherman came upon his friend, Robert Kemp Goodloe, trying to protect two Mexican drummer boys from a couple of Texas regulars who wanted to use their bayonets on the youths. "They're my prisoners," Dr. Goodloe was shouting. But Goodloe had only a carbine, which had to be reloaded after every shot, and a Bowie knife, and the Mexican boys might well have died if Sherman hadn't ridden up and told the regulars not to kill them. Sherman took the two young boys as his prisoners and told them to follow him.

Colonel Delgado survived because of a single kind-hearted Texan. Delgado had chosen to run to the east, toward the marshes on San Jacinto Bay. Said the Colonel:

About a musket shot from our camp was a small grove on the bay shore. Our disbanded herd rushed for it, to obtain shelter from the horrid slaughter carried on all over the prairie by the bloodthirsty usurpers. Unfortunately, on our way we came to a bayou, not very wide but rather deep. The men, on reaching it, would helplessly crowd together and were shot down by the enemy, who was close enough not to miss his aim. It was there that the greatest carnage took place.

Delgado saw Almonte swimming across the bayou with his sword in one hand. Delgado also crossed the bayou but ran out of his boots in the mud. Barefooted, he ran into a grove, where he witnessed the death of one of his friends, Col. Jose Batres, a native of San Antonio.

Texan Surgeon Labadie was there, too, and tried to save Batres, whom Labadie in his account called Colonel Bertrand. The Mexican officer was bogged to his knees and begging for his life. Just as Labadie stuck out his left hand, intending to pull Batres to firmer ground, three Texas riflemen came trotting up. Labadie cried, "This man is my prisoner. Don't shoot! Don't shoot!" But one of the riflemen shot Batres through the forehead, and Labadie's extended left hand was splattered with the Colonel's blood.

Delgado would have gotten the same medicine if the courageous officer who had been Byron's friend, Capt. John Allen, hadn't ridden up in time to save Delgado and the hundred and fifty other fugitives in the grove. Said Delgado:

> It would have been all over for us had not Providence placed us in the hands of the noble captain of cavalry, Allen, who by great exertion saved us repeatedly from being slaughtered by the drunken and infuriated volunteers.

Private Erath, the scholarly Viennese, said that an unidentified Mexican colonel stood on the bridge of dead men over the bayou and

> flourishing his sword, made a grand appeal to rally his men, but he was shot down, and the Mexicans who had turned to face us again resumed their flight, only to be overtaken and shot down. I do not like to dwell on these scenes.

Private William Foster Young, a powerfully built, thirty-six-year-old soldier who rode a tremendous gray horse, said the battle was like a target shoot. "We drove them into a marsh and I sat there on my horse and shot 'em until my ammunition gave out. Then I turned the butt end of my musket and started knocking them in the head." Old Jimmy Curtis and some of the other wild frontiersmen in Billingsley's outfit paused in the slaughter long enough to lift a few scalps.

Even though the Mexicans who had fled to the swamps were simply being slaughtered by this time, not all of the fighting had ended. Deaf Smith was riding his weary horse among Turner's infantry when, as he reached the Mexican works, the horse stumbled over a Mexican body and Smith went flying over the animal's head. Deaf wasn't hurt much, but he fell right at the feet of a battling Santanista lieutenant, and when he tried to shoot the Mexican, his pistol missed fire. As the lieutenant slashed at the old scout, who still lay on the ground, Deaf flung his useless pistol into the lieutenant's face. The Mexican missed on his first slash but then he had Smith helpless. John D. Nash, another member of Karnes's company, came to Smith's rescue by putting spurs to his horse and running over the Mexican officer. Smith leaped on his dazed adversary and killed him with his own saber.

Deaf got a new mount the same way Houston had earlier in the battle. Private Prospero Bernardi, a forty-two-year-old native of Italy in Turner's company, had caught a saddled Mexican horse. Bernardi, who'd fought as a boy in the Napoleonic wars, preferred to be an infantryman, so he gave the pony to old Deaf. No sooner had Smith mounted this fresh horse than he snapped off his newly won saber in the act of killing an enemy colonel. He then took the rifle and pistols of a slain Texan, Lt. George Lamb, who'd fallen near the Mexican cannon.

John Robbins, a big, athletic Texan, was knocked from his horse by a Santanista foot soldier who was swinging a lance like a club. Like Smith, Robbins fell into a fight. He got to his feet quickly after the fall and found himself in a hand-to-hand battle with a powerful Mexican officer. The lancer who'd unhorsed Robbins could easily have slain him during this wrestling match, but instead, he dropped the lance, jumped on Robbins's horse, and fled the field. He must have gotten away, for Robbins never saw his horse again. The Texan finally outwrestled his opponent, got out his Bowie knife, and cut the officer's throat.

"Claret, thick as cornstalk, gushed from Mexicans all over the field," said one Texas soldier.

This undisciplined, personal kind of combat wasn't at all pleasing to Houston. The General ranged all over the battleground roaring orders to ears that couldn't and wouldn't hear in the midst of this blood bath. Later, Sam's political enemies claimed that he ordered the troops to halt right at the height of the victory. According to Rusk what actually worried Houston was that, after the Texans had fired all their ammunition and broken half their rifle butts on Santanista skulls, a big column under Urrea or Filisola might show up on the prairie. Houston later said that one hundred well-disciplined Mexicans could have wiped out the Texans after they broke ranks and began running around shooting and clubbing and stabbing.

That wonderfully ungrammatical soldier, Pvt. Bob Hunter, told how Houston tried to stop the slaughter and get his army under control. Bob said the dead Mexicans lay

> 3 and 4 deck around the 12-pounder. They did not git
> to fire there cannon but 3 times. Our men then took there

gun loded & turned it on them & shot them with there own gun & they wanted to giv up. Gen'r'l Houston giv orders not to kill any more but to take prisners. Capt Easlen [First Lieutenant William Mosby Eastland of Heard's company] said Boys take prisners, you know how to take prisners, take them with the but of yor guns, club guns, & remember the Alamo, remember Labaher, & club guns right & left, & nock there God damn brains out.

The Mexicans would fall down on there knees & say me no Alamo, me no Labaher. They was a mudy laggune a bout 4 or 5 hundred yeards south of the Battlefield about 15 or 20 yeards wide & the Mexicans broke. They run for that laggune & man & horse went in head and years to the bottom, about 18 feet boly [boggy] mud.

It was said that Saint Anna's money chest was thowed in there & a parsel of us Boys went and cut out some poles 6 or 7 feet long, probed down to finde the money & we could not finde bottom & we got some poles 10 or 12 feet long. We could feel dead horses and I expect men but no bottom & we give up. That laggune was full of men & horses.

Dr. Labadie said that in the midst of the heaviest fighting Houston was roaring: "Parade, men! Parade, men!" And Labadie said that when the soldiers ignored their General and went on gleefully killing Santanistas, Houston bawled out, "Gentlemen! Gentlemen! Gentlemen!" until some of them stopped the slaughter long enough to listen to him. Then he continued, "Gentlemen, I applaud your bravery. But damn your manners!"

Amasa Turner, a canny, thirty-six-year-old infantry captain originally from Massachusetts, said of the reports later circulated by Houston's political enemies to the effect that the

General ordered a halt before the battle was won: "The report wasn't true and I believe it was maliciously spread by Col. Robert M. Coleman." Coleman, one of the officers who had often criticized Houston before, later published a broadside against the General. Turner said that while Houston didn't want a general halt, he did want at least one company under discipline. Not only would the army need a controlled nucleus in case Filisola or Urrea appeared with another Mexican army, but Houston wanted a disciplined guard for the spoils of Santa Anna's camp. Turner described the first steps toward the restoration of order this way:

The enemy didn't have time to form behind their works before we were among them. The hand-to-hand-combat that followed threw our battle line into great confusion, though. Many of the company commanders made efforts to form their commands after passing the breastworks but failed to do so. I managed to keep something like a line and we joined the rout in something like the order of a company.

After a few hundred yards of pursuit at double quick step, I heard the command given: "Halt! Halt!" I looked around and saw Colonel Millard come up on horseback, calling, "Halt! Captain Turner, halt your command, sir!"

I stopped my company and formed my line. Here, I will remark, my company was the first to halt and after we stopped not a single gun was fired by the enemy. Before Colonel Millard had time to give me his orders, Colonel Wharton rode up from the rear, also, and cried out: "Regulars, why have you stopped? On! On!" Wharton was about to pass when Millard spoke to him. I did not hear their conversation. The result, however, was that

Colonel M. detailed my company to return to the Mexican camp and place a guard around it.

At this time, I saw General Houston and his staff walking their horses slowly from the same direction that Colonel Millard and Colonel Wharton had come from. Houston and his staff returned to the Mexican camp with my company. I had my men halt around the 12-pounder and stand at ease.

Houston said to Wharton: "God damn it; quit trying to command." Wharton answered nothing. He took a swig from his water gourd and then galloped away.

Not much later, Dr. Labadie walked up and offered to dress Houston's wound. Blood was oozing both from the bullet hole in the ankle and from the top of his boot, and the General looked to be in intense pain. "No, I will have it attended to when I get back to our camp. I can last until then," said the General, and he asked whether Labadie had suffered any damage in the assault.

Amasa Turner said: "Houston's staff seemed to scatter and leave him as we came in the Mexican camp. He rode up in front of my company and stopped his horse."

Ordinarily, the General's eyesight was normal, so the mistake he made when he reached the Santanista camp is surprising. But the sun had already gone down behind the great trees, and perhaps the pain from Houston's wound misted his eyes. Captain Turner said

Houston threw up his hands and exclaimed: "All is lost! All is lost! My God, all is lost!" I saw that he was looking at General Rusk, who was marching several hundred Mexican prisoners on their way to our camp on Buffalo Bayou.

There was a spy glass lying on the ground near
Houston's horse. I took it up and handed it to him. I
said: "Take this general and you can see what's really out
there on the prairie. Just then my first lieutenant, Bill
Miller, said: "General, Colonel Rusk has a very respectable army, eh, sir?" "Is that Rusk?" said the general. "It
sure is, sir, I said."

Amasa wrote later that he was "of the opinion that when
the general first saw Rusk and the Mexicans on the prairie
he thought it was Filisola's column coming from the Brazos."

President Burnet said he was told later that Rusk's prisoners
were part of the Guerrero battalion which "Almonte, with
cool intrepidity and adroitness, kept intact and was retreating
in good order beyond the boggy bayou on the south of the
hostile camp." Burnet said he heard that Almonte collected
between "450 and 500 strong" and was marching them in a
body to surrender. Rusk, who was on the spot, said it was more
like two hundred fifty men. When the Secretary of War saw
Almonte come out of the woods followed by the body of un-
armed men, he had to restrain the few Texas soldiers with him
from shooting into the Mexican formation.

"There were at that place not exceeding 15 Texans and none
of us could speak the Spanish language well," said Rusk. "The
prisoners were asked (in halting Spanish) if any of them could
speak English." The officer answered in Spanish that they
could not. Rusk's narrative continues:

> The Mexicans were then told in Spanish that they should
> form two and two deep and march with us to camp. They
> formed and commenced to march. Our few men were
> distributed around them as a guard. Most of them were
> very tired and such was the condition of the Mexicans,

also. As we proceeded in this way, one of our soldiers, who was so tired he could hardly walk, cursed and threatened in English a Mexican who had dropped out of line. [God damn you—I'll cut off your ears!] The officer repeated this threat immediately in Spanish to the offending Mexican soldier. I concluded that he, at least, must understand English very well, and that it was probably Almonte whom I saw before me. I, therefore, observed to him: "You must be Colonel Almonte." He replied in English: "You speak well, sir." I then rode up to him and gave him my hand, saying to him, "It affords me great pleasure to see you, colonel." With great presence of mind and customary politeness, he responded: "The pleasure is reciprocated."

They had a conversation as they walked along. Almonte said that defeat "was not an extraordinary event in the life of a soldier of fortune. He spoke freely and without reserve" with some of the Texans in the guard whom he'd met when he visited the province two years before. Rusk said "there is no doubt that Almonte's philosophic and cheerful temper" made the angry Texas guard deal more kindly with the prisoners.

Rusk's small group of guards soon had a lot of reinforcements, including Houston and his staff, Colonel Sherman, and the ubiquitous Dr. Labadie. Labadie asked Rusk: "Where is Dr. Mott?" "Oh, poor fellow, he is shot," answered the cabinet member. And he asked Labadie to hasten back to camp, where Dr. Mottley had been carried, and see that he was getting proper attention.

Sherman said he rode part of the way back to the Texan camp with the wounded General, and that:

General Houston rode up and offered me his hand, congratulating me on our success. And he remarked that he hoped I was now satisfied, evidently alluding to the complaint I had made in regard to his conduct toward me on the day previous. I replied that I was satisfied with this day's work. I said that I'd heard the general had been wounded. He replied *a mere scratch.*

Captain Turner claims that Houston was in a less cheerful mood at the time. Turner said that when the General's staff rejoined him, Houston cried out: "Have I a friend in this world? Colonel Wharton, I am wounded, I am wounded; have I a friend in this world?" According to Turner, Wharton made a rather strange reply. He said: "I wish I was (wounded?). Yes, General, I hope you have many friends."

Calder, an impartial witness, said that when Houston arrived in camp, he was still making light of his hurt ankle. Said Calder:

> As we reached the precincts of our camp, I met General Houston and Rusk. Rusk inquired about Houston's wound. Houston replied that it was slight. Rusk insisted on helping the general from his horse, and called on me to assist him. I was about to do this when David Rusk came up. And the brothers helped Houston down. The general appeared to suffer a great deal of pain when being moved, but called repeatedly for Almonte to be brought before him.

The acting surgeon general, Dr. Alexander Wray Ewing, took off Houston's blood-filled boot and found that the injury was serious indeed. It was later diagnosed as a compound fracture of the right tibia and fibula, just above the ankle.

No one bothered to record whether or not Dr. Ewing removed a bullet from Houston's ankle. Years later Sam's son,

Col. Andrew Houston, said it was "a copper ball from a Mexican escopette." The barrage of bullets that wounded Houston and killed two of his horses caused several historians to suggest, without giving their sources, that the General was actually shot by a disgruntled member of his own army.

In Mirabeau Lamar's private papers the Georgian poet, with mock seriousness, deplores the alleged effect on Houston's personality of Pope's *Illiad,* which he memorized during his exile with the Indians. Lamar observes that the *"Illiad* is a poem where chicken-hearted heroes are under the protection of demonic immortals. With dread that he [Houston] might defraud the eager band of victory at San Jacinto it was said that an excellent marksman of Captain William S. Fisher's company in the early part of the action thought it safest to temporarily depose Achilles [Houston] by a touch on the heel."

Houston *was* shot in the Achilles tendon, and Captain Fisher's Company I *was* equipped with muskets. Algernon P. Thompson, a private from New York City, might be a suspect. He was transferred into Fisher's company that day because he had a musket and bayonet "for the sake of uniformity of arms." Later, Thompson, a prominent attorney, was the ghost author of a bitter pamphlet against Houston. But most of the evidence suggests that this yarn of Houston's being shot by a Texan was just another campaign slander thought up by his enemies during the quarter century that old Sam dominated Texas politics.

Despite the seriousness of his wound, Houston continued to demand to see Almonte. The General was eager to question the Mexican officer about Santa Anna's whereabouts, but as it happened, Almonte told Houston nothing more than what the rebels already knew: that the President of Mexico had ridden from the battleground toward the Brazos at about 4:45 P.M.

During the early evening of the twenty-first the Texans found time to count their casualties. Only Pvt. Lemuel Stockton Blakey of Billingsley's outfit and Second Lieutenant George A. Lamb of Captain William Ware's company had been killed in the battle. Seven more were to die later of wounds, and among these was Dr. Mottley. The last words of Rusk's young aide and loyal friend were, "Nothing, nothing, nothing."

It was estimated that the Santanistas lost 630 killed and 208 wounded. The prisoners, including the wounded, numbered 730. Santa Anna's army had been almost annihilated. Yet Sam Houston, as he sat that night by a roaring fire and chewed tobacco and cursed his shattered ankle, knew that San Jacinto would not be a real victory until the President of Mexico was among the prisoners.

Old Whip

*In 1838 I rented the historic Allen Vince Place on
the bayou of that name. I have often seen the fine
black horse, taken from Vince, on which President
Santa Anna attempted to escape from the Texans.*

—F. R. Lubbock, Governor of Texas, 1861–1863

HENRY KARNES and the tireless Deaf Smith led the
pursuit of Santa Anna out over the darkening
prairie to the south of the battlefield. A horseman
named Pvt. William S. Taylor described the first part of the
search. According to Taylor, the cavalry had been much better
disciplined throughout the battle than the infantry, and when
Karnes saw the Mexican leaders escaping on horseback, "he
called for all those having loaded guns to follow him in pursuit." The response was prompt. Besides Smith, who after his
part in the fighting had reclaimed his own horse, there were
about seventeen other volunteers, including Alex Alsbury,
Washington and Fielding Secrest, Shell Tunage, Thomas and
John Robbins, W. T. C. Pierce, Thomas House, and Elisha
Clapp. In some places, said Taylor, the prairie "was knee deep
to our horses in mud and water." Two or three miles from the
battlefield, four of the Mexicans struck off from the main body
as if to go around the head of Vince's Bayou. The others continued on the road directly to Vince's Bridge. As Taylor later
wrote:

165

Elisha Clapp had a very fleet horse and he started after them [the four Mexicans who'd sheered off farther south]. Clapp soon came upon them and fired his rifle, killing one of them. The others turned to give him battle. Clapp was compelled to retreat, not wanting to cope with three Mexicans when his gun was unloaded. The Mexican dragoon nearest to him discharged his escopete at the Texan, but the ball missed although Clapp heard the whistle of it by his head. But he returned to us unhurt.

After that, there was no pursuit of the three dragoons going for the head of Vince's Bayou, and Taylor said:

As I afterward learned the three made good their escape to Filisola on the Brazos where they reported that Houston's army was 4,000 strong. While pursuing the main body of fugitives toward Vince's Bridge we overtook numbers of them, their horses being too tired to enable them to escape. We felt compelled to kill them even though many got on their knees and cried for quarter, saying: "Me no Alamo! Me no La Bahia!" meaning they weren't in on either of these horrible massacres. As there were but 18 of us as against some 60 Mexicans when we started the chase, it was impossible for us to take prisoners and we had little disposition to do so. For about half the distance from the battleground to Vince's Bridge the road was strewed every few hundred yards with dead Mexicans.

When we got within a half mile of Vince's Bridge, Captain Karnes ordered those in advance to halt until the rear could come up. Karnes said that Santa Anna was, no doubt, with the other Mexicans and that when they reached the bridge and found it destroyed they would certainly make a fight. We then rode in a body, prepared for a battle. But when the Mexicans reached the bridge and found it burned, it seemed that they'd scattered, some going up and some down the bayou.

Some 300 or 400 yards from the bridge we saw a large black stallion which the Mexicans had stolen from Mr. Vince. And sitting on the black stud was a fine-looking Mexican officer in a pretty uniform. Captain Karnes, supposing it was Santa Anna (as it was rumored that the President had escaped on Vince's stallion) made for the officer. When Karnes came up to him on the banks of the bayou, the officer dismounted. Karnes asked if he were Santa Anna. He replied that he was. I suppose he thought quarter would be given. Whereupon, Captain Karnes struck at him with his sword, a glancing blow on the head. The Mexican jumped into the bayou, saying at the same time that he was not Santa Anna. Whereupon some pistols were discharged, killing him in the bayou.

The identity of this officer is not known. Whoever he was, he must have found Old Whip wandering loose some time after the battle. Since Deaf Smith had made two hard gallops to the bridge that day, Karnes told the old scout to take the still fresh-looking black stallion. Karnes then sent half his men upstream and the others down. "We continued the pursuit, killing all we overtook," said Taylor.

It was near sundown when the eighteen Texans returned to the wrecked bridge. Several hundred yards upstream from the bridge they found four riderless Mexican horses which they hadn't seen before. Tracks indicated that the riders had jumped into the bayou, and on the other side of the water were further tracks, and fresh ones, leading to a big grove of trees. By that time, it was too dark to search the grove, but since Karnes had a feeling that Santa Anna was hidden there, the Texans crossed the bayou and surrounded it. Alex Alsbury, who spoke the best Spanish, "called out to Santa Anna to come out and deliver himself, and his life would be spared."

Karnes knew he did not have enough men to place an adequate guard around the thicket, and he had fears that the President might ecape from the thicket during the night and make it to Filisola's camp, twenty miles away. There was no answer to Alsbury's cries, "yet we were satisfied that Santa Anna was in there," said Taylor.

"Mr. Smith," said Karnes, "I hate to impose on you. But you got the best horse. Would you go tell General Houston to fetch us down some more help to the bridge? Tell him we think we got that God damned old rascal, Santa Anna, hemmed up."

Deaf Smith must have ridden fast from Vince's Bayou. Calder, back at Houston's camp, said:

> Soon after dark, Mr. Smith rode up to company's quarters on the large black stallion on which [Calder learned later] Santa Anna had fled the battlefield. The horse was covered with mud. Smith said Santa Anna had tried to cross Vince's Bayou by fording but had bogged the animal and went ahead on foot.
>
> Our noble old scout, Smith, was in high spirits and felt no doubt about securing the president next day if he could get 100 mounted men that night to act as a line of patrol and prevent his [Santa Anna's] escape across the prairie during the night. Our entire command volunteered and 25 were accepted.

After Smith had made his report to Houston, the men Karnes had sent for were dispatched and the hundred mounted guards Calder mentions were positioned.

By that time, order had been substantially restored in the Texan camp. Some seven hundred thirty Mexican prisoners cowered in a crude stockade, made from debris of the battle, with *The Twin Sisters,* loaded and ready to be fired, pointed at them. Whole trees had been put on the huge bonfires used to light the area, and for extra light the Texans used long white candles which they had found among the Santanista spoils. As the guards walked slowly around and around the prisoners' compound, each one carried a lighted taper. The sight of this moving chain of light around the prisoners gave the whole scene an eerie look.

Prisoner Delgado said:

I have no doubt that the Texans, amidst the hurrahs and exultations of their triumph, were lavish with insults. However, not understanding their language, we didn't feel them.

But one of our own countrymen, who had joined the enemy's cause, assailed us in the Christian language with such a volley of threats, insults and abuse that the tongue of that vile and recreant Mexican seemed to have been wrought in the very caves of hell and set in motion by Lucifer himself. "Now you shall see," he cried, "contemptible and faithless assassins, if you do not pay with your vile blood for your murders at the Alamo and La Bahia. You shall pay with your heads for the arson, robbery and depredations you have committed in our country, etc."

Our thirst was quenched with an abundance of water which Captain John Allen and others allowed to pass from hand to hand, until all were satisfied. A crowd of Texans gathered around us, asking with persistent impertinence: "Where is General Santa Anna? Where is

Cos?" We knew not the fate of these gentlemen. But to rid ourselves of their repeated questions, we answered: "Dead! Dead!" I still wore my embroidered shoulder straps on my jacket. These attracted the Texans' attention and they would say to me: "You general?" I would answer: "Me no general." When one of them angrily tore off my shoulder straps I was glad of it, as they ceased to question me.

Delgado said the immense fires convinced him

and several of my companions that we were to be burnt alive in retaliation for those who had been burnt in the Alamo. Oh, the cruel and bitter moment. So we felt considerably relieved when they let us go to the fires to warm ourselves and to dry our wet clothes.

You should have seen those Texans, or rather phantoms converted into moving armories—some wore two, three and even four braces of pistols, a cloth bag of very respectable size filled with bullets; a powder horn; a saber or Bowie knife, besides a rifle, musket or carbine. Everyone had in his hand a burning candle. The heat of their hands and the breeze melted the candles very fast; and yet that illumination was kept up all night. Was this display of light to prevent us from escaping? Fools! Where would we go in that vast country, unknown to us, intersected by great rivers and forests, where wild beasts prowled.

Some of the Texans called the corrallike structure where the Mexican captives were held "the bull pen," but this description was not altogether accurate, for some of the prisoners were women.

Nepomuceno Navarro, a handsome twenty-five-year-old

private in Captain Seguin's company, paid particular attention
to two young sisters among the women in the stockade.
Navarro's stare terrified the Mexican girls. He was only ad-
miring them, but the dark-haired, blue-eyed soldier in his
rags and greasy buckskins must have looked to the women
like just another Texan. When he smiled, though, one of the
girls took heart enough to appeal to Navarro, apparently
without much hope that he would understand her:

*"Senor God Damme, no me mata por el amor de Dios y
por la vida de su madrecita!* [Mr. God Damn, don't kill me
for the love of God and for the life of your dear mother!]"

Navarro replied in reassuring Spanish that no harm would
come to any woman, and he added that her new life might
be better than the one she had led as a Santanista camp fol-
lower and drudge. The girl turned to her sister and said gladly:
*"Hermanita, mira! Esse Senor God Damme habla la lingua
Christiana como nosotros!* [Look here, sister! This Mr. God
Damn speaks the Christian language like us!]"

While the kinder-hearted Texans were reassuring anxious
prisoners, arrangements were being made for guarding the
spoils of the battle. Colonel Ned Burleson placed George Erath
and another private in Billingsley's company, William Simmons, in charge of guarding some of Santa Anna's baggage.
Included in this loot were the President's silver dinner service
and a silver-mounted chamber pot. Of more immediate interest
were two 6-foot-high mounds of "baskets of champagne" and
huge stocks of food "part of it already cooked."

"George and Bill, you stay here all night and take charge of
this baggage. You may take anything to eat and allow others
to have eatables. But don't let anything else of value be carried off," said Burleson.

Erath and Simmons, a steady, middle-aged man and a
future comptroller of the Republic of Texas, passed out bottles

of champagne to soldiers who happened that way. They thought Colonel Burleson would agree that champagne could be classed among the "eatables." Erath said he drank no champagne at all and Simmons "made modest use of it." Word soon spread in the army about the champagne and the two sentries had plenty of company, "especially officers," during the all-night vigil.

Near the two guardians, dead and grievously wounded Mexicans sprawled over one another in a gruesome mass, from which came agonized cries of *"Agua!"* Erath said he and Simmons fetched water to the wounded enemy, "but they were all dead by midnight."

The bright moonlight shining on the Plain of San Jacinto on the night of April 21 illuminated a grisly scene. The bodies of six hundred thirty Santanistas lay as they had fallen, on the plain, in the surrounding woods and bayous, scattered over the nine miles from the battlefield to the wrecked bridge at Vince's Bayou. Throughout the night, great packs of wolves that had gathered made a horrible din as they fought over the Mexican corpses.

Houston slept little that night. Most of the night, he stayed up talking with Almonte, Deaf Smith, and others of his men about the missing Santa Anna. Just before dawn, a search party of thirty horsemen was formed, with Ned Burleson in command. Burleson, famed as an Indian fighter, was a good frontier-style man hunter.

Before the resolute Colonel left, Houston told him: "You will find The Hero of Tampico, if you find him at all, retreating on all fours in high grass. And he will be dressed as badly, at least, as a common soldier. Examine every man you find very closely."

Had Houston known as he spoke of Santa Anna's whereabouts and condition at the time, even he might have been surprised at the accuracy of his guess.

When Santa Anna had accepted the horse Juan Bringas's servant offered him during the battle the day before, His Excellency had made his first mistake. Or perhaps the original mistake was that when on the eighteenth he had graciously spared Mrs. Brown and her son Jimmy, he ought to have gone a step further and let them keep their horse. When Santa Anna fled the battleground, it was Old Whip he rode, and the frightened dictator gave the big stud his head. Old Whip's homing instinct took him to the Vince's corrals near the destroyed bridge. Vince's Bayou was wide and deep, and His Excellency feared water. So he rode Old Whip into a trap.

Had Santa Anna taken a more southerly course over the prairie he would have met no serious water hazards, and he might have made it to Filisola's column on the Brazos in a few hours. Within two days, he could have been back with thousands of fresh troops, including those of the undefeatable Jose Urrea. And the battle might have been fought over again at San Jacinto with a different result. Instead His Excellency was trapped in a pocket of overflowing bayous and creeks around the wrecked bridge. His secretary, Ramon Caro, followed the dictator from the Mexican camp, and according to Texas reports General Cos was also with his brother-in-law.

When Caro reached Vince's Bayou, he was so confused that he thought it was the Brazos. Certainly, the swollen bayou could have been mistaken for a river that late afternoon when the fugitives rode up to the bridge that Deaf Smith and his boys had burned only a few hours before. Caro claimed that neither he nor Santa Anna had to dash through enemy ranks to get away and that the Texas pursuers were never within rifle range. "Thank God we were not among the last who fled, for few of those survived," said the secretary. "We continued at full speed until we reached the bridge on the Brazos, eight miles away, only to find it burned."

Caro's account makes no mention of Santa Anna's bogging Old Whip. According to the secretary, they entered a thicket, dismounted, and turned their horses loose. They had two reasons for preferring to travel on foot. One was that they were in very marshy country and could make better progress without horses, and the other was that the shoulder-high sedge grass offered fair cover for men on foot. Santa Anna evidently thought he would do best by himself, for Caro said that after they dismounted "His Excellency left me."

Old Whip went off, with his reins dragging, over the boggy turf. The big horse, for years after a famous sire in the San Jacinto country, had completed his mission. The President of Mexico was in a trap from which a man with a distaste for swimming couldn't very well escape.

Santa Anna had snatched up a few things when his party with Emily, the pretty slave, had been so rudely interrupted. When he jumped on Old Whip he had on white silk drawers, a linen shirt with diamond studs, and red morocco slippers. He carried with him, for some reason, a white cotton sheet, a box of chocolates, a gourd water bottle half full, and a fine gray cloth vest with gold buttons. When he dismounted from Old Whip he took a blanket which Colonel Bringas had tied behind the saddle.

When Karnes and his men shouted into the thicket near the burned bridge, Santa Anna was not there, although Caro was. Cos swam the bayou and headed for the Brazos on foot. Santa Anna spent the night in tall grass near the bayou. He doesn't mention it in his accounts, but he must have heard Alex Alsbury calling his name in Spanish. Early on the morning of the twenty-second, by crawling around in the grass and work-

ing up nerve enough to ford a waist-deep creek, he found
his way to the slave quarters, deserted, of course, on the Vince
ranch. He took off his wet silk drawers and put on the cast-
away clothes of a slave, including a blue cotton round jacket,
pantaloons of domestic cotton, and a smelly hide cap. He still
wore the linen shirt with the diamond studs and the morocco
slippers. He'd eaten the chocolates, but he made a bundle of
the sheet, silk drawers, and water bottle. Bringas's blanket he
used for a serape.

Had the President walked from the Vince ranch through
the tall grass toward the head of Vince's Bayou he still might
have gotten away, but he'd lost his sense of direction, so instead he crept along the bayou in the general direction of the
Texan camp.

In Colonel Burleson's party was a twenty-one-year-old from
Captain Heard's company named Joel W. Robison. As
Robison tells it:

> We picked up two or three cringing wretches before we
> reached Vince's Bayou that morning. Colonel Burleson
> gave each of them a few lines in pencil stating that they
> were his prisoners. He then sent them back to our camp
> without guard. The colonel, with the greater part of the
> detachment, went up toward the head of the bayou. Six
> of us went down the bayou and, finding no Mexicans,
> decided to head back to camp.

The others in this six-man group were the Kentucky com-
pany's color-bearer, Sergeant Sylvester, and Privates Sion
Record Bostick, Alfred Miles, Charles Thompson, and Joseph
Vermillion. Robison was the only one who could speak much
Spanish. These men had started back on the road between
Vince's Bridge and the Lynchburg Ferry, which ran through

fields of sedge grass as high as the sides of a horse, when Sylvester spotted some buck deer. While the others waited for him, he galloped into the high grass. He drew rein about four hundred yards from the road and began to draw a bead on one of the bucks, but something startled the animals and they ran off. A moment later, the head of a man in a hide hat appeared across the waves of grass. The flag-bearer shouted to his companions and at the same time put spurs to his horse.

Santa Anna ran only a few paces and then fell to the earth, covering himself with his muddy blanket. Sylvester's galloping horse almost trampled His Excellency. Then Bostick rode up, dismounted, kicked Santa Anna to his feet and searched him for weapons. Bostick wanted to shoot him, but, as Santa Anna later told Houston, Sylvester interceded. When Robison rode up and started talking to the captive in Spanish, Santa Anna kissed the Texan's hands.

Robison saw the fine shirt and the diamond studs under the rough clothes, and he asked:

"You are an officer?"

"No, soldier."

"Where do you think Santa Anna and Cos have gone?"

"Maybe they go to the Brazos," replied the prisoner.

Alfred Miles, a brawny, tough fellow from Richmond, Virginia, said: "Robison, tell him to jump up behind me. I got the biggest horse. We better let him ride until he gets to the road. We might lose him in this tall grass."

Once they'd reached the road, Miles pushed Santa Anna off the horse. The party continued on its way with Santa Anna being driven along like a sore-footed cow. Robison said:

Santa Anna walked slowly and apparently with pain. He groaned and complained. Miles, who was a rough, reckless fellow, carried a Mexican lance he'd picked up during the morning. With this he occasionally pricked the prisoner to quicken his pace, which sometimes amounted to a trot.

Finally, Santa Anna fell in the road and begged Miles to let him ride again. He stood up and grabbed the muscular Virginian by one hand, which he began kissing. Miles drew back his hand and cried: "If this crazy son-of-a-bitch doesn't stop this kissing, I'm going to kill him."

Santa Anna then appealed to Robison in a torrent of Spanish. He said he was a cavalryman and not used to walking. Then, incredibly, the Texans almost let Santa Anna get away. Five of the six favored letting the prisoner walk on to the Texas camp alone and turn himself in, both to be rid of his complaining and to free themselves for the more rewarding pastime of hunting deer. Only the exasperated Miles balked.

"Let's kill the son-of-a-bitch," he said. "Then we can go hunting."

But this suggestion, too, was rejected. As Robison said, "My compassion for the prisoner moved me to mount him behind me."

Perhaps a few of the six Texans did continue their hunt, for Sylvester and Miles were not in the party that brought the prisoner into camp. Santa Anna said later that the color-bearer had been the kindest of all his captors, but certainly, Joel Robison also treated *El Presidente* well. As Robison described the trip to camp:

He [Santa Anna] was disposed to converse as we rode along. He asked many questions. The first was: "Did General Houston command in person at the action yesterday?" He also asked how many prisoners we'd taken and what we were going to do with them. When, in answer to an inquiry, I told him that the Texan force in the battle

was less than 800 men, he said I was surely mistaken—
that our force was certainly much greater.

I asked him why he came to Texas to fight against us.
He replied he was a private soldier and bound to obey
his officers. I asked if he had a family. He said he did. I
asked if he expected to see his family again. He only
shrugged his shoulders.

The prison compound was in a state of excitement. Some
of the Texas guards had been teasing the prisoners and, as
Delgado said:

They told us in broken Spanish that their officers were
holding a meeting to decide whether we should be shot
before notifying their government or whether the execution should be postponed until ordered by the superior
authority. Such was the state of our affairs when assembly,
roll call, or something else was beaten. Over a hundred
Texans stood in line; they loaded their guns, and then
stood at ease. We felt rather nervous. I, for one, was as
cold as ice, believing those in favor of immediate execution had carried the point and the fatal moment had come.
Soon, however, our confidence returned when a good man
(they are to be found everywhere) told us to cheer up as
Houston, Rusk, Allen and others, whom I respect for it,
had opposed the motion.

It was soon after, at 2 P.M., that His Excellency arrived at
the prison area, as Delgado said "under charge of a mounted
soldier."

Robison said he was astonished

to hear the other prisoners exclaim: *"El Presidente! El
Presidente!"* by which we were made aware that we had
unwittingly brought in the Napoleon of the West. The

news spread and we'd scarcely dismounted ere we were surrounded by an excited crowd.

Moses Austin Bryan said that several of the prisoners were imprudent enough

to remark, *"El Presidente,* General Santa Anna!" and some of the Mexican officers said, *"Ini la boca!"* meaning, "Shut your mouth!" This let it out that it was Santa Anna and Colonel Hockley and Major Ben Fort Smith took charge of him and led Santa Anna to where General Houston was lying.

The guard hurrahed and the army took it up. I went from my camp fire to where General Houston was, a distance of 30 or 40 steps. Houston was on a mattress brought from Lorenzo de Zavala's house. Colonel Hockley said: "General Houston, here is Santa Anna!" Santa Anna said in Spanish: *"Yo soie Antonio Lopez de Santa Anna, Presidente de Mexico, Commandante en Jefe del exereito de opperacions y me jouje a la dispasicion del vahinte General Houston y quinos ser tabado comedene ser an General quando is prisonerno* [sic] *de guerra."* The English being, "I am Antonio Lopez de Santa Anna, President of Mexico, Commander-in-chief of the Army of Operations and I put myself at the disposition of the brave General Houston. I wish to be treated as a general should when a prisoner of war."

Rusk and Lorenzo De Zavala, Jr., were walking up to see Houston when Santa Anna was led up. Said Rusk:

Santa Anna recognized young De Zavala at once and advanced to meet him. Among other things he exclaimed: "Oh, my friend, my friend! The son of my early friend!" With other exclamations in the same strain he embraced young De Zavala, with high indications of apparent feeling, and I think dropping a tear. De Zavala returned his greeting with that deference which would have been due to his former rank and power; but at the same time there came from his countenance an expression I have scarcely seen equalled on any occasion. His look seemed to wither Santa Anna. And staring the president full in the face, he replied: "It has been so, sir." Santa Anna showed plainly that he was much mortified.

Santa Anna was more than mortified when he stood before Houston, ringed in as he was by curious Texans, most of them in favor of executing him on the spot.

Later, Houston recalled: "I was lying on my left side in a kind of daze, when I felt some person clasp my right hand. I looked up as Santa Anna stood before me. He announced his name and rank."

As Santa Anna stood before the wounded giant under the oak tree, The Hero of Tampico was trembling. His right hand was on his heart. The Texas soldiers pressed close. Old Jimmy Curtis yelled: "I'm going to kill him and skin him for Wash Cottle!" Another soldier jeered: "So that's the big dog of the tanyard!" Private James W. Winters described the scene: "I was digging graves for our dead near the prisoners' corral when Santa Anna was brought in. Some called out, 'Shoot him! Hang him!' Houston ordered the men who made these threats to be taken away."

Some of the Texans, according to Delgado, wanted to "fire salutes and to make other demonstrations to celebrate the capture of so lofty a person, but Houston courteously forbade it. From this time on we [the prisoners in the compound] were left alone. His Excellency had become the center of attraction."

Santa Anna's arrival excited reactions other than anger in

some Texans. For example, Colonel Somervell, who years later was to offend Prince Carl of Solms-Braunfels by his rude glee when he saw the prince, leader of a Texas German colony, being lifted into his pants, was never a man to restrain himself when something struck him as ridiculous. Somervell laughed uproariously at the sight of *El Napoleon del Occidente* in his hide cap and slave's clothes.

"Quiet, God damn it! Quiet!" boomed Houston.

Santa Anna took off his hide cap.

Houston's Spanish wasn't adequate for the occasion, so first Bryan and then Almonte and young De Zavala acted as interpreters.

"Ah, General Santa Anna, have a seat!" said old Sam. He motioned to an ammunition box nearby. Houston had propped himself against the oak in a seated position. Earlier in the afternoon he had been gnawing on an ear of corn and cursing his aching ankle. Then he'd fallen into a troubled doze. But now he felt a lot better, and the wound was forgotten for the while. He cut himself a chew of tobacco.

The Mexican President sat down on the box. He clutched his knees to control his *muy agitado,* and asked that his *cofre de medicamentos* be brought to him. Almonte brought the box containing Santa Anna's opium supply. At the same time, Houston ordered that Santa Anna's silken marquee and other camp effects be brought up by some prisoners and set up about thirty yards from the Texas General's own bedroll.

Santa Anna opened the medicine box with a convulsive motion of his hands and swallowed a piece of opium. The drug calmed him and restored some of his old self-assurance. He had full command of his voice when he said: "That man may consider himself born to no common destiny who has conquered The Napoleon of the West. And now it remains for him to be generous to the vanquished."

"You should have remembered that at the Alamo," answered Houston.

"I summoned them to surrender," said Santa Anna. "They refused. The Alamo was taken by storm. The usages of war justified what I did. I was acting under the orders of my government."

"Why, you ARE the government of Mexico," said Houston. "A dictator, sir, has no superior."

"I have orders among my papers, General Houston, from my government commanding me to exterminate every man found in arms in the province of Texas and to treat all such as pirates. You have no government and you are fighting under no recognized flag."

"The less you say about your own crimes, the better it will be for you, sir," Rusk interjected.

"We flatter ourselves that we have a government," said Houston, "and we'll soon have a flag."

Houston had been speaking in calm and courtly fashion, but his big voice began to have angry tones as he asked the Mexican: "If you feel excused for your conduct at the Alamo, you don't have the same excuse for the massacre of Colonel Fannin's command. They had capitulated on terms offered by your general, Urrea. And after the capitulation they were perfidiously assassinated."

Almonte translated this to Santa Anna slowly, as if he were speaking to a child. The President began to tremble again. He clutched his knees once more, and he said: "I was not told that your men at Goliad had capitulated. General Urrea told me he conquered them in battle. He had no authority whatever to receive their capitulation. If the day ever comes that I can get Urrea into my hands, I will execute him for not telling the truth."

Santa Anna helped himself to another piece of opium and

fell silent. While His Excellency tried to regain control of himself, Almonte remarked to Houston: "You were lucky, General, you didn't fight us on the twentieth. Our men were ready then and so anxious to fight we could hardly keep them in ranks. Why did you wait, General, until after Cos had reinforced us to attack?"

"Why take two bites for one cherry?" replied Houston. But then he demanded sternly: "Must I be questioned by an inferior officer in the presence of his commanding general?"

Abruptly, Santa Anna found his voice and began to curse Almonte in voluble Spanish. He accused the aide of losing the battle by his lack of vigilance. Almonte, growing equally excited, tried to defend himself. Houston was affronted by this exchange, and the Texas General roared: "Quiet, God damn it! Quiet!" Bryan and De Zavala translated this order to Santa Anna.

In the conversation that followed, Santa Anna analyzed the battle to Houston in much the same way Almonte had. Santa Anna told Houston: "It is hard to believe that the same troops who fled yesterday in dismay and terror at your first fire are the same ones I could scarcely restrain the day before from attacking you. They were old soldiers, who fought bravely with me in Zacatecas. It was destiny!"

Moses Bryan said that Thomas Rusk did as much talking as Houston during the two-hour conference with Santa Anna. According to Bryan, His Excellency ultimately said he "would stop the war and send Filisola and the other troops out of Texas."

"Filisola wouldn't obey you," suggested Rusk. "You're only a prisoner now."

"My officers and men are so attached to me they will obey any order," answered Santa Anna.

"Then tell Filisola and all of the troops with him to surrender," said Rusk.

"I will do nothing to disgrace myself and my nation,"
answered Santa Anna, with more spirit than he'd shown since
his capture. "I am but a single Mexican. You can do what
you wish with me."

Bryan said:

> Colonel Almonte modified this reply of Santa Anna's.
> Almonte said that while Santa Anna was willing to order
> General Filisola to march out of Texas, he could not con-
> sent to order him to surrender; that the Mexican forces
> were far superior to the Texan.

Santa Anna's account went like this: "He [Houston] proposed that I issue orders for the surrender of all the troops
under my command. I refused, emphatically, to do this." Santa
Anna said that he agreed to send a message to Filisola ordering all Mexican troops to retreat as far as West Texas just so
that his armies in the field would know that *El Presidente* was
still alive. He added that he really wanted Filisola to attack
the Texans and "vindicate the honor of our arms."

Houston agreed, as a temporary solution, to a limited withdrawal of Mexican troops rather than absolute surrender or a
full-scale retreat, and Caro was summoned to prepare Santa
Anna's dispatch to Filisola. Several copies of this document
were made. It read:

> Your Excellency: The small division under my immediate
> command having had an unfortunate encounter yesterday
> afternoon, I find myself a prisoner of war in the hands of
> the enemy, who have extended to me all possible con-
> sideration. Under these circumstances I recommend your
> Excellency to order General Gaona to march back to

San Antonio and wait orders, as Your Excellency will also
do with the troops under your immediate command; at
the same time warning General Urrea to retire with his
division to Victoria; since I have agreed with General
Houston upon an armistice, pending certain negotiations,
which may put an end to the war forever.

Almonte asked how the dispatches should be dated, and
Houston replied: "Lynchburg, I believe, is the name of this
place."
   "No, sir," John Wharton said. "It is called San Jacinto."
   "Then let it be dated San Jacinto," said Houston.

10

The Aftermath

While Santa Anna was held a prisoner, his friends were afraid to invade Texas because they knew not at what moment it would cause his sacrifice. His political enemies dared not attempt a combination in Mexico for a Texas invasion, for they did not know at what moment he might be turned loose upon them. So it guaranteed peace to Texas so long as he was kept prisoner.

—SAM HOUSTON, EXPLAINING WHY HE DIDN'T KILL SANTA ANNA

WORD of the battle and its outcome spread quickly to the refugees nearest the battlefield. On the twenty-first, Miss Dilue Rose's sorrowing family were about twenty-five miles from San Jacinto, at a town called Liberty. The same morning, Dr. and Mrs. Rose had buried their youngest daughter in Liberty, and they intended to rest there for the night.

As Dilue wrote in her diary:

On Thursday evening [April 21], all of a sudden we heard a sound like distant thunder. When it was repeated, father said it was cannon and that the Texans and Mexicans were fighting. He had been through the War of 1812 and knew it was a battle we were hearing. The cannonading lasted only a few minutes. And father said the

Texans must have been defeated, or the cannon would not have ceased firing so rapidly. We left Liberty in half an hour. We traveled nearly all night. We were wretched as we could be; for we had been four weeks from home and there was not much prospect of ever returning. We had not heard a word from brother or the other boys that were behind us driving the cattle. Mother was sick and we had buried our dear little sister at Liberty.

We continued our journey through mud and water. And when we camped in the evening 50 or 60 young men came by who were going to join General Houston. One of them was Harvey Stafford, our neighbor, who was returning from the United States with volunteers.

The young men went a short distance from us and camped. Then we heard some one calling in the direction of Liberty. We could see a man on horseback waving his hat; and as we knew there was no one left at Liberty, we thought the Mexican army had crossed the Trinity. Harvey Stafford and the other young men were ready with their guns.

When the lone rider got near enough we understood what he said. It was, "Turn back! The Texan army has whipped the Mexican army and the Mexican army are prisoners! No danger! No danger! Turn back!"

When he got to our camp he could hardly speak he was so out of breath. When Harvey Stafford and the other young men began to understand the glorious news they wanted to fire a salute, but father made them stop. He told them to save their ammunition, for they might need it.

Father asked the rider for an explanation. And he showed us a dispatch from General Houston giving an account of the battle and saying it was safe for the people to return to their homes. The courier had crossed the Trinity River (which was ten miles wide at Liberty) in a canoe, swimming his horse. He had left the battlefield the day after the fighting. He said that General Houston was wounded and that General Santa Anna had not been captured.

The courier was an Irishman and had been an actor. He stayed with us that night and told various incidents of the battle. There was not much sleeping that night. Mr. McDermot not only told various incidents but acted them. The first time that mother laughed after the death of my little sister was at his description of General Houston's helping to get a cannon out of a bog.

We were on the move early the next morning. The courier went on to carry the glad tidings to the people who had crossed the Sabine. We took the lower road and went down the Trinity. When Mr. McDermot left us the young men fired a salute.

By dawn of April 22, the battlefield, still strewn with corpses, was visited by its first curiosity seeker. Mrs. Sophia Suttonfield Auginbaugh, who later proudly claimed to have been the first Texan woman to venture into the camp after the battle, was a native of Indiana. She was an attractive, capricious young woman. A year before, she had separated from Jesse Auginbaugh, her schoolteacher husband who was said to be a former Prussian officer. Some time later, after spicy debate, the Texas Congress was to grant her a divorce on grounds of desertion, but when she turned up in Houston's camp on the twenty-second, she was still a married woman. There is some doubt as to Auginbaugh's sympathies during the Revolution, and in Almonte's journal there is a reference to a lone Prussian, who could have been Jesse, walking into

Santa Anna's camp on the Brazos. But there's no doubt that
Sophia was loyal to the Texas cause.

This intrepid lady must have found Houston, whom she'd
met during his stay in Nacogdoches, in a sorry state. By sun-
rise on the twenty-second, the wounded General must have
been worn out from exertion and loss of blood, and in his
eagerness to discuss ideas for Santa Anna's capture with Smith
and Almonte that night, he had gotten hardly any sleep. According to Mrs. Auginbaugh, she did some practical nursing
for Houston, sponge-bathing his face and combing his hair
for him.

Even though on the morning of the twenty-second Santa
Anna was still at large, the Texan soldiers found time to think
of other matters besides his capture or the probability of another battle with the powerful Mexican forces if *El Presidente*
should succeed in reaching Filisola's camp.

Late on the evening of the twenty-first, word had spread
through the Texan camp that one of the victims of the day's
action had been a woman. Second Lieutenant William W.
Summers and Pvt. Sam Woods of Capt. Amasa Turner's company saw her body by Peggy Lake on the twenty-second.
Summers said that she was young and long-haired and finely
dressed. Though the Texans were fresh from slaughtering
hundreds of Santanistas, these blood-stained avengers were
horrified over this report that someone in their army had killed
a helpless girl prisoner by plunging his saber into her breast.

It wasn't just whispered—it was shouted throughout the
Texas camp that the killer was Col. John Forbes, Commissary
General of the Texas army. Forbes was thirty-nine, a stout
man of medium height with sandy hair and mutton-chop
whiskers of the same color. He was a native of Ireland. Like
Sidney Sherman, he'd been a successful businessman in and

around Cincinnati, Ohio, before he came to Texas. The year before Forbes had been judge of the municipality of Nacogdoches. He'd helped Houston make the treaty with the Cherokee Indians that kept these warlike people neutral through the critical months of the Revolution. Later, Forbes was to be Mayor of Nacogdoches and to win many state honors.

No commissary general could have been popular in Houston's half-starved, ill-clad army. And it would be hard to find an army less amenable to authorities in general than the rebel Texans. Private Joel Robison, the Spanish-speaking lad who brought in Santa Anna, said that Forbes made a lot of enemies "because of his strict discipline and enforcement of military usage." What Robison must have meant was that Forbes *tried* to enforce military usage. But even before the battle, Forbes had been the object of catcalls and jokes from the disrespectful Texan enlisted people. On the morning of the twentieth, Commissary Forbes had been sleeping soundly by Buffalo Bayou, his saddle mule hobbled nearby, when someone yelled a false alarm that the Mexicans were attacking the camp. Colonel Forbes awoke with a start, jumped up, leaped onto his mule, and began to flog the creature frantically. Because of the hobbles, the mule could only jump around. The Commissary General was surrounded by laughing men. After this prank, one man would call out:

"Who rode away on a hobbled mule?" and another would reply loudly, "Colonel Forbes done it."

On the night after the battle and for several days thereafter, the jibes directed at Forbes were uglier.

"Who killed the woman?" one Texan would yell.

"Colonel Forbes done it!" a fellow soldier would roar in reply.

Often these shouts were exchanged in the Commissary General's hearing. Certainly, Forbes suffered under these accusations, yet the determined officer refused to be distracted from his duty, which was keeping an eye on the spoils.

The days following the battle brought personal sufferings to Mirabeau Lamar, too, but not because of hostility from the men. The young Georgia Colonel was as much of a hero as ever in the eyes of his comrades-in-arms after the battle.

Like Rusk, Lamar had a close friend who had been critically wounded in the fighting. His name was Pvt. Benjamin Rice Brigham, and he was a member of Calder's company. He was nineteen years old.

The evening before the battle, the enthusiastic youngster had appealed to his friends in the company for someone to substitute for him on guard duty, saying: "Boys, I've stood guard for two nights in a row and am detailed again tonight. I want to be fresh for that battle tomorrow. I'd sure give somebody a pretty to take my place."

Francis J. Cook, another young private, agreed to do Brigham's guard stint that night, and Lamar's friend had gotten his rest. The boy fell during the charge on the Mexican works, and on the twenty-second lay close to death.

The arrival early that afternoon of Joel Robison with Santa Anna must have thrust all other concerns from the minds of the Texans, for whether or not the soldiers expected that the fighting would end because they held the Mexican dictator, none of them could have failed to understand that the capture of the arch-criminal behind the Goliad massacre was and would remain the climax of the Revolution.

How much the army as a whole knew of what was going on during Houston's two-hour talk with Santa Anna would be hard to say, but it is certain that some among the men were privy to the conversation between the two commanders. Deaf

Smith sat nearby throughout the conference, listening with cupped ear.

When Caro had prepared Santa Anna's dispatch for Filisola, Houston summoned Smith and entrusted to him the delicate job of delivering the order. Smith was given at least two copies of this document. The canny scout needed no briefing. Deaf and two companions took off that night for the Brazos. They were halfway between Harrisburg and Fort Bend on the morning of April 23 when they suddenly came upon a lone Mexican rider. They knocked him off his horse and then caught and questioned him. He turned out to be a courier from San Antonio, bringing City of Mexico dispatches intended for Santa Anna. He had been riding along in the open so casually because he had thought that the Santanistas had control of the Brazos country.

Deaf confiscated all the dispatches intended for Santa Anna. Then he told the thoroughly scared courier about Santa Anna's defeat and capture and showed him the President's letter to Filisola. He put a copy of the letter in the Mexican's wallet and told him to deliver it to Filisola at Fort Bend.

Evidently it was Smith's plan to slow-trail the messenger to Filisola's camp, but, very close to Dr. Pleasant Rose's deserted farm near the Brazos late on April 23, he encountered another lone Mexican. This one was a small, dapper man traveling on foot and carrying a fine china pitcher of water and an ear of corn. Smith didn't know it then, but his new captive was Santa Anna's brother-in-law, General Cos. Soon after this, Smith happened upon a fellow member of the spy company, Dilue Rose's uncle, Jim Wells. No doubt Miss Dilue heard the story she committed to her diary from Wells. It reads:

Smith carried Cos to Stafford's Point where he got another horse, and then took Cos back to the San Jacinto

battleground. Mr. Smith said that when he captured
General Cos, whom he did not know, he asked the prisoner if he had been in the battle. General Cos said he
had been in the battle but he escaped after dark on the
evening of the 21st, and that he abandoned his horse at
a burned bridge. Smith then asked him if he had seen
General Cos, and the prisoner said he had not. The old
scout continued: "I am Deaf Smith, and I want to find
General Cos. He offered $1,000 for my head, and if I
find him I will cut off his head and send it to Mexico."
When they arrived at the battlefield, Smith was very
much surprised to find that he'd captured Cos.

The scout made no effort to harm the General, though,
once he had him identified.

Labadie was making a list of the prisoners when Cos was
brought in. "I soon found difficulty making out my list because
of the eagerness of our men to see General Cos," said the doctor. One Texan, after looking at Santa Anna's brother-in-law,
said: "Why, he's just a God damned little scrub of a thing!"

Delgado wrote:

The presence of General Cos created such a sensation
among the conquerors that they crowded and quarreled
for a sight of him. They would even push off the guard
around the prisoners. The general found it expedient to
lie down, wrapping his head in a blanket. Scoundrels
were not wanting who would have murdered him.

Among the Yankees, according to Delgado, "was a hunch-
back who spoke Spanish and took a wicked pleasure in bringing us unpleasant news." This fellow said that all the prisoners
were to be executed "if Santa Anna doesn't put an end to the
war and remove every Mexican from Texas." Labadie, Cap-

tain Allen and other Texans assured them that their lives were safe as long as they remained quiet.

Although Smith had not set out for Filisola's camp until late on April 22, Santa Anna's second-in-command already had a rough idea of the battle's outcome many hours before the dictator was captured. Colonel Mariano Garcia, the commander of Cos's straggling rear guard on the morning of the battle, had not arrived at Vince's Bayou until after Smith's men had burned the bridge. Garcia's unit apparently camped near the bayou, where they heard the noise of battle and then intercepted fleeing Mexican survivors. The company Garcia commanded was an infantry unit, and it seems that the Colonel himself had the only horse. He scribbled a penciled note describing the Mexican defeat to Filisola and lent his mount to a courier, who delivered the message in the early morning hours of April 22.

At Fort Bend on the twenty-first, Filisola had almost a thousand troops on the east side of the Brazos ready to march to the President. When Garcia's messenger arrived, the wary Italian General hastily ordered these to return to the west bank, where they joined Gaona's division. This combined force quickly retreated fifteen miles to the west, to Elizabeth Powell's tavern. Evidently, the cautious Filisola was afraid the Texans would press the offensive, and he didn't want to be surprised at Fort Bend.

Not until 3 P.M. on April 22 did Filisola get around to sending Urrea a message: "The President has suffered a misfortune. . . . It is necessary, therefore, for you to do everything you can to reach this place [Mrs. Powell's] with all your force as soon as possible."

Urrea, who wasn't friendly with Filisola, said he got this order between 9 and 10 A.M. on April 23. He set out up the west side of the Brazos at once. On the way, Urrea picked up two or three survivors of Santa Anna's division, and they told him that the President had been killed. Near Mrs. Powell's, Urrea said, his scouts

> overtook my brigade while on the march, bringing with them a presidial soldier with papers for Senor Filisola from His Excellency, General Santa Anna. This courier informed me that he had set out from San Antonio de Bexar with mail for His Excellency, the general-in-chief, and when he arrived at the Brazos in search of our army he met A CERTAIN SMITH and two other Texans, who by the orders of General Houston was looking for Senor Filisola to deliver to him the dispatches of His Excellency, General Santa Anna; that the said men [Smith and the two other Texans] had taken the correspondence for General Santa Anna and had given him the one for Senor Filisola. From this information, I learned that His Excellency was a prisoner. All the members of the brigade under my command were overjoyed to hear this news for we had been told that he had been killed in battle.

Urrea sent two of his aides to escort the courier at the gallop to Filisola, and the message from Santa Anna reached the temporary staff headquarters at Mrs. Powell's hours before Urrea's unbeaten brigade arrived. Filisola, Gaona, and Sesma were already there.

Mrs. Powell's was the scene of a ranting council of generals. Urrea said later that he advised for a force of three thousand backed by a rear guard of fifteen hundred to cross the Brazos and attack Houston's army. In justifying the proposal later, he remarked:

> Can the success of such a combination be doubted? It seemed certain that Houston had only about 720 men

and they had an equal number of prisoners to guard. Under such circumstances, it is impossible to believe that nearly three thousand men, all in fighting trim, could not have obtained a complete victory.

Urrea accused Sesma of having avoided combat with Houston in cowardly fashion during the Texans' long retreat, and he charged that General Gaono had no real excuse for having tarried so long on the upper Colorado River.

Filisola had a good argument for the retreat Santa Anna had ordered. The new commanding General said that if the Mexicans went on the offensive, Houston would merely kill all the prisoners, and that then the mobile rebels could easily continue keeping one or more of the raging rivers between them and the government forces. Filisola himself reminded his colleagues that he was Italian-born, and said that he would be glad to turn over the supreme command to one of the native Mexicans. No one, not even Urrea, took him up.

Perhaps all the generals at Mrs. Powell's realized that the average Mexican soldier had had a bellyful of this wilderness called Texas. Santa Anna had said, just after the victories at the Alamo and at Goliad, that "it was then, with sorrow on the part of the troops, that thought was given to the need of garrisoning this vast territory to hold our conquest; and the mere idea of remaining in Texas dismayed the triumphant Mexican soldiers more than defeat."

According to Gaona, even Urrea finally voted for the retreat, and the Mexicans headed for West Texas as Santa Anna had ordered them to do.

In the Texan camp on April 23, while the Mexican generals and their 4,500 well-equipped men were beginning their retreat, Houston's eight hundred ragged rebels settled down in earnest to the labors of the victorious.

One of the most pressing of their chores was the care of the spoils. Houston, in his official report on the battle, said there were "about 600 muskets, 300 sabers, 200 pistols, several hundred mules [Rusk said there were 700 mules] and horses and near $12,000 in specie." There were also some seventy or eighty loads of ammunition and powder, which had been hauled from Santa Anna's camp to the Texas bivouack, stacked close to the prisoners' stockade.

During the morning of the twenty-third, the interest of the Texan soldiers in their loot nearly caused the destruction of the whole camp. Dr. Labadie was searching the pile of plunder for some sheets for bandaging when he saw a few enlisted men nearby examining some of the Mexican pistols. As the doctor watched, one of the pistols exploded, "causing it to discharge a ball which grazed the chin of Colonel Robert Eden Handy," who was taking an inventory of the spoils. The ball also gave the handsome Handy a flesh wound in the left arm. Labadie said "a burning wad from the pistol fell on some cartridges and caused more than 20 ammunition boxes to explode, scattering fragments in every direction.

Colonel Delgado, watching from the stockade, said "the fire extended to the pans of the stacked muskets, which exploded like infernal machines. The prairie, too was set on fire, and the covers of other ordnance boxes began to burn." The prisoners were permitted to move swiftly from the scene under guard. Delgado described their flight:

We had run a considerable distance when we turned around and saw the fire had been extinguished. We could not help applauding the resolution and bold determina-

tion with which some of these extraordinary men had
rushed into the flames and smothered them with their
feet and blankets and some water drawn from the bayou.
[Dr. Labadie started a bucket brigade.] We had a narrow
escape. I thought at one time that the conquerors of San
Jacinto would be blown into eternity; not, however without some regret on my part to have to go with them,
owing to their stupid carelessness.

Delgado had noticed that "repeatedly the Texans went about
the combustible matter and even handled it with glowing
pipes in their mouths."

Judging by Pvt. Bob Hunter's report, when the ammunition
dump exploded, some Texans thought they were under attack
from Filisola, and Santa Anna may have thought so too. Said
Hunter:

I & Meredith Tunget was on gard that day, & we was
garden Sant Anna. We was by the log that was bifore
Sant Anna doore [the entrance to his tent] when the firing
commenced & Sant Anna broke for the doore. We jurked
up our guns & presented them to his breast, tolde him to
halt. He got within 2 feet of the doore & stopt. He looked
up strate in our eyes. We had our guns cocked on him.
Every body jumpt for his gun. We thot that Colonel
Ugawtechea [Colonel Domingo de Ugartechea] & General Fillasola & General Woll had come from Richmond
and attacked us . . . There is one [thing] about it, I know
we was pritty badly scared.

Houston had more to worry about than the carelessness of
the men wandering around near the explosives that day,
though certainly the explosion and fire must have distracted

him temporarily from his other problems. One particularly difficult decision faced him after the battle. In Santa Anna's captured papers, Houston found the names of prominent Texas Tories. Many of the Santanista collaborators had relatives who had fought well for the rebels, so, out of wisdom and kindness, Houston never released the names of these Tories. Instead, he sent out a company under Capt. Dan Kokernot to inform the known Tories "along and beyond the Trinity River" that they were now working for a lost cause. Kokernot must have had a good number of serious talks with the Tory leaders, but he, too, kept their names secret.

On the twenty-third, Houston began dictating his official report of the battle for Burnet, but because of his wound, which was growing steadily more painful, and the heavy demands on his time during those hectic days, he didn't finish his account until the twenty-fifth.

The first member of the government to arrive after the battle was Vice-president De Zavala, who appeared on the twenty-third. The earnest Latin official had not come to celebrate. When he had set out from Galveston Island, he had intended to join Houston's army with reinforcements and fresh supplies. With De Zavala were Emily's master, James Morgan, a Texan named John J. Linn, who was in charge of the cannon and supplies, and an armed company. This force had embarked from Galveston Island in the steamboat *Cayuga,* and had only learned of Houston's victory at New Washington when they stopped at Morgan's plantation and talked with some of the servants. The steamer had then forged on to San Jacinto, its passengers in a much altered frame of mind.

As the *Cayuga* neared the rebel camp at around 5 P.M. on the twenty-third, Labadie said the first thing the Texans saw was smoke rising from San Jacinto Bay. Rusk took all the mounted men in camp and galloped toward the smoke column to investigate. Rusk met the steamer at Lynch's Ferry. Linn later said:

> Colonel Rusk greeted me with the exclamation: "Linn, we've got him now!" meaning Santa Anna. We steamed up Buffalo Bayou and were soon at the camp of the army. Our arrival with the much-needed supplies was the signal for general rejoicing as the men had lived for several days on fresh beef without salt. I delivered to Old Bennett [Valentine Bennett of the Texas army commissary department] an abundance of flour, coffee, sugar, soap, powder, lead, etc.
>
> Tom McKinney [one of the financiers of the Texas Revolution] and I went to visit the field of battle. The ghastly spectacle of 600 Mexican corpses festering in the sun met our gaze. The pockets of every one had been turned in the search for plunder. In passing the breastworks I noticed a man who was extracting the teeth of dead Mexicans. He was a dentist from the United States. [Sam Houston later implied that this was Dr. Labadie.] I suggested to General Houston that several hundred prisoners under strong guard should bury the enemy slain. Houston repeated my suggestion to Santa Anna, who replied that he was wholly indifferent and cared not what disposition was made of the bodies.

Linn, who spoke Spanish well, said that Santa Anna "volunteered the information" that he'd often had "similar problems" during his military career. The year before, for instance, he had ruthlessly slaughtered hundreds of Zacatecas rebels, and *El Presidente* regarded this slaughter as analogous to the defeat of his army. "Santa Anna said he found incremation a ready solution. But here the matter ended."

Linn said he was a witness when Mrs. Peggy McCormick came back and took a horrified look at her once-beautiful San Jacinto ranch. Private Bob Hunter described the scene like this:

> Mrs. Mc Cormac an irish woman come to camp to see Gen'r'l Houston. She wanted to know if he was going to take them ded Mexicans off my Leg [league of land]. They Hant me the longes day I live. Houston told [her] no. He wanted Sant Anna to bury them & Old Sant Anna would not. I & Meredith Tunget stud gard on Sant Anna, it come to our lot to gard him several times. Sant Anna said that it was not a Battle, that he cald it a massacre. Plage gon him what did he call the Alamo & Labahie.

Houston replied to Mrs. McCormick's request that the slain Mexicans be removed with what Linn called "mock seriousness." Old Sam said: "Madam, your land will be famed in history."

"To the devil with your glorious history!" replied Peggy McCormick.

Delgado said that when on April 23 the steamboat carrying De Zavala arrived, "the artillery on the boat, consisting of two guns, fired a salute of five rounds. The troops in camp formed a line and received the visitors with hurrahs."

One of the first things De Zavala did at San Jacinto was to inquire about General Castrillon. The Texas Vice-president was an old friend of the General's. When De Zavala heard of his cultured friend's death, he set out to look for the body. He was shocked to see the Spaniard still lying nearly nude on the plain beside the scalped carcasses of two gunners. He had his servants carry Castrillon's body across the bayou to the De Zavala ranch, where the General was buried in the Vice-president's family plot.

Another funeral held late on the twenty-third, or the day after, was that of Mirabeau Lamar's good friend, Benjamin Brigham. Brigham, one of the Texans who'd been wounded in the battle, died the same day De Zavala arrived. Colonel Lamar was deeply moved by the sight of his young friend's body. His emotion prompted him to write a poem on the subject, which began:

> Beautiful in death
> The soldier's corse appears,
> Embalmed by fond affection's breath
> And bathed in his country's tears.

Despite the various distractions of the day, some on Houston's staff besides the General himself managed to give some thought to the culmination of the campaign itself. The most impetuous suggestion came from the aggressive Col. John Wharton, who went to Houston and offered to ride out to Filisola's camp and propose armistice terms to the Mexican General. Apparently, Houston himself agreed to this proposal, but Rusk and others opposed arranging such terms with the enemy without the sanction of Burnet and the cabinet. Houston did not argue the point—perhaps because he agreed with Rusk, or perhaps because he was too busy and too ill to be bothered with a dispute on the subject. Instead he simply ordered Wharton to abandon the plan.

Rusk, unlike Houston, had somehow found time before De Zavala's ship arrived on the twenty-third to complete his brief report of the battle for Burnet, and he and the commander in chief decided to dispatch this message at once instead of waiting until Houston's was ready. Although the government was then only forty-five miles away, the messengers would have a difficult trip, for the journey had to be made by boat and only small open craft were available.

Rusk chose as his couriers Pvt. Benjamin C. Franklin and two other soldiers whose names have been lost. At the last minute, the three soldiers' company commander, Bob Calder, volunteered to go along too. Calder had no special interest in bearing messages to Burnet, but he did have a fiancée whose family had sought refuge on Galveston Island, where the Texan government had temporarily established itself.

The four messengers set out around noon on the twenty-third in a leaky rowboat, somehow forgetting to take provisions for the trip. The water in San Jacinto Bay was fairly calm, and the soldiers made good progress with two men rowing and two bailing, until they reached Galveston Bay. There they encountered a storm, and the little boat was tossed around fearfully. They pulled in close to the shore and continued their journey with Calder, wading in the shallow water, towing the boat while his three companions gave him what help they could with the oars. When they saw the *Cayuga* heading for San Jacinto Bay, they signaled frantically, but the big boat either failed to see them or feared to venture into the shallow water. The *Cayuga* steamed on past, and the four men in their leaky, foundering rowboat were left alone, no better off than before.

By the morning of April 25, Houston and Santa Anna had agreed on further measures to avoid, for the time being, new battles between the two armies. Santa Anna had drafted a new dispatch for Filisola ordering the Mexican troops to retire to the Rio Grande. This message was to be handed to Filisola in person, and Ned Burleson was instructed to deliver it.

Colonel Burleson, with three hundred horsemen including Deaf Smith, set out on April 25 in the early morning in search of Filisola's camp. Burleson's men had to ride hard to catch

up with the fleeing Santanistas, and even the resourceful Smith
had trouble finding the four thousand Mexican troops. They
caught up with Filisola just before he reached the Colorado
River, and they actually located his camp by an accident.
Walter Lane, who was on the expedition, said:

> We camped on the San Bernard one evening a few days
> after the Battle of San Jacinto. Some of our men, who
> were bathing, swam over and happened to go through a
> skirt of willows on the other side and saw Filisola's army
> encamped on the prairie. They came back and gave the
> alarm. Colonel Burleson and some others swam their
> horses over. We were drawn up opposite the ford with
> orders, if we heard anything, to swim over and succor
> them. In about an hour they came back. Filisola, after
> reading Santa Anna's letter and order, told Burleson he
> would give an answer next morning.

One of the Texans who rode into Filisola's camp with
Burleson didn't return. Instead, Alex Alsbury of the spy company got a pass from Filisola so he could ride on to San
Antonio to see if his wife and child, of whom he had heard
nothing since Mrs. Dickenson had told him they'd survived
the Alamo siege, were safe. When, after a perilous trip among
the confused and fleeing Santanistas, Alsbury arrived in San
Antonio, he found that his family had come to no harm.

By nine o'clock on the morning after the Burleson-Filisola
conference, the Texans had still not received Filisola's promised reply. Walter Lane said:

> Our officers went across the San Bernard again. In a few
> minutes Deaf Smith came back and said that Filisola had
> retreated during the night and his camp was vacant. We

swam over to see the enemy's camp. They had left tents, wagons, muskets, lances and everything they couldn't carry conveniently on pack mules and had cut out, burning the carriages of six pieces of artillery and throwing the guns into a pond.

Lane picked up a lance and "exercised my juvenile arm" by hurling it at the canvas tops of covered wagons. From the wagons came loud howls: "Don't kill us, God Damn Soldiers!" About twenty sick and wounded Santanistas were in the wagons. Said Lane:

We treated them kindly and fed them. We sent a detachment to follow Filisola and see that he didn't damage the settlements any more during his retreat. He made a straight march for the Rio Grande and didn't draw rein until he got into Mexico.

Some of the Texan settlers who had fled during The Runaway Scrape were beginning to return to their old homes as the Mexican armies withdrew from the area between the Brazos and the Colorado, where most of the refugees had lived. Many of the families had suffered dreadfully during their flight.

As the Rose family made another trying journey from Liberty to Lynchburg, they met a family of refugees named King. These people were grieved over a particularly horrible disaster, for not long before the Roses joined them, Mr. King had been devoured by a huge alligator.

Dilue and her parents reached Lynchburg on the night of April 25. By then, Nathaniel Lynch had the ferry back in operation. "We crossed the San Jacinto the next morning and stayed until late evening on the battlefield," said Miss Dilue.

"General Santa Anna had been captured. There was great rejoicing at the meeting of friends." Dilue wanted to go see the famous prisoner, but she said:

> Mother would not go because she said she wasn't dressed for visiting; but she gave sister and me permission to go look at the President of Mexico. I had lost my bonnet crossing Trinity Bay and was compelled to wear a table cloth on my head. I couldn't go see the Mexican prisoners with a table cloth on my head for I knew several of the young men in the army.

The Rose family did visit the graves of the two Texans who died on the battlefield. Said Dilue:

> There was none of them that I knew. The dead Mexicans were lying around in every direction. We were glad to leave the battlefield for it was a grewsome sight. We camped that night on the prairie and could hear the wolves howl and bark as they devoured the dead.

Houston, Rusk, and the others at the Texan camp had resolved to wait until Burnet arrived before working out a peace treaty with Santa Anna, but even though the Santanistas had shown nothing if not eagerness in the matter of retreating, Houston believed a new outburst of fighting was possible. The Texan army was still vastly outnumbered by the Mexican troops in their territory, and Filisola had given Houston no real indication that he would not turn back and attack once he had had a chance to organize the forces that had so recently come under his command.

The Texans had no way of knowing how Rusk's four emissaries to Burnet had fared, but they certainly realized that the trip to Galveston Island in a craft no more seaworthy than the one Calder and his men had used would be slow. The days between the twenty-third, when the message had been sent to Burnet, and Burnet's arrival were necessarily anxious ones for Houston. Moreover, the General was feverish, for his wound had become infected.

In one respect, Houston's position was immeasurably improved after the battle, for though he still had in his command men like Mirabeau Lamar and Sidney Sherman, who would not be reconciled to his leadership and remained steadfastly his enemies, the rank and file of his army had reconsidered, and almost overnight Houston had become their hero. This new popularity did not distract the General from his responsibilities, but because of his illness and the number of demands on his time, a certain amount of mismanagement was inevitable, especially in connection with the spoils.

Although Houston already had an estimate of the spoils by the twenty-third, his colonels felt called upon to verify the General's figures by recounting the money. Dr. Labadie said:

> Twelve thousand dollars in specie was captured and it was decided it should be distributed among the captors. The money was counted so often and by so many that, naturally, it stuck to their fingers till but $7,000 was left. I was told that General Houston cursed them in his peculiar way for their rascally conduct and swore the money should be counted no more.

Dr. Labadie said that he never got his share of the $12,000 and charged that "Colonels Burleson and Forbes brought an account of $15 against me for sheets I had used for the wounded."

Sidney Sherman said that he, Burleson and Forbes were appointed

> on a committee to count the money. I had nothing further to do with it. I think $3,000 of it was voted to the Texas

Navy. I do not remember the amount of the spoils but my impression was that each man was to receive about $11. I know that I never received any share of it. Commissary General Forbes was the principal man in keeping and distributing the money.

Captain Heard said that he believed that there were about forty-five boxes, each containing about $1,000 of "silvery money." Heard said "there was a general suspicion and belief that John Forbes secreted and stole a considerable amount of money and goods which had been taken from the Mexicans, and appropriated same to his own use." Heard said his men got $10.25 each. Captain James Gillaspie said each man in his company got $11.75.

Said Dr. Robert Kemp Goodloe:

My captain, Henry Karnes, told me that each soldier was supposed to get $12. Actually, every man in Karnes company received only $4 and we didn't get that until we were at Victoria in West Texas during the pursuit of Filisola and the main Texas Army overtook us. We were told that Commissary Forbes had gone East with the money.

Private Campbell Taylor said he got $8 or $9 as his share. He said "the day for distribution of the money was put off, from day to day, and each time the amount was reported it grew less and less. The opinion prevailed through the army that the spoils were being absorbed by Forbes, who had charge of them."

Amasa Turner said his men each got $6.

Houston said later:

I never saw a dollar of the money. I appointed Colonel Sherman and other officers to divide the spoils and had

nothing further to do with it. I understood that $12,000
was found in Santa Anna's chest. That a number of the
spoils were purloined I have no doubt. Four hundred
and some odd dollars worth of spoils were purchased on
my account by John A. Wharton, for which I paid into
the Treasury of Texas in 1838 upwards of $400. I was
wounded and lying on my blanket after the battle and
did not hear all the rumors and slanders of the camp.

It is possible, though this story can hardly be verified, that
the captured specie amounted to even more than the $12,000
figure originally given to Houston. Henderson Yoakum, a
Texas historian who knew many of the men of San Jacinto,
said that Santa Anna's war chest contained more than
$18,000.

On the twenty-sixth, the spoils were auctioned off. Santa
Anna's silken love bower went to Emily's master, Colonel
Morgan. Forbes wasn't the auctioneer, but he kept the books
and often handed up such portable articles as Santa Anna's
silver chamber pot to the auctioneer. Each private soldier was
given $16 credit to buy auctioned articles. The auction was
held near the prison compound, and that close observer, Colonel Delgado, reported: "It was hard to see them breaking our
trunks open and everyone of them loaded with our shirts,
trowsers, coats and other personal possessions. I saw my boots
sold at auction while my blistered feet were wrapped in pieces
of rawhide."

Delgado wrote that he and most of the prisoners were
wearing lice-ridden castoff clothes. "His Excellency, the general-in-chief, alone, had the good fortune to preserve most, if
not all, of his baggage."

Seven hundred mules, about one hundred horses, and many
Mexican saddles were sold to the Texan soldiers. Delgado said

that a sort of rodeo followed the livestock auction right there on the corpse-strewn battleground. Said Santa Anna's former aide:

> It was quite amusing to see these gentlemen putting riding saddles on fractious and wicked mules which knew nothing beyond the pack. They would adorn the mules with green and red cords which our voltiguers and grenadiers had worn on their caps, placing these on the animals' ears, manes and tails. They also bedecked the mules with epaulets of our officers, caring little if one was white and the other yellow. Just so the epaulets glittered, that was enough. They also delighted in covering their animals with all sorts of trappings and colors after the fashion of our bullfight clowns.

The Mexican Colonel said the "trials of horsemanship lasted the whole day" and many a Texan was thrown heavily. After the rodeo performance, Delgado thought: "How strange these men! Many of them act and feel like the wild Comanche!"

There is no doubt that one of the slanders circulating in the Texans' camp reached Houston's ears. Commissary General John Forbes, who bore not only insinuations that he was appropriating the spoils, but also the more sinister accusation that he had cold-bloodedly murdered the Mexican woman found dead after the battle, went to Houston and asked for a court of inquiry on the murder charge right there on the battleground. This inquiry was held, probably on April 28, with Houston's old antagonist Sherman, who was no particular friend of Forbes, as President of the court. The official report of the court was that

after a strict, thorough and full investigation of all matters bearing on this case, we find no evidence whatever in
support of such charges or any grounds for censure
against Colonel Forbes in the action of the 21st. On the
contrary, the court finds his conduct on that occasion to
have been characterized as that of a courageous as well
as humane soldier.

This should have settled the matter. Yet twenty-two years
later, Dr. Labadie, in his first-person account of the battle
written for the *Texas Almanac,* again implied that Forbes
had killed the girl prisoner and had also stolen some of the
$12,000 found in Santa Anna's war chest. In 1859, Mayor
Forbes filed a $25,000 slander suit in the district court at
Nacogdoches against Labadie. There followed years of taking
depositions from men who'd fought at San Jacinto, including
a lengthy and lofty one from Sam Houston.

The most damaging testimony against Forbes came from
Thomas F. Corry, who'd been a nineteen-year-old private in
Captain David Murphee's company. Corry was also from
Cincinnati and had known Forbes there. Corry said that
Forbes had treated him with great politeness when the youth
joined the Texas army at Groce's. The Commissary General
took Corry to General Houston and introduced them. As
Corry described the death of the Mexican girl:

On the 21st, about an hour before sundown, and after
the Mexicans had been completely routed, I found myself on the margin of San Jacinto Bay. I was among some
Texas soldiers, strangers to me, who were shooting Mexicans who were trying to swim across the bay or hide in
the marshes.

As this work did not suit my feelings, I left and soon

after met Forbes. He was alone and on foot and he had his drawn sword in his hand.

Corry said that he and Forbes stopped there and spoke in friendly fashion for a few minutes. Then, "there came from the timber onto the prairie where we stood two men in the uniforms of Texas regulars, bringing with them two prisoners, a man and a woman."

At a considerable distance, probably too far away to see that one of the prisoners was a woman, there appeared a Texas colonel on horseback, riding at the gallop. Corry said that this dignitary was "Colonel Somervell or Colonel Burleson, I don't remember which." The Colonel pulled rein and cried out to the regulars: "Kill them, God Damn them! Remember the Alamo!" Then the Colonel went off at a gallop. Said Corry:

> The two regulars immediately attacked the man prisoner with their bayontes. I tried to save the man's life. At the same time, Colonel Forbes thrust his sword through the woman's breast, the blade entering in front and coming out her back. As the sword was withdrawn, she fell forward upon her face and, quivering, died without a groan.
>
> She made no effort to escape or ask for mercy. I have always thought she felt that, as a woman, she was safe.
>
> This dreadful deed paralyzed me. The man was killed, too. I said to Forbes: "Damn you, you have killed a woman." He, without uttering a word, stooped down and touched her on the shoulder with the tips of his fingers and gave out a sound of sorrow, a sound which sounded like, "tut-tut!" I left him instantly. I do not believe Forbes was in the battle. He was, from his office, a noncombatant. And when I met him he was coming from the direction of our camp.

I have never spoken to Forbes from that day, although I met him frequently around the camp and afterwards on the streets of the City of Houston in 1839. My own indignation has never ceased.

I told the facts to Dr. Booker [Dr. Shields Booker, surgeon of the Second Regiment] about 10 minutes later. Booker damned Forbes and said he would spread it all over camp. That evening, and for several nights after tattoo had been beaten, cries would be heard all over camp: "Who killed the woman?" And the answer would be: "Colonel Forbes." Forbes must have heard this, night after night.

The murder of the woman was the most horrible thing I have ever witnessed in a life of much adventure.

Sam Houston said in his deposition that he hadn't read the Labadie account of the battle in the *Texas Almanac*. The General said he'd wait to read it "along with Baron Munchausen when I have utter leisure." Houston also said:

An envious and slanderous report of Colonel Forbes was circulated in camp, something about killing a woman. Colonel Forbes came to me and asked for a court of inquiry. He was found not guilty of every imputation of unsoldier-like or improper conduct. I believe it was all a fabrication and not one word of truth.

Colonel Sherman, in his report as President of the court of inquiry made on April 28, 1836, had completely exonerated the Commissary General. In his 1859 deposition, Sherman said that Forbes had admitted to the court of inquiry that he killed the woman, "but claimed he was excusable for doing so in battle. No person, to my knowledge, showed any interest in prosecuting the matter against Forbes."

Sherman said that neither Corry nor Pvt. Robert M. Cravens, who also claimed to have seen Forbes kill the woman, stepped forward to testify. Corry, when questioned on this point in 1859, said he didn't even know that the court was held. Sherman recalled that

> the commissary general had one witness at the court of inquiry, a Mexican woman prisoner, wife of a muleteer. She testified as to Forbes' humanity and kindness to her and other women made prisoners. She spoke of him caressing her fondly. This created some amusement.

Sherman said he'd ridden by McCormick's (or Peggy) Lake

> after my regiment had defeated the division opposed to us. There I saw lying dead a woman. I asked: "Who killed her?" Several answered at the same time, "Colonel Forbes." I asked why. The same men replied that he [Colonel Forbes] was anxious to bloody his sword.

Sherman said he believed the object of the court of inquiry was to show that Forbes would not kill a woman prisoner intentionally, and that none of his accusers came forward, so the Commissary General was acquitted.

Private Thomas H. Mays of Capt. Jesse Billingsley's company testified that Forbes fell behind on the initial charge against the Mexican camp and hid in the tall grass of the prairie and behind a rise "until he heard the shouts of victory." In his testimony, Mays mentioned Pvt. Robert Cravens, who claimed to have seen Forbes kill the Mexican girl. Said Mays:

> When about 250 or 300 yards from the breastwork I was cut down by a musket ball which entered my left thigh. While on the ground, R. M. Cravens, who'd just fired off his gun, stopped near me to reload. I found my thigh wasn't broken. Just then Cravens directed my attention

to four or five of our men in the act of rising out of some
grass to our rear and protected by a rise. Cravens and I
began calling them damned cowards. One was Commissary General Forbes.

Private William B. Stout said that "just before the Mexicans
broke and ran," he saw a figure he took for Forbes lying in the
grass about fifteen to twenty yards to the rear of the line of
charging Texans. A man on Stout's left saw the prone Commissary General, too, and "remarked that Colonel Forbes had
been killed."

Young Walter Lane testified:

I saw Forbes while we were chasing Mexicans. Four or
five of us caught up with some Santanistas whom we
took prisoner. One prisoner was wounded and lying on
the ground. Forbes came up with sword in hand and
tried to run it through the man on the ground. A Texan
standing by cursed Forbes for his brutality and said that
the commissary general had already killed a woman.
Forbes denied this. The Texas soldier said it was the
truth and raised his gun on Forbes.

Captain Amasa Turner later said: "I think some of them
were not disposed to do him [Forbes] justice in anything. And
this may have been occasioned by the honest and faithful
discharge of his duties as commissary general."

Despite the evidence Labadie brought out in 1859, Forbes
was ultimately exonerated in this belated investigation, too.
Perhaps there was no real case against Forbes, or possibly Dr.
Labadie simply got scared, but in any case, the doctor ad-
mitted to the court that all he said about the Commissary
General was from "hearsay," and the case was dismissed with
Labadie having to pay $141.07 court costs and Forbes $78.97.

While Houston's army occupied itself with quarrels and accusations, Rusk's four soldiers in their leaky rowboat pressed on toward Galveston Island. Their first night out, they reached Spillman's Island, about five miles down the bayshore from New Washington. Here they found deserted plantations and supplied themselves with live chickens, a side of good bacon, and some corn meal.

On the third day of the trip, they reached the plantation of Monroe Edwards, a gambler, forger, and slave trader, at Redfish Bay, about twenty miles shy of Galveston. There was no one left at the plantation except a wild-looking slave who spoke no English, but the slave gave them provisions, including a box of fine Havana cigars.

The water grew calmer. Calder did no wading and towing now. He gave an inspired hand with the oars, but even he was tiring, and the others were just about exhausted. As they neared the island, the young Captain was doing all the rowing.

At sundown of the fourth day they reached Virginia Point, just across a wide lagoon from Galveston. They had a tantalizing view of shipping in Galveston Bay. Three ships of the Texas Navy were there, led by Commodore James Hawkins aboard the flagship, *Independence*. The others were the *Invincible*, Captain Jeremiah Brown, and the *Flash*, Captain Luke Falvel. They were there to protect the refugees or to help them escape.

With Galveston in sight, the four men in the rowboat were too weary to go on when the sun went down on the fourth day of their journey. Even Calder had given out. They pulled in to Virginia Point and spent the night under wet blankets, once moving their camp because they'd stirred up a nest of rattlesnakes. On the morning of the fifth day they crossed the lagoon in a 40-degree norther.

As they pulled alongside the *Invincible*, said Calder:

Through his speaking trumpet, Captain Brown hallooed to us: "What's the news?" When I told him about the battle his men literally lifted us on board in the midst of wild excitement. Brown took off his hat and gave us three cheers and threw his hat into the bay. He cried to his men: "Turn loose long Tom!" And they fired a cannon twice. Then Brown said: "Hold on men, Old Hawkins [the senior Texas Commodore] will put me in irons again!"

The ship captain took the four heroes of San Jacinto to his cabin "and treated us to the best liquor on the ship." They were in a very mellow mood when they started for the island in Brown's gig. The flagship of Commodore Hawkins, the *Independence,* was anchored between the *Invincible* and the landing. Hawkins had been watching the strange behavior of the *Invincible* through his glass. When the gig drew near, the Commodore also shouted through his speaking trumpet: "What's the news?"

"When we were sufficiently near to be understood another scene of wild excitement ensued," said Calder. Commodore Hawkins insisted that they come aboard the *Independence* and have another round of drinks and something to eat. "The welkin rang," said Calder. "Hawkins fired 13 guns. I suppose this was for the 13 original United States colonies as Hawkins had been with the U. S. Navy before he came to Texas."

They were downing great drafts of rum when Commodore Hawkins mentioned that Captain Calder had better go ashore and tell the news to the President "for Burnet was a great stickler for official prerogative, and would be miffed if anyone on the island got the news before he was officially notified of the battle and its result."

Calder and the other three then resumed their journey to

the island. On the shore Mary Douglass, Calder's pretty fiancée, was waiting and the three privates found members of their families or friends among the refugees. It wasn't until hours later that they thought of taking Rusk's report to the President.

Calder said that "Santa Anna was expected every day on the island." And on that April 27, many of the refugees, including the Douglass family, were ready to sail away on the schooner *Flash* when the happy news arrived. The President had strict rules on the island. No drinking of liquors was permitted. Even so, Captain Calder was full of good spirits when he marched into the President's marquee. There he said he and the three privates

> were received with stately courtesy which, at first, we did not understand, thinking a little more cordiality and less formality would have suited the case. This, however, gradually, subsided. And before the interview was closed, the president treated us with grave though genial courtesy.

Bob Calder and Mary Douglass were later married and had six children. The couple lived long and happy lives.

One of the dispatches Houston had sent much earlier to refugees around San Jacinto telling of the victory had by this time reached the United States Army forces under General Gaines on the Neches River. Probably on the same day that Rusk's report reached Burnet, Gaines selected a young lieutenant named Ethan Allen Hitchcock as his own messenger to relay the news to Andy Jackson in Washington, D. C. Hitchcock, a grandson of the Ethan Allen of American Revolution renown, set out from the Neches around April 28 on the long, hard journey.

On April 30, Filisola's emissary to the Texan camp, Brig. Adrian Woll, rode in under a flag of truce. According to Urrea, he himself had wanted to make such a visit earlier

> on the pretext of taking to His Excellency his mail and bringing back the armistice. The army could await the result of my mission on the Brazos, from where, once information as to the weakness and impotency of the enemy was obtained after my return, it (the four-thousand-man army) could march upon the Texans.

But apparently Filisola would have none of any such plan. Instead, no emissary was sent until after Filisola had crossed the Colorado, and then Woll, whose command of English was excellent, was selected to make the trip. This soldier of fortune from France was allowed to interview Santa Anna and other prisoners hurriedly. Delgado said that

> tears of indignation gushed forth from General Woll's eyes at the wretched and degraded condition of his brothers-in-arms. This gallant general, our good friend, was hardly allowed to embrace two or three of us, with a few hurried words, as we were surrounded by strict and insolent guards.

Woll was kept in detention for eight days, probably because Houston was still afraid Filisola's column might turn around and attack if they had reliable information as to how weak in numbers the Texas army was.

Actually, whatever Urrea's hopes had been earlier, there was little danger that the Mexican army would again go on the offensive. The campaign had been hard on the morale of the soldiers even when they had been victorious, and the retreat had utterly destroyed their interest in fighting Texans.

If the rebels were inclined to ascribe the meek withdrawal of their once-powerful foe entirely to the battle of San Jacinto, they flattered themselves, for as Samuel Asbury, a contemporary Texas historian, observed:

The Battle of San Jacinto wasn't the real climax of the Texas Revolution. The last real great action of the revolution was the Battle of Texas Elements before which Filisola's 4,000 troops went down to complete destruction AS AN ARMY. On the two forks of the San Bernard River and on the Colorado, the rain and the cold and the wind and the mud and the flood destroyed that fine army.

The canny Indians, too, believed that the fleeing Mexicans suffered infinitely more from the unfamiliar climate and the new hazards it brought than from their one defeat in battle. The Texas settlers on the Red River, who got their first news from the Indians, were told: "Tiebo-Mex get sick and go home. Their horses sick, too."

In Houston's camp, frequent rainstorms followed by periods of hot sunshine had made the battlefield stench unbearable by May 1. So the Texan army, now a grand caravan with few pedestrians, moved seven miles in the direction of Vince's Bayou to the plantation buildings of Dr. George Moffit Patrick. Here there were three frame houses in which the officers found quarters, and the men put up rude shelters. The feverish Houston was given the luxury of a cot.

Some of the officers were routed out of the houses on May 4 by the appearance of the travel-worn Texas ad interim government. President Burnet and his suite arrived on the busy steamboat *Yellowstone*.

The President wasted no words of praise on the wounded General. Now it was obvious that Burnet was Houston's implacable enemy out of sheer jealousy. Secretary of the Navy Potter, undoubtedly with Burnet's support, suggested that Houston should be court-martialed for mismanagement of the San Jacinto campaign. The Potter-Burnet theory was that Houston could have just as easily whipped the Mexican hosts on the Colorado ard saved the country between the Colorado and the Brazos from being overrun by the enemy.

Rusk, De Zavala, and others saw to it that Potter's suggestion was ignored. Anyway, Houston's tremendous popularity with the majority of the soldiers would have saved him from a court martial. As Pvt. George Erath said: "Like the rest of the army I had criticized the general during the retreat. But after San Jacinto I was well reconciled to Houston's management of the campaign." William H. Wharton, statesman brother of John Wharton, wrote about this time that Houston was so popular with the soldiers that he could easily have become dictator.

The President and his cabinet spent little time at the army's headquarters. By May 5, Houston's wound was so much worse that Surgeon General Ewing was afraid the General would get lockjaw and die if he didn't get better medical attention. The doctor suggested that Houston be sent to New Orleans by way of Galveston. So on the fifth of May, Houston resigned his commission and turned his command over to Rusk so that he could return to Galveston with Burnet, who was leaving in only two days.

Santa Anna and others of the more prominent Mexican prisoners were to be taken back to Galveston with the Texas government officials. Late on the evening of May 7, Burnet and the cabinet, including the new Secretary of War, Mirabeau Lamar, went aboard the *Yellowstone*. When Thomas Rusk and his brother David carried Houston, on a cot, down to the dock, Burnet informed them, to their astonishment, that as Houston was no longer in the employ of the Republic, he could no longer have passage on government ships. But here, J. E. Ross, Captain of the *Yellowstone,* came to the rescue.

"This ship is not sailing," the rugged old Captain informed Burnet, "unless General Houston is on it." A few minutes later, the Rusk brothers carried Houston aboard the *Yellowstone.*

The long-suffering Delgado was among the prisoners on the steamer. His guards were "those lambs," the Kentucky company. The Mexicans were herded on deck with a "volley of God dammes and other abusive expressions." Pedro Delgado said that his guards, both enlisted men and officers, quickly got into a fierce fistfight on the main deck aft. Burnet and the cabinet came out of a stateroom, and the President shouted:

"Stop this dreadful noise, sirs!"

Said Delgado:

They would no more pay attention to the voices of their President or other members of their so-called government than they would to the barking of dogs. Captain Allen finally broke up the fight on the deck by choking some of them. Very early on May 8th, after striking a bell three times, as is customary on the vessels, the machine was set in motion and we glided toward Galveston. As the steamboat passed the battlefield of San Jacinto, the troops on board were formed, facing to the field, and they presented arms, the drums beating a march. They remained in that position until they lost sight of the field.

Epilogue: Sad and Happy Endings

A reward will be paid for delivery to me [John Rice Jones] on Bailey's Prairie, Brazoria County, of a Negro named Joe, belonging to the estate of the late William Barret Travis. Joe took off with one Mexican and two horses, saddles and bridles. The Negro was in the Alamo with his master when it was taken, and was the only man from the colonies not put to death. Joe is 25 years old, about five feet six or seven inches in height, very black and of good countenace. Forty dollars reward will be paid for Joe and $10 for the Mexican.

—MAY 27, 1837, ADVERTISEMENT IN THE TEXAS "TELEGRAPH AND REGISTER," THE REPUBLIC OF TEXAS'S ONLY NEWSPAPER

D R. PLEASANT ROSE, Miss Dilue and the rest of the family returned to their home on the Brazos on either the first or second Sunday of May, 1836. They found that hogs running loose had done more damage to the farmhouse than had Santa Anna's army. The Mexicans had torn up some of the flooring, apparently while searching for eggs. They'd left the front door open and hogs had entered. Said Miss Dilue:

When we got to the front door there was one big hog that would not go out until father shot at him. Father's book-

case had been knocked over and his books, some medicines and other things were scattered around and hogs
had been sleeping on them. We children began picking
up books. We could not find those that Colonel Travis
had given us, but did find broken toys that had belonged
to our dear little sister who died while we were running
from the Mexicans.

The first thing father did after breakfast was to go to
the cornfield that Sunday morning. He had planted corn
the first of March and it needed plowing. He didn't wait
for Monday, or to put the house in order, but began to
plow at once. His field was in the Brazos bottom and he
had hidden his plow . . . Mother was almost in despair.
Father was cheerful and said Texas was going to make a
great nation.

Bob Hunter, the diary-keeping private, and his brother,
John, were the first of the Hunter family to return to their
farm on the Brazos. As Bob describes it:

I went to Lieut. McCalister & [got] a furlow to go & see
our place. Brother John & myself went ther and fond
Moseley Baker ther with his hole company & his horses
all in the yeard & one end of the corn crib tore down &
all his horses in the corn, & 30 or 40 hogs in the corn,
& I got to snorting and cussing & Moseley Baker wanted
to know what athority I had to order him off the place.
I tole him it was my father's place & I had a right to take
care of it. Capt. James Perry come up behind me and
slapt me on the shoulders & said, go it, Bob. Capt. Perry
said, Capt. Baker this is Dr. Hunter's Son & he has a
right [to] defend his property & futher Capt. Baker all
the famelys in this country is depending on this corn for

bread . . . They [Baker's company] left that evening & Capt. Perry, Brother John & myself set in & put the corn back & pached the crib as well as we could & fixt the fences and drove out the cattle . . . When the people got home, some fond something they had left and some fond nothing. Down the Brassos corn sold for $1 a bushel, up, after the battle.

Within days after the *Yellowstone* reached Galveston, Houston left for New Orleans to have his badly infected leg wound treated. For six weeks he was seriously ill, and he was not active for another month and a half after that.

With old Sam out of the way, Burnet must have hoped that things would go smoothly for him, but such was not the case. From Galveston, the ad interim government moved to Velasco, where the Brazos meets the Gulf, and settled down to consider the case of the Republic of Texas versus Lopez de Santa Anna. The judicial-minded Burnet turned his cabinet into a court of justice, and Santa Anna was charged with murder. Mirabeau Lamar, the new Secretary of War, and Navy Secretary Potter argued violently that Santa Anna should be executed immediately. For the first time, Lamar and Potter fell out with Burnet, for the President believed, as Houston had, that Santa Anna should be spared, at least for a while, "as a hostage for peace." Rusk, the new Commander of the army, sat in on the case, and, as Lamar wrote: "coincided with the President in his views and made a few remarks in support of them."

The cabinet, except for Lamar and the cantankerous Potter, agreed with Burnet. So, instead of putting their captive to death, on May 14 at Velasco the Texans signed not one but two treaties with Santa Anna.

The first treaty, which was made public, provided that all

hostilities should cease, all Mexican troops should retreat beyond the Rio Grande, and prisoners should be exchanged. This treaty also stipulated that Santa Anna would be returned to Mexico as soon as possible, after having promised that he would never again take up arms against Texas.

The second treaty was a secret one, and it differed from the first only in that there were more details on the promised conduct of Santa Anna once he was back in Mexico. He was to use his influence on the Mexican government for an acknowledgment of Texan independence, and to make arrangements so that Texan diplomatic and trade missions could visit the City of Mexico.

If this second treaty was to serve its purpose, it was imperative that Santa Anna be returned to Mexico before his dictator's organization had broken up.

The oratory of Potter and Lamar had inflamed many of the Texan army officers against Burnet. That level-headed San Jacinto Captain, Amasa Turner, talked Henry Millard and others out of trying to overthrow Burnet's government, but the army persisted in demanding Santa Anna's execution. The courageous Burnet defied them. One night during this crisis, Mrs. Burnet sat up all night with a loaded pistol so her husband could get some sleep.

On June 1, 1836, in accordance with the treaties, Santa Anna was taken aboard Captain Jerry Brown's *Invincible* off Velasco. With Santa Anna were Almonte, Caro, and other aides. The captive President sent a farewell message to the disgruntled Texan army units at Velasco: "I have been a witness to your courage on the field of battle, and know you to be generous. Rely with confidence on my sincerity, and you shall never have cause to regret the kindness shown me. In returning to my native land I beg you to receive the thanks of your grateful friend."

Adverse winds prevented the *Invincible* from sailing for the next two days. On June 3, 1836, several hundred armed volunteers from the United States arrived under three men named Thomas Jefferson Green (not the artilleryman Tom Green of the battle of San Jacinto), Memucan Hunt and James Pinckney Henderson. They came on a steamboat, called the *Ocean,* and they were looking for trouble. Mirabeau Lamar described this episode:

Whilst The Invincible was still anchored off Velasco, with Santanna on board, Green, Hunt and Henderson arrived with their volunteers. These gentlemen took, at once, an active part with the mob against Burnet and greatly encreased the public ferment by their violent speeches. They demanded that Santanna be brought on shore. The President refused. The mob, headed by Green, Hunt and Henderson, gathered around the President's house. The volunteers were paraded under arms. In this situation, Burnet came out and addressed the croud, defended his views and insisted that the Treaty should be carried out and the faith of the nation preserved. He was followed by [Attorney General Peter William] Grayson, who spoke to the same effect. [John A.] Wharton then made a long and independent speech. He vindicated the Treaty and repelled most vehemently the interference of the military in the affair. Wharton protested especially against the interference of armed strangers who had just landed on our shores. He could not brook the idea that they should become the dictators of the country and set the government at defiance. The mob headed by Green & Henderson finally prevailed. Brown sent in word from the Invincible that he wouldn't sail even if ordered to do so by the President. Burnet then saw the impossibility of carrying out the treaty. Hardeman, Hunt, Henderson and Colonel Ben Fort Smith went on board after Santanna. He [Santa Anna] was landed and marched under the execration of the populace to McKinney's store.

Tom McKinney, owner of the store and one of the Revolution's financiers, commented: "My God! What a burlesque of government!"

De Zavala asked to be excused from further connection with the Burnet government, which he said had lost the "moral support" of the Texas people. Actually, Burnet had behaved with great courage. And his impassioned speeches, and those of young John Wharton and Grayson, probably saved Santa Anna from being lynched.

Santa Anna was imprisoned in Texas for many months, during which time his influence in Mexico waned. The City of Mexico government announced that all of his acts as a captive were illegal. And, anyway, Texas hadn't fulfilled all the provisions of the Velasco treaties, for the Mexican President had not been returned to his own country.

Burnet had other troubles besides his disagreements with Mexico. There was no money in the treasury, and next to the President, the tax collectors had the most dangerous jobs in the new nation. The army continued to give trouble. Private Peter Hansborough Bell, later a governor of Texas, said:

President Burnet and his cabinet have incurred such a mass of odium that [should] they send one of the Old Patriarchs [apparently he meant a Biblical character] here on the most sacred mission he would be viewed with suspicion. God in his wisdom & perfection could not please the dissatisfied spirits of the Army.

The Texas army had grown tired of guarding the herd of prisoners, so most of them had already been farmed out to work on farms and ranches. The big plantation owners, swarming back over Lynch's Ferry, seized the most skilled ones. The planters needed laborers, for hundreds of slaves had run off during the flight of the civilians before Santa Anna's army.

Miss Dilue Rose's father, although he had owned no slaves before the Revolution, got a very scholarly Mexican officer for a peon. Soon, however, the officer was instead teaching the Rose children French and other languages. Although the prisoners were not formally returned to Mexico, they were all released. Many, including the Rose family's learned servant, chose to settle in Texas.

Burnet enjoyed during his administration only one stroke of good luck and that came, unexpectedly, from the United States of the North. Ethan Allen Hitchcock, the messenger carrying news of Houston's triumph to Andrew Jackson, had arrived at the White House grounds on May 16. Although Houston hadn't bothered to sign the message that Hitchcock carried to the United States capital, President Jackson recognized the General's handwriting. Jackson must have had trouble adjusting himself to what had happened at San Jacinto, for he didn't release the story until May 21.

The Texas cause was popular in most parts of the United States. Even the Abolitionists had developed a sympathy for the faraway rebels after they heard of Santa Anna's cruelty at the Alamo and the Goliad massacre. There were wild celebrations throughout the United States after May 21 when the battle account appeared in the public prints.

Aaron Burr, who was eighty years old and near death in

Staten Island, New York, commented bitterly on Houston's popularity. In 1806 Burr had been tried for treason because he too had had a scheme to appropriate a part of Mexico, together with United States lands in the West, and make the combined territories an independent nation. Burr remarked cynically: "I was born thirty years too soon. What was treason in me thirty years ago is patriotism now."

The Mexican minister to Washington was angered by the celebrations in the United States over Houston's victory, and reminded Andrew Jackson that Mexico had a treaty of amity with the United States of the North. But Jackson and his government apparently didn't take the minister's anger too seriously.

On June 18, 1836, Henry Clay offered a resolution to the United States Congress that the independence of Texas be recognized. Although the resolution was not adopted until March of 1837, the fact that it was offered did serve to bolster the Texan position in relation to Mexico, and it must have cheered the hard-pressed Burnet.

The first Texan President was no doubt very weary of his office when, on July 23, he issued a proclamation for a general election on the first Monday of September, 1836. There were three candidates for the Presidency: Stephen F. Austin, Henry Smith, and Sam Houston. Although Houston claimed to be reluctant to run because he was still convalescing from his wound, he won easily. He got 4,374 votes to 745 for Smith and 587 for Austin.

Houston and the first Congress took office in October. The new President made Austin Secretary of State and Smith Secretary of the Treasury. He also relieved Rusk of the command of the unruly Texas army, which now numbered about twenty-five hundred, and returned him to his old post as Secretary of War.

When Rusk accepted the cabinet post, a new problem arose. A wild fellow named Felix Huston, said to be a distant relative of the President, had brought about five hundred volunteers to Texas from Mississippi soon after San Jacinto, and as soon as Rusk left the army, this Huston took over. The soldiers "elected" him their General.

Sam Houston and the Texas Congress nominated Albert Sidney Johnston, as the senior General, but when Johnston tried to take over command of the army he was challenged to a duel by Felix Huston and accepted. Johnston was severely wounded, but later recovered and returned to duty.

Then the Texan President resorted to what Burnet called his "Indian cunning" to dispose of Felix. The self-appointed Commander of the Texan army was infected with what old Sam styled "the Matamoros fever." Felix wanted to lead another expedition against that Mexican metropolis on the Rio Grande. The President asked Huston to come to the Texas capital and discuss the Matamoros operations. Houston entertained the young General without stinting, even letting the guest have his bed while old Sam slept on the floor. At the same time, Secretary of War Rusk was riding to all the army camps giving most of the troops furloughs. When Felix Huston returned from the capital he found that his army had been reduced by about two thousand men. Deprived of his army, he lingered for a few years in Texas, participating in Indian wars from time to time but never again making his ambitions felt as he had when he first arrived. In 1840 he went home to Mississippi and never returned to Texas.

Houston had inherited one problem from the Burnet administration—Santa Anna himself. His Excellency's supporters in the City of Mexico were rapidly losing official status, and a bitter rival of Santa Anna's named Anastacio Bustamente had gained much of the power Santa Anna's sympathizers were losing. Houston realized that Santa Anna was becoming less and less valuable as a hostage, so he decided to send The Napoleon of the West back to Mexico as soon as possible.

Houston's plan was for Santa Anna to be sent first to Washington, D. C., for a conference with President Jackson. From Washington he would be shipped to Vera Cruz. Andrew Houston, old Sam's son, said: "The purpose of the Texan President was for the Mexican people to see the apparent respect shown to Santa Anna as their President and for Santa Anna to be impressed with the power of the United States."

The captives, Santa Anna and Almonte, traveled under guard, passed over the road between Vince's Bayou and Lynch's Ferry on their way to Washington in late 1836. The skeletons of His Excellency's army still lay on the field at San Jacinto, but there is no evidence that Santa Anna was affected by this grisly sight.

Not long after His Excellency reached Washington, he was released and sent back to Mexico on a United States ship. Although he was received coolly when he got home, the old Santa Anna luck held. In December, 1838, he joined in the defense of Mexico against a minor invasion launched by the French in retaliation for the mistreatment in Mexico of some bakers who were French nationals. This wrangle was called The Pastry War. In a comic opera battle with the French invaders, Santa Anna lost a leg. His Excellency also lost the battle, but his defeat was not much publicized because the French got bored and left the country. Santa Anna capitalized on the occasion by making a death bed speech in which he reminded the world that he had always been ready to shed his blood for his country. When he recovered from his leg amputation he visited the City of Mexico and was again received as a national hero.

A state funeral was held for his lost leg and a great monument was raised over the spot where it was buried. In 1838 he became acting President. By characteristic plotting against the elected President, he overthrew that dignitary in 1841. For the next four years he was again nominally President and actually supreme dictator, but in 1845 he was the victim of a liberal counter-revolution and was exiled to Havana, Cuba.

When the war between Mexico and the United States started in 1846, Santa Anna made a secret agreement with President James K. Polk, as a result of which he was permitted to go through the United States blockade and return to Mexico. This was a smart move on the part of President Polk, for Santa Anna immediately took command of the Mexican armies and started losing battles. His Excellency refused the Presidency to take command of the northern Mexican armies and was promptly whipped by Zachary Taylor at the battle of Buena Vista. He fared even worse against Winfield Scott at the battle of Cerro Gordo farther south in 1847. After this encounter, Santa Anna had to flee the battle scene on a horse, leaving his cork leg behind in his luxurious coach.

Another exile followed, but nothing seemed to discourage Santa Anna. The conservatives called him back in early 1853, and for the last time he became President and dictator. He provoked a liberal counter-revolution by selling to the United States 45,535 square miles of Mexican territory, the so-called Gadsden Purchase of territory now in New Mexico and Arizona, and he was thrown out of the country again.

Santa Anna's career was now over, but he wouldn't admit it. He even incorporated himself and sold stock on his chances of again becoming dictator of Mexico. In the 1860s he tried to return to Mexico twice and was turned back both times, once by the French and once by the United States Navy.

Finally, in 1874 when he was old, and nearly blind, and without funds, he was allowed back into the City of Mexico, and there he died in 1876.

Although he was President of Mexico four times after his San Jacinto defeat, Santa Anna never showed much inclination to mount another real invasion of Texas, any more than Napoleon thought of taking a second shot at Russia. There were a few Mexican raids in Texas during the ten years that the former Mexican subprovince was a republic, but Santa Anna's mischievous leadership kept his country in such a turmoil that no serious efforts could be organized for the purpose of regaining the lost land. Mexico never did recognize Texas as a nation.

Almonte, Delgado, Caro, and Cos all got safely back to Mexico. Almonte's career was particularly colorful. He was Mexican Secretary of War during the conflict with the United States, and thereafter he was Mexican minister first to Great Britain and later to France. He died in Paris in 1869, exiled there because of his part in aiding French invaders and putting the unfortunate Hapsburg, Ferdinand Maximilian, on the Mexican throne for a while.

Sam Houston was the political colossus of Texas for more than twenty years after the battle of San Jacinto. He was twice elected President of the Republic. After Texas was annexed to the United States, both Houston and Thomas Rusk enjoyed long terms as United States Senators. And when he was an old man, Sam was elected Governor of Texas.

Soon after San Jacinto, the Congress of Texas gave Houston a divorce from Mrs. Eliza Allen Houston. His Cherokee wife,

Tiana Rogers, died in 1839. In 1840, Houston was married to an attractive, cultured, twenty-one-year-old Alabama girl, Miss Margaret Lea. Despite the twenty-six-year difference between their ages, theirs was a very happy marriage. Sam wrote beautiful love letters to his wife when he had to be away from his family, and she wrote poems in praise of her husband. She made him give up drinking. At her insistence, Ned Burleson's cousin, Rufus Burleson, a Baptist minister, baptized old Sam in a creek. After the General had been immersed in the water, Rufus Burleson said: "Your sins are now all washed away." Houston looked into the creek and said: "God help the fish!"

Hard as Margaret Houston tried, she couldn't make her husband stop swearing. One day they were riding along and the General's horse stumbled. When he exclaimed: "God damn a stumbling horse!" Margaret made him dismount, get on his knees, and pray for forgiveness. Margaret can scarcely have blamed herself for her failure to reform her husband's language, for even on the floor of the United States Senate, Houston was sometimes guilty of blasphemy. A book called *Famous Senators*, published in 1850, observed: "Houston would sit in the Senate and whittle and mutter discontent at long-winded speakers, whom he would sometimes curse violently for their intolerable verbosity."

Houston and Rusk were among the few Southern senators who urged concessions to avert the War between the States. Texas was believed to be pro-Southern, yet Houston made speeches all over the state calling secessionists "reckless agitators." In 1859 he was elected Governor of Texas on a campaign to save the state "from the perils of anarchy and civil war."

On April 21, 1860, Houston was nominated for President of the United States by something called "The People's Party."

The nomination convention was held on the San Jacinto battle-ground, and Houston's supporters had a "San Jacinto Campaign Song" which began:

> There's a right and wrong in politics
> And right is on our side.
> So we've harnessed up the wagon, boys,
> To let the Nation ride!
> The Union is our wagon
> And it isn't any sham
> For it's crowded with people
> And the driver's name is Sam!

Houston never campaigned for President of the United States. What's more, in 1861, he did a most unpolitical thing: Governor Houston refused to take an oath of allegiance to the Confederate States of America. Houston maintained that since Texas had seceded it had reverted to its old status as a republic. He was deposed and went to live in the Steamboat House in Huntsville, Texas. Although he predicted the defeat of the Confederacy, he did let one of his splendid sons become a soldier for the South.

The Big Drunk did not live to see his prediction come true. A couple of weeks after Vicksburg fell in 1863, Sam Houston died at his farm in Huntsville.

Santa Anna and Houston had relatively happy lives, by their ambitious politicians' standards. Not all the principal actors in the San Jacinto drama were as fortunate. Take Deaf Smith, for example, who made as big a contribution to the April 21 victory as any man.

The hardships of the campaign took a lot out of old Deaf. In 1837, while scouting on the Medina he was taken ill and thought he was going to die. He told his friend Jim Davis that he wanted to be buried standing on his head, "because mine was an abnormal birth. I came into this world feet first and I've had bad luck ever since." Smith recovered and the same year led an expedition to the Rio Grande, where he defeated a squadron of Mexican dragoons. He lost a lot of horses though, and failed to realize an ambition to fly "the flag of independence" from the spire of the cathedral at Laredo.

Smith and his family were given their pick of fine houses in San Antonio which had been confiscated from Santanistas. They chose the Ramon Musquiz house where Mrs. Dickenson and the other non-combatant survivors of the Alamo had been quartered immediately after the battle. Deaf and Lupe and the children had about a year of happiness. Then Smith died of consumption.

In honor of the great scout, an area of 1,057 square miles of fertile farm country in the Texas Panhandle is called Deaf Smith County.

Many of the Latin leaders of the Texas Revolution had a difficult time under the Republic, although Sam Houston was always a sympathetic friend. De Zavala died on his plantation across from the San Jacinto battleground in late 1836, and he was buried near General Castrillon in the family plot there.

Don Juan Seguin and Tony Menchaca became political leaders in San Antonio just after the Revolution. Seguin was mayor and Menchaca an alderman and mayor pro tem. Don Juan, who'd gotten along so well with the old-time Texas settlers and fought so bravely at San Jacinto, had trouble with anti-Latin newcomers from the United States. When in September, 1842, General Woll led fifteen hundred Mexicans in a surprise raid on San Antonio and packed off fifty-six Texas prisoners, Seguin was accused of aiding the invaders. The fifty-six kidnapped Texans included San Jacinto veterans Tony

Menchaca, Dr. Booker, Alex Alsbury, and James W. Robinson. Dr. Booker was shot by a drunken guard and "died in great bodily pain and mental agony," according to another prisoner. Not long after this raid, Woll—a Frenchman by birth—was run out of Mexico, and except for Booker all of the San Jacinto veterans among the fifty-six prisoners got home safely.

Seguin left Texas after being implicated in the Woll attack. In the war between the United States and Mexico, Houston's brave Latin-company commander served as a colonel under his old enemy, Santa Anna.

The city of Seguin, on the Guadalupe River near San Antonio, is now a prosperous metropolis of about fifteen thousand people. In 1839, it was surveyed by the San Jacinto gunner, Ben McCulloch, who named it in honor of his friend, Don Juan Seguin.

Soon after San Jacinto, Mirabeau Lamar tired of his post as Secretary of War and tried instead to make himself a Major General in command of the Texas army, but the troops wouldn't accept him. Thereafter the frustrated Lamar turned politician, and in later years held just about every job from public weigher to President of the Republic.

He had spectacular runs of luck. For instance, he was elected President in 1838 almost unanimously. Both of the other candidates, Peter Grayson and James Collinsworth (a San Jacinto soldier), committed suicide just before Election Day. Lamar made some spectacular mistakes, too. In 1836–37, when Houston served his first term as chief executive, the Republic of Texas spent around $200,000 on its "Indian Policy." Old Sam understood how to deal with the Indians; he used cheap presents and honest promises. As a result, there was no major war with the Indians during Houston's first administration.

While Lamar was in office, the Republic spent about $2,000,000 fighting Indians. At one time during Lamar's administration, the Comanches were raiding as far south as the Gulf Coast, and they had fires blazing for three hundred miles in the outboard Texas settlements. In 1839, while Houston was away from the Republic, Lamar undertook a war against Sam's friends, the East Texas Cherokees, and the ancient war chief, The Bowl, was killed in battle. The Cherokees were chased over into Indian Territory after a slaughter. Lamar's Indian policy was still haunting Texas in 1959, when the Cherokee Indian Nation of Oklahoma asked for conferences with Governor Price Daniel of Texas over two million acres of land in East Texas on which the Indians say they still have a claim. The Cherokees maintain that they are entitled to compensation of $1.25 an acre for the territory they lost in 1839.

Lamar was probably urged on to his harsh action against the Cherokees by the Indian-hating Burnet, then Lamar's Vice-president, who claimed that: "Had the Mexicans been victors at San Jacinto it is quite probable that the Cherokees would have bathed their tomahawks in the blood of our wives and children."

Lamar did do constructive things, too, while he was President. He originated legislation that caused lands to be set aside for public-education-system endowments. He founded the Philosophical Society of Texas, the forerunner of the present-day organization of the same name.

If Lamar was one of Texas's worst published poets, he was also the state's best unpublished historian. He never got around to putting together a great history of the land he loved, but his notes are of immense historical value.

Lamar died in 1859 at Richmond, Texas, soon after he'd returned from twenty months of service as United States minister to Nicaragua and Costa Rica. A 934-square-mile county between the Red and Sulphur Rivers in northern Texas is named in his honor.

Tragedy came to the Wharton brothers. John Austin Wharton died of cholera only two years after the battle, and was eulogized as "the keenest blade on the Field of San Jacinto."

His statesman brother, William H. Wharton, was captured in 1838 in a Mexican raid and imprisoned in a Matamoros jail. He was rescued from his dungeon by Padre Muldoon. It seems that Miguel Muldoon went to visit Wharton, bribed the guards, and smuggled the Texan out in a priest's robe. For this good deed, Muldoon himself was imprisoned by Santa Anna in 1842, and the "Friar Tuck of the Texas Revolution" was never heard of again after that 1842 arrest.

El Colorado Karnes survived one more fierce battle with the Comanches, but in 1839 he died in San Antonio, as a result of getting up too soon from a sick bed. A 758-square-mile county in southwest Texas is named for him.

By the time Moses Lapham came home from the war, his admired Mrs. Demis Borden had died from the hardships of The Runaway Scrape. Moses again became a surveyor, and went back to West Texas to work. Not long after, he was killed by the Comanches. His good friends the Borden boys wrote a sorrowful letter to Lapham's father in Ohio, commenting that young Moses "was always ready to fight for Texas."

The Comanches also killed Alfred Miles, the tough lad who had prodded the captive Santa Anna with a lance. Miles took several warriors with him before he was slain and scalped on the headwaters of the Brazos.

David Burnet made little headway in politics when he opposed Houston. "Mr. Burnet couldn't be elected fiddler-general to the Old Chief [Houston]," said Henry Millard, the head of the regulars at San Jacinto. Colonel Millard made this prediction when Burnet was running against Houston for President in 1841. Houston won, two to one. Millard might have been somewhat prejudiced, though, for he had been one of the leaders of the army group that wanted to impeach Burnet right after San Jacinto and execute the prisoner, Santa Anna.

Burnet never profited much from his intense labors for Texas. He was in particularly distressing financial circumstances during the War between the States. Moreover, the old patriot from New Jersey saw his last surviving son march off in a Confederate uniform, and the boy was killed in combat. Since both Houston and Burnet had opposed secession and since Houston, too, had a boy in the Confederate army, this tragedy softened Burnet's attitude toward his old enemy considerably. Soon after, Burnet went to live for several years with Sidney Sherman.

In 1866 Burnet was elected to the United States Senate, but the fates were still working against this man. He wasn't permitted to serve because Texas was still an unreconstructed state. David Gouverneur Burnet died in 1870, after outliving all the other Texan leaders of the Revolution. A 1,003-acre county and its county seat in the pleasant hill country of Texas are named for the Revolutionary President.

Several weeks after San Jacinto, Robert Potter, Burnet's old friend, became commander of the Port of Galveston. While he held this post Potter married a lady he had met during the Revolution. Mrs. Solomon Page was one of those whose home life had been shattered by The Runaway Scrape. She took it ill that her husband went to the army and left her to get their two small children to the safety of Galveston Island as best she could. On the island, she was taken under the protection of Secretary of War Potter, and their relationship proved so satisfactory that after the war, she cheerfully committed bigamy in order to marry him.

Perhaps though, Mrs. Page was unaware that her marriage to Potter was illegal, even though she had never divorced her soldier husband. She'd had a civil marriage to Page while Texas was a part of Mexico, and the persuasive Potter told her that only marriages presided over by a priest were legal under Mexican law. In any case, Potter and his new wife were apparently very happy in their bigamous union.

When Houston became the first elected Texas President, Potter moved from Galveston to one of his land grants on Caddo Lake near the Louisiana border. Here he was elected first to the Texas Congress and then to the Senate. He was soon mixed up in a nasty East Texas feud called The Regulator-Moderator War. Potter was a Regulator and particularly bitter against a Moderator leader named William Pinckney Rose. Rose, nicknamed The Lion of the Lakes because of his talent for guerrilla fighting, was supposed to have been involved in the death of an East Texas sheriff of Regulator propensities. Senator Potter is said to have persuaded his friend, President Lamar, to post a $500 reward for anyone who captured or killed William Pinckney Rose.

In March, 1842, Potter led a posse to Rose's ranch and tried to earn the $500 reward. Rose was warned just before his enemies appeared, and hid under some brush, in company with a few nervously clucking hens. After a diligent search, Potter's party failed to find The Lion of the Lakes and rode away.

Soon afterwards, a committee of Moderators led by Rose called at the Potter ranch headquarters on a bluff over Caddo Lake. Mr. and Mrs. Potter were there alone. Harriet Potter, a very brave lady, tried to fire a small cannon, loaded with buckshot, which was kept on the front porch to greet Moderators and other rude guests, but she couldn't find any matches to ignite the artillery. Meanwhile, Potter picked up a rifle and ran from his dwelling, apparently in a gallant effort to draw the enemy fire away from his lady. The athletic Senator sprinted down the side of the bluff to Caddo Lake. The Moderators fired at him six times and missed. Potter was an excellent swimmer, so he laid his rifle against a tree and jumped into the lake. He might have escaped if he hadn't come to the surface too close to shore. His wife said that a Moderator named John Scott seized Potter's rifle "and as Colonel Potter's head rose out of the lake, Schott (Scott) fired," killing her husband. Later, when she recovered his body, she found in his pockets the matches for which she'd been searching so desperately.

Mrs. Potter said that after the shooting, Rose turned to her "with a cruel sneer and said: 'Now, what do you think of your Pretty Bobby?' " She claimed that Rose would have killed or wounded her if John Scott hadn't protected her.

Rose, Scott and the others were indicted and kept in jail for months. One of the lawyers for the defense was Thomas Rusk. Finally, in 1843, the case was dismissed before it was scheduled for trial.

Potter's will was as weird as his personality. He gave the latest Mrs. Potter a league of land, but it was far from the home place on Caddo Lake. The provisions of the will gave the league near Caddo Lake to the wife of a prominent Texas politician. Another Potter-owned league of land was willed to the wife of a second prominent politician. Most 1842 Texans interpreted the will to mean that the former Secretary of the Navy had had romantic relationships with the two surprised heiresses, for in his will Potter wrote that he was giving the ladies the land out of "gratitude for the delight I've had in conversations" with them. Dr. Samuel Asbury, who has studied Potter's life closely, believes that politics rather than romance motivated the strange provisions of the will. "Had Potter lived he would have run for the Texas presidency in 1844. He was a magnificent stump speaker and had an almost hypnotic effect on many voters," said Asbury. "I believe that Potter left the leagues of land to those two politicians' wives in return for a promise that the politicos would support Potter when he ran for the presidency."

Harriet Page Potter married for a third time, but for years she was involved in court cases over Potter's estate. Ultimately, the illegally married widow lost. These cases are still cited in Texas trials where common-law marriages are involved. Harriet had reasons for being bitter against Potter, yet, judging by her loving references in her memoirs, she never ceased to love Pretty Bobby. A 901-square-mile Panhandle county, of which Amarillo is the capital, was named in 1876 for Robert Potter.

Tom Rusk was almost as popular as Houston throughout his political and military career. Old Sam and Tom had a falling out in 1839 when Rusk, at President Lamar's order, led the army that drove the Cherokees out of Texas, but in 1844 Houston and his former friend had a bizarre private conference after which they were again on excellent terms. The meeting that led to their reconciliation took place on top of a twenty-five-foot-high pile of green lumber in a Shelby County pine forest. Oran Roberts, a one-time Governor of Texas, believes that it was during this conference that Rusk and Houston formulated the plans that enabled them to be repeatedly elected as a team to the United States Senate after Texas joined the Union. Roberts said the two old fighting men sat up there on the lumber pile and whittled and, toasting their renewed friendship with frequent pulls from one whiskey bottle, plotted their political course.

"Houston and Rusk occasionally had small differences, yet everybody knew that they were really firm friends," Dr. Asbury wrote.

Rusk's record in the Senate was brilliant as Houston's, but in 1857 the honest and faithful Rusk, deeply grieved by the death of his wife, shot and killed himself in his home at Nacogdoches.

Many of the *Soldados God Dammes* lived normal, happy lives after San Jacinto.

Moses Austin Bryan founded a dynasty of bankers and business leaders. Private Robert Justus Kleberg became a celebrated lawyer and judge. His son, Robert Justus, Jr., married the King Ranch heiress, and that agricultural empire has been run by the Kleberg family for many years. John M. Allen, the gallant friend of Lord Byron's who saved the lives of so many prisoners at San Jacinto, became the skipper of a far-ranging Texan gunboat, the *Terrible,* after the war. In 1839, Allen was elected Galveston's first mayor, and thereafter he was reelected whenever he wanted the job.

The flag-bearer at San Jacinto, Jim Sylvester, whose pursuit of a few deer had flushed Santa Anna, was a Galveston alderman and mayor pro tem during one of the Allen administrations. For his services to the Republic, Sylvester was given 640 acres in what is now the heart of Dallas, Texas, but before he joined the Texas army, Sylvester had been a wandering printer, and he continued to be one. He swapped his Dallas acreage for a flea-bitten gray mule and rode the animal off to a new job on the New Orleans *Picayune.*

After San Jacinto, Colonel Burleson resumed his "normal

career," fighting Indians. One orator said that the women and children of Texas slept easy at night for the next twenty years because they knew old Ned Burleson was on the frontier doing battle with the Comanches and other savage tribes. Between Indian wars, Burleson held several public offices. In 1841, he was elected Vice-president under President Houston. When old Ned, often dressed in buckskins, presided over the Senate, he simply used common sense as a substitute for an understanding of parliamentary rules. Burleson founded one of the state's most distinguished families. One of his descendants, grandson Albert Sidney Burleson, was Postmaster General of the United States from 1913 to 1921. A county of 679 square miles in Central Texas is named for the staunch commander of Houston's First Regiment.

Sidney Sherman and Andrew Briscoe were the men who dreamed about and then built the first Texas railroads. In 1840, Briscoe started a railroad from Harrisburg to the West. His blueprints called for the line to run to San Diego, California, but Briscoe built only a few miles of track. Hard times all over the world stopped his railroad building, but he later became a successful merchant and banker. Briscoe County, an 887-square-mile spread of country partly on Llano Estadado (The Staked Plain) and partly in the breaks of the Palo Duro and Tule Canyons, commemorates this San Jacinto officer.

In 1843, Sidney Sherman organized the railroad company which laid track as far as the Brazos River. This Harrisburg-to-the-Brazos line on which Briscoe and Sherman worked so hard is now a part of the Southern Pacific, and its route between San Antonio and Houston is almost the same as that followed by Santa Anna to San Jacinto.

General Sherman was still a fighting man in the Civil War. A 914-square-mile county in the Texas Panhandle and a prosperous city of more than 30,000 near the Red River were named for the brave officer.

The battleground itself became a tourist attraction immediately after the battle, much to the annoyance of Peggy McCormick. Not long after the fighting ended, Mrs. McCormick petitioned the Republic of Texas for damages done by the two armies to her ranch. She asked payment for one hundred forty head of cattle, seventy-five bushels of corn and two horses, but she never got any money from the Republic. Most of her land she ultimately sold. Sometime in the 1850s, Peggy McCormick was apparently burned to death in her home, although rumor had it that she had been robbed and murdered before the house was burned. Young Mike McCormick, whose warning to Burnet at New Washington had saved the President's life, became a pilot for vessels going through the river and Buffalo Bayou. In 1875, he was drowned in the bayou, at about the same place where his father had been drowned fifty years before.

San Jacinto was tragic ground for the McCormick family.

Great oak trees, their limbs flowing with Spanish moss, still rise from the shorelands of Buffalo Bayou and the San Jacinto River and Bay, and there are still islands of timber on the Plain of St. Hyacinth. But there are not nearly so many trees now as there were in 1836. The broad bayou, the river, and the bay are now part of a busy thoroughfare for ocean-going vessels called the Houston Ship Channel. Smoke rises out of all the horizons around San Jacinto from chemical plants and factories, although the prairie just southwest of the battleground is yet ranch country.

There's still a ferry at Nathaniel Lynch's old stand of business on the San Jacinto River, though today the craft in use are two swift-motored "jeeps" operated free by the state. Near the ferry, a rise of land in Lynchburg from which Santa Anna's Texan sympathizers spied on Houston's army is called Tory Hill. A wooden bridge again spans Vince's Bayou, and nearby a marker indicates the spot where the President of Mexico was captured, cowering in the tall salt grass.

The McCormick League was just another piece of Texas ranch country until 1883, when the State of Texas bought ten acres of the battlefield for a park. Today, the park is 402 acres. Markers commemorating important sites were first installed in 1894 by a committee of survivors of the battle, who carefully located key spots.

On a pitch of high ground in front of Santa Anna's campsite there is a noble shaft of steel, concrete, and fossilized buff limestone. It is 124 feet square at its base and it rises up 570 feet. At its apex is a 220-ton Texas star. This is the San Jacinto Monument, fifteen feet higher than the Washington Monument.

The names of most of the men known to have fought with the Texas army appear on plaques in the main halls of the San Jacinto Monument. At the base of this memorial is a museum, and in the tranquil rooms of the museum, mementos of the violent, bitter war rest in glass cases: the coppershot that killed one of Moseley Baker's men in the shooting at the San Felipe crossing of the Brazos; the uniform of Sidney Sherman, carefully cleaned since that muddy, bloody April 21 when it was worn by the commander of the Second Regiment; the much more resplendent uniform of a Santanista colonel.

Other relics of that grim battle are in equally sedate surroundings. The Kentucky company's colors now stand in the House of Representatives in the Texas capital at Austin, but some prudish seamstress restored it since Sylvester carried it across the rising plain at San Jacinto, and the then proudly near-nude Miss Liberty now wears flowing purple and white robes. And in a Dallas museum called the Hall of State there is a glass picture frame containing four dried oak leaves and a yellowed fragment of a love note. Those four leaves were green on Saturday, April 23, 1836, when the wounded commander of the rebels fashioned a victory garland. That yellowed piece of paper was smooth and white on that happy morning, when the triumphant General wrote on it:

To Miss Anna Raguet,
Nacogdoches,
Texas
  These are the laurels I send you from the Battlefield of San Jacinto.

> Thine,
> Houston

Chapter Notes

CHAPTER 1

Page 9, paragraph 1: Historians disagree about the quality of the army Santa Anna led into Texas in 1836. H. M. Henderson, in a 1956 issue of the *Southwest Historical Quarterly,* said: "Not disparaging the Texans, one must admit that the Mexican soldier at San Jacinto was far below average, did not compare with the Texans in any respect." The old-time Mexican-history authority, Hubert Howe Bancroft, on the other hand, called Santa Anna's expeditionary force "the flower of the Mexican army." And Capt. Reuben Marmaduke Potter was much impressed with it and said it contained many American and European soldiers of experience.

Page 10, paragraph 2: Although Santa Anna, at 5 feet 10 inches, was one of the tallest men in his army, many of the Texans who saw him at San Jacinto described him as a small man.

Page 10, paragraph 3: George Erath, a Texas private who helped guard Santa Anna's baggage after the battle of San Jacinto, said that the Mexican President was outfitted "like a European prince."

Page 13, paragraph 4: Federalist Generals Jose Antonio Mexia and Juan Alvarez also failed in rebellions that year, but the Zacatecas uprising was the most serious threat to Santa Anna's government.

Page 14, paragraph 1: This order discharging most of the state militia was the Congressional Act of March 31, 1835.

Page 14, paragraph 1: The leader of the Zacatecas army was Gov. Francisco Garcia. In this campaign Santa Anna used several of his leading officers as spies. They pretended to desert the President's army and Garcia gave them positions on his staff, but during the battle they switched back to Santa Anna's side.

Page 14, paragraph 2: A "hearsay" report of the United States Secretary of War said that the big Texas landowner, Enrique Neri, who was called the Baron de Bastrop, lured the rebels into the Royalist trap. However, it was certainly through Bastrop's influence that Austin was able to open the first Anglo-American colony in Texas, and in most Texas histories Baron de Bastrop is treated as a hero.

Page 16, paragraph 2: General Filisola was very critical of the route Santa Anna selected from Saltillo to Bexar. Filisola wanted to go by way of Mier (across from Roma, Texas) and Goliad, a much more southernly route near sea supply routes. The army suffered terribly from thirst on the march from Saltillo to Laredo. An unusually severe cold wave, with some snow, hit the Rio Grande country during the Santanistas' march. Half a hundred yoke of oxen died from the cold and from fatigue, according to Filisola. A 437-man brigade of cavalry under Gen. Juan Andrade got lost in the brush country for several days.

Page 16, paragraph 2: Almonte says the bulk of the army reached a point "half a league from Bexar" on February 23.

Page 16, paragraph 2: Jose Tornel says that Santa Anna marched to Bexar because "it was the only city in Texas whose population was Mexican in its entirety and could be relied upon to lend cooperation." As it turned out, this wasn't true.

Page 17, paragraph 4: Tony Menchaca's account of the mock marriage begins like this: "In the year 1836 Santa Anna deceived Melchora Iniega Barrera, a young woman of 17 and very beautiful who belonged to one of the best families of San Antonio. Santa Anna, not being able to obtain the favors of Senorita Melchora said that he would marry her. He arranged for one of his sergeants to disguise himself as a priest, and in this manner the marriage was celebrated."

Page 19, paragraph 2: From San Antonio on March 7, Santa Anna also issued a proclamation to citizens who had fled San Antonio: "Citizens! The causes which have conducted to this frontier a part of the Mexican army are not unknown to you: a parcel of audacious adventurers, maliciously protected by a neighboring republic, dared to invade our territory with an intention of dividing among themselves the fertile lands that are contained in the department of Texas; and even had the boldness to entertain the idea of reaching the capital of the Republic. It became necessary to check and chastise such enormous daring, and in consequence some exemplary punishments have already taken place. I am pained to find among those adventurers the names of some colonists to whom had been granted repeated benefits, and who had no just motive of complaint against the government of their adopted country. Bexians! Return to your homes and dedicate yourselves to your domestic duties. Your city and the fortress of the Alamo are already in possession of the Mexican army."

Page 23, paragraph 2: The official Texas figure was that 342 prisoners were shot at Goliad. Colonel Portilla says that 445 were marched out to be shot. Another Mexican officer wrote: "At 6 o'clock in the morning the execution of 412 American prisoners was commenced and continued until 8 o'clock when the last of the number was shot. This

day, Palm Sunday, has been to me a day of most heartfelt sorrow:
The prisoners were all young and of fine florid complexions."

CHAPTER 2

Page 27, paragraph 1: The Heroes of San Jacinto by Dixon and Kemp
lists only twenty members of Seguin's company, but both Juan Seguin
and Menchaca say there were about thirty there. The names of many
Texas fighters at San Jacinto were never on official rolls.

Page 37, paragraph 3: Elisha Pease, a secretary at the Convention, said
it was understood that Childress brought a draft of the Declaration of
Independence to Washington-on-the-Brazos.

Page 52, paragraph 3: The discord between Houston and Moseley
Baker started at a convention in late 1835 when Baker, in a fiery
speech, urged that Governor Henry Smith and his council be impeached. Houston defended Smith's government and attacked Baker.
According to Joseph J. Linn, Sam referred to Baker's alleged forgery
back in Virginia of a check for $5,000. Linn said that Baker later paid
back all the money.

CHAPTER 3

Page 55, paragraph 2: Dr. Johnson Calhoun Hunter was a medical
doctor from North Carolina who'd been in Texas since 1821. His son,
Robert Hancock Hunter, who was born in Circleville, Ohio, on May 1,
1813, wrote his account of his family's activities during the Revolution
in 1860. It was published in a pamphlet by Beulah Gayle Green in
1936.

Page 57, paragraph 2: Miss Dilue Rose was married on February 20,
1839, to Ira A. Harris. Her reminiscences and those of her father,
Dr. Pleasant W. Rose, were first published in a newspaper, the Eagle
Lake, Texas, *Headlight,* and in the 1900–1901 *Quarterly* of the Texas
State Historical Association. Mrs. Harris died at Eagle Lake on April 2,
1914.

Page 60, paragraph 2: Miguel, or Michael, Muldoon was the son of an
Irish soldier of fortune and a Spanish girl. According to his Mexican
citizenship papers, he was born in Ireland, but most reports have said
that he was born in Spain while his father was a fugitive from the
English. In 1829 Muldoon was the chaplain of the foundation Texas
Irish colony, San Patricio de Hibernia, near present-day Corpus Christi.
In 1831 he became curate of Stephen F. Austin's colony with head-
quarters at San Felipe de Austin on the Brazos River.

CHAPTER 4

Page 67, paragraph 1: Bill Simpson escaped from his Mexican captors.

Page 67, paragraph 5: In his memoirs, Francis Lubbock, a one time Governor of Texas who came to the state in 1836, has an interview with Mrs. Powell in which she said that she stayed at her home all during the Revolution. Clarence Wharton, in *The History of Fort Bend County* says that Mrs. Powell left her home with other refugees during The Runaway Scrape.

Page 69, paragraph 3: Santa Anna might have been referring to the snow-capped mountains of what is now New Mexico, which were then in Texas.

Page 69, paragraph 3: Filisola with 1,800 men and Gaona with 725 probably joined Sesma at the Brazos on April 14 and 15. At the same time about 400 Santanistas were on the Colorado with General Woll. John Henry Brown, a Texas historian who knew many of the men who fought in the Revolution, says that Santa Anna had 7,478 men in Texas in mid-April of 1836.

Page 70, paragraph 1: Some Mexican sources called *The Golden Standard* a 9-pounder.

Page 70, paragraph 3: Gail Borden, Jr., in partnership with his brother, Thomas Borden, and Joseph (Don Jose) Baker, began publication of their paper on October 10, 1835. Gail Borden sold his interest in 1837 to become the Sam Houston–appointed collector of customs at Galveston. Borden turned inventor in the 1840s. One of his inventions was a land or sea boat (or wagon) powered by sail. In 1856 he got American and British patents for a process for condensing milk in vacuum. He died in Borden, in January, 1874.

Page 71, paragraph 5: Juan Nepomuceno Almonte was said to be the son of the Rev. Jose Maria Morelos, one of the leaders of the Mexican rebellion against Spain. Father Morelos was captured and executed by the Spanish. When he was twelve in 1815, Juan Almonte was sent to the United States to be educated.

Page 72, paragraph 2: Anahuac, on the mainland, was then the principal port of Galveston Bay; there were only a few crude buildings on Galveston Island. Both the settlers and the Mexican army men sometimes meant Anahuac when they referred to "Galveston."

CHAPTER 5

Page 80, paragraph 1: Houston wrote to the *ad interim* government on April 13: "Taunts and suggestions have been gratuitously tendered to me, and I have submitted to them without any disposition to retort either with unkindness or imputation." Houston's plan for the San Jacinto campaign is hinted as early as November 13, 1835, in a letter to James Fannin when he said: "Remember our maxim, it is better to do well late than never." Also, on March 15, he wrote from his camp on the Navidad River: "My morning report on my arrival in camp at [Gonzales] shewed 374 effective men, without two days provisions, many without arms, others without ammunition. We could have met the Enemy and avenged some of our wrongs, but detached as we were, without supplies for the men and remote from succor, it would have been madness to have hazarded a contest. I had been in camp only two days and had succeeded in organizing the troops, but the first principles of drill had not been taught to them. If starved out, and the camp once broken up, there was no hope for the future. By falling back, Texas can rally and defeat any force that can come against her."

Page 92, paragraph 4: After the Revolution, Mrs. Mann started one of the city of Houston's first hotels, the Mansion House. In 1839 she was found guilty of forging the name of William Barret Travis on a legal document, a strange verdict since she couldn't write. She was sentenced to death, but Sam Houston's law firm, together with a delegation of citizens and the newspaper, *The Morning Star,* got President Mirabeau Lamar to give her a full pardon. She died in November, 1840, leaving large properties to her sons.

Page 95, paragraph 2: Lorenzo De Zavalla, Jr., returned to Mexico some time after the Texas Revolution.

Page 96, paragraph 5: Andrew Jackson Houston, the General's son, said that more than one hundred of the men left in the camp opposite Harrisburg were "disabled from the measles." Houston left all the wagons except one for carrying ammunition in the camp across the bayou from Harrisburg.

Page 99, paragraph 7: Washington Winters said the men began pulling the two cannon manually after they left Harrisburg. According to Winters, Houston's army crossed the bayou two miles below Harrisburg, just below the point where Sims Bayou joins Buffalo Bayou. "We fixed up an old ferry boat with flooring from Mrs. Batterson's house and with some new lumber we found there, and we took over the cannon," said Winters. "It took all day for the army to cross. I think Houston intended to fight and fight to the finish."

CHAPTER 6

Page 105, paragraph 2: Moses Austin Bryon described this incident: "Erastus Smith, afterwards known in the army as Deaf Smith, had been on the Little River killing buffaloes for their hides. He arrived in camp and informed the General [Stephen F. Austin] that he wanted permission to go into the town of San Antonio to see his family and that he didn't want to take any part in the war because his wife was a Mexican." Austin gave him permission. When Cos's sentries drove him back toward the Texas camp, said Bryan, "My brothers William J. Bryan, and a man named John W. Hassell, being on the picket guard of our army and seeing Smith running, spurred their horses to meet him and when Cos's soldiers were near enough, my brother and Hassell fired and caused the enemy to retreat. Smith then went into the General's tent and said: 'I told you yesterday I didn't want any part in this war ... but since they [Cos's men] have used me so treacherously, I now offer you my services. I can be of use to you as a guide or spy, as I know this whole country, have hunted over it for about 12 years.' "

Page 106, paragraph 4: The free Negro, Hendrick Arnold, seems to have been vastly respected by most soldiers in the Texas army. During the Texan attack on San Antonio in December, 1835, one division of the rebels refused to make the assault on the city until Arnold arrived to guide them. Arnold guided the division commanded by Ben Milam. Arnold's name is not listed in the Karnes spy company, although he served throughout the San Jacinto campaign and his comrades attested that he was in the battle of San Jacinto. He died in a cholera epidemic in San Antonio in 1849.

Page 110, paragraph 3: Moses Austin Bryan was born at Herculaneum, Missouri, on September 25, 1817. Moses came to Texas in January, 1831, and in early 1832, he accompanied his uncle, Stephen F. Austin, to the Mexican city of Saltillo.

Page 112, paragraph 1: At this stage of the San Jacinto campaign, Uncle Jimmy Curtis and Noah Smithwick were members of a ranger company which a fabulous character named Robert McAlpin Williamson was recruiting for the Texas army. An illness had caused Williamson's right leg to stiffen in an L-shape, drawn up at the knee, so he attached a pegleg to his right knee. His Latin-American friends in Texas therefore called him "Senor Three-Legged Willie." He was a well-educated lawyer whose vigorous support of the Revolution caused the Santanistas to put a price on his head. Ultimately, Williamson's rangers were split up in other companies and Three-Legged Willie fought at San Jacinto as a trooper in Lamar's cavalry.

CHAPTER 7

Page 123, paragraph 2: This Benjamin Harrison, aged thirty-five, wasn't lying to General Urrea. He was the son of William Henry Harrison.

Page 131, paragraph 1: Reuben Potter said he learned in 1838 from one of Santa Anna's sergeants, who'd issued the ration list for the Santanista army on the morning of the twenty-first, that the Mexican President had thirteen hundred men at San Jacinto after the Cos reinforcement.

Page 134, paragraph 5: Reuben Potter, who knew many of the Texan and Mexican leaders of 1836, wrote in the *Magazine of American History:* "The assertion that Houston would not have fought at San Jacinto when he did had his army not compelled him to, does not harmonize with his disregard of the war council's vote [against an immediate attack] or his action immediately after." Houston no doubt exulted in the fact that the vote of the council was less daring than his own determination.

CHAPTER 8

Page 141, paragraph 4: Ben McCulloch was a well-read native of Rutherford County, Tennessee. He formed a friendship with David Crockett and planned to accompany Crockett to Texas, but something happened to delay his trip and keep him from going with Crockett. He did reach Texas in time for the battle of San Jacinto.

Page 150, paragraph 5: Alphonso Steele died near Kosse, Texas, on July 7, 1911, at the age of ninety-four. He was said to be the last known survivor of the battle of San Jacinto.

Page 158, paragraph 1: Houston, in his official report, says that the conflict lasted "about 18 minutes from the time of close action until we were in possession of the enemy's encampment." Houston said the battle commenced at half-past four. The anonymous sergeant in the Santa Anna army, quoted by Capt. Reuben Potter, also says that the "whole surviving force of Santa Anna was scattering 18 minutes after the Texans charged."

Page 158, paragraph 1: "If Santa Anna had had 300 of his best cavalry in reserve—and he would have had if Urrea's division instead of Cos' had reinforced him—then I fear the infant Republic of Texas would not have lived to a marriageable age and could not have been annexed," said Reuben Potter in his account of the battle of San Jacinto. Potter meant that the rather disorganized charge of the Texans could easily have been broken by three hundred disciplined dragoons.

CHAPTER 9

Page 165, paragraph 1: William S. Taylor was a stout supporter of Sam Houston. Later he wrote: "I have often been mortified at the slanderous lies published about General Houston's conduct at the Battle of San Jacinto."

Page 172, paragraph 2: The unnamed Mexican sergeant at San Jacinto whom Reuben Potter wrote about in his account of the battle said that he got a glancing blow on the head during the fight and fell between the bodies of two dead Santanistas. This sergeant then "enacted the role of a corpse until he heard a voice say in Spanish: "All the wounded who are able may now arise. Their lives will be spared!" The speaker was Lorenzo De Zavala, Jr., who conducted the sergeant to the prison compound.

Page 176, paragraph 2: Sylvester says that Santa Anna also kissed his hands.

Page 181, paragraph 1: Moses Austin Bryan described Santa Anna's attire differently from most other eyewitnesses. Bryan said that *El Presidente* was wearing a brown linen outfit, old brogans, and a black sailor cap.

CHAPTER 10

Page 188, paragraph 4: C. A. Spears, a Sherman, Texas, banker who has been investigating the life of Sophia Suttonfield, says that her career makes those of fictional heroines like Scarlett O'Hara seem tame by comparison. She was Mrs. Sophia Suttonfield Auginbaugh Coffee Butts Porter when she died in her huge mansion, Glen Eden, on the Red River near Sherman in 1899, in her eighty-fourth year. Before the Civil War she entertained such personages as U. S. Grant, Robert E. Lee, Albert Sidney Johnston, Sam Houston, and some famous Indian chiefs. Besides the mysterious Auginbaugh, her husbands were Col. Holland Coffee, a trader with the Indians at Fort Preston (near what is now Sherman, Texas), Maj. George N. Butts, and Judge James Porter. Coffee was killed in a duel with a gunman who had shown some slight impoliteness to Sophia. During the States War, William Clarke Quantrill's men were quartered for a while near Glen Eden. At a party at the mansion, one of Quantrill's lads shot a ribbon out of Sophia's hair. She went right on dancing in unconcerned fashion. Major Butts, her third husband, threw the pistol shooter and his friends out of the house. A few days later, Butts was found shot to death, apparently from ambush. Her fourth husband, Judge Porter, was a Confederate colonel from Missouri who was bound for Mexico to join Emperor Maximilian's forces when he met Sophia, then in her forties but still very attractive. He decided to stay in Texas. He is the only one of her husbands known to have died a natural death.

Page 219, paragraph 3: Sam Houston wrote of Woll's visit: "General Woll came into the encampment at San Jacinto without my knowledge. Nor was I apprised of his presence until he and his aide traversed our lines. I ordered them to my presence and instructed them that such conduct would not be tolerated and caused them to be placed under vigilance. Woll's subsequent conduct was so obnoxious to the [Texan] army that, from desire for his personal safety, I did not permit his release until he could go in perfect safety."

Principal Sources

HISTORIES OF TEXAS (Title not given if History of Texas)

Hubert Howe Bancroft, *The North Mexican States and Texas;* John Henry Brown; Carlos Castaneda, *Our Catholic Heritage in Texas;* Henry Stuart Foote; Herbert Gambrell; William Kennedy; Peter Molyneaux; Ralph W. Steen; Homer Thrall, *A Pictorial History of Texas;* Dudley G. Wooten; Louis J. Wortham.

HISTORIES OF MEXICO

Lucas Alaman, *Historia de Mexico;* Hubert Howe Bancroft, *The North Mexican States and Texas;* John A. Crow, *Mexico Today;* Henry B. Parkes, *A History of Mexico;* Carlos Pereyra, *Tejas: La Primera Dismembracion de Mejico;* Allesio Robles, *Coahuila y Texas en la Epoca Colonial;* Jose Vasconcelos, *Breve Historia de Mexico.*

MISCELLANEOUS BOOKS

Memoirs of George W. Erath, Austin, 1928; Charles Francis Adams (editor), *Memoirs of John Quincy Adams;* Samuel E. Asbury (editor), *The Private Journal of Juan Almonte;* D. W. C. Baker, *Texas Scrap Book;* Eugene C. Barker, *The Life of Stephen F. Austin, Readings in Texas History, Stephen F. Austin Papers,* and *Samuel Houston Papers;* William Bollaert, *William Bollaert's Texas;* Dr. Rufus Burleson, *Life and Writings of Rufus Burleson;* John Henry Brown, *The Life of Henry Smith;* Wilfred Hardy Callcott, *Santa Anna;* Jose Thomas Canales (editor), *Native Latin American Contribution to the Colonization and Independence of Texas;* Carlos Castaneda, *The Mexican Side of the Texas Revolution;* Davy Crockett, *The Life of Davy Crockett, The Original Humorist and Irrepressible Backwoodsman [To Which Is Added An Account Of His Glorious Death At The Alamo While Fighting In Defence Of Texas Independence];* H. B. Cushman, *History of the Texas Indians;* Sam Houston Dixon and Louis Wiltz Kemp, *The Signers of the Texas Declaration of Independence* and *The Heroes of San Jacinto;* J. Frank Dobie, *The Flavor of Texas;* Grant Foreman, *Pioneer Days;* Llerena Friend, *Sam Houston: The Great Designer;* Herbert Gambrell, *Mirabeau Buonaparte Lamar, Troubadour and Crusader* and *Anson Jones, The Last President of the Republic;* Ramon Caro, *Verdadera Idea de la Primera Campana de Tejas;* Vincente Filisola, *Memorias para la Historia de la Guerra de Tejas;* Philip Graham, *The Life and Poems of Mirabeau Buonaparte Lamar;* J. Hefter and Mrs. Angelina Nieto, *El Soldado Mexicano;* B. G. Green (compiler), *Narrative of Robert Hancock Hunter from His Arrival in Texas, 1822, Through the Battle of San Jacinto, 1836,* published by Cook Printing Company, Austin, Texas, and Copyright 1936 by B. G. Green; Frank C. Hanighen, *Santa Anna;* William Ransom

Hogan, *The Texas Republic;* Andrew Jackson Houston, *Texas Independence;* Marquis James, *The Raven;* Anson Jones, *Republic of Texas;* John J. Linn, *Reminiscences of Fifty Years in Texas;* Francis R. Lubbock, *Six Decades in Texas;* Chester Newell, *History of the Revolution in Texas;* Harriet Smith (editor), *Mirabeau Lamar Papers;* Noah Smithwick, *Evolution of a State, or Recollections of Old Time Texas;* Lon Tinkle, *Thirteen Days to Glory: The Siege of the Alamo;* Jose Valades, *Santa Anna and the War in Texas;* Walter Prescott Webb (editor), *The Handbook of Texas;* Clarence Wharton, *San Jacinto: The Sixteenth Decisive Battle* and *Remember Goliad!;* Amelia Williams, *A Critical Study of the Siege of the Alamo;* Volumes of the Texas *Almanac,* 1857 through 1872, which includes an English translation of Pedro Delgado's reminiscences of the San Jacinto campaign in the 1870 *Almanac.*

PERIODICALS

Eugene C. Barker, "The Heroes of San Jacinto" and "The Texas Declaration of Causes of Taking up Arms Against Mexico," from *Southwest Historical Quarterly,* 1931. Eugene C. Barker, "The San Jacinto Campaign" and Dilue Rose Harris, "The Reminiscences of Mrs. Dilue Rose Harris," from Volume IV of the *Southwestern Historical Quarterly.* Andrew Forest Muir, "The Mystery of San Jacinto," from *Southwest Review,* 1951, and "The Lady Was for Burning," from *Southwest Review,* 1959. Reuben Marmaduke Potter, "Battle of San Jacinto," from *Magazine of American History,* May, 1880; James Presley, "Santa Anna in Texas: A Mexican Viewpoint," from *Southwestern Historical Quarterly,* 1959; Reminiscences of Moseley Baker, J. H. Kuykendall, Dilue Rose, Pleasant Rose, Santa Anna, and Amasa Turner from Texas State Historical Association *Quarterlies,* 1900 through 1901. "Battle of San Jacinto by One Who Fought In It," Anonymous, from *United Service Magazine,* 1837, reprinted by *Living Age,* 1844.

NEWSPAPERS

Files of *Galveston News* and *Dallas News; El Mosquite Mexicano; Telegraph and Texas Register. Austin City Gazette;* Houston *Morning Star;* Eagle Lake *Headlight.*

PAMPHLETS AND UNPUBLISHED PAPERS

Robert M. Coleman, "Houston Displayed: or, Who Won the Battle of San Jacinto? by a Farmer in the Army." Alphonso Steele, Autobiography of Private Alphonso Steele, Last Survivor of the Battle of San Jacinto, together with Mr. Steele's Account of the Campaign and Fight." Publications of the Texas Folk Lore Society. The Samuel Asbury Papers in the University of Texas Library; David Burnet Papers in the Rosenberg Library, Galveston; H. A. McArdle Papers in the Texas State Archives; John S. Ford Journal, in the Texas State Archives; Santanista Pvt. Cubas Lozano letters, courtesy of Nestor

Garcia; Mirabeau Buonaparte Lamar Papers, in the Texas State Library; Anthony Menchaca Papers, in the San Antonio Public Library; James Morgan Papers, in the Rosenberg Library, Galveston; James Sylvester Papers, in the Rosenberg Library, Galveston; Moses Austin Bryan's unpublished memoirs, owned by Mrs. C. R. Bryan, Jr., of Houston; unpublished anecdotes on Houston by Senator Tom Love of Dallas. Original court records of Forbes vs. Labadie slander suit, furnished by District Clerk Matt C. Gartman and District Attorney Robert Murphey of Nacogdoches; also a typescript of the case assembled by R. B. Blake. Unpublished anecdotes on the Texas Republic period by Bill Kittrell of Dallas.

Frank Tolbert has been a professional writer since leaving college (Texas Tech and the University of Texas), although his major studies were anthropology, archaeology, and geology. He got his start at national magazine writing with sports articles for *Collier's*. He was a sports columnist for the Fort Worth *Star-Telegram* until December of 1941, when he joined the Marine Corps and asked to be assigned to a raider battalion. The editor of the Marine Corps magazine, *The Leatherneck*, saw one of Tolbert's *Collier's* pieces and he was forthwith put on a train for *The Leatherneck's* Washington office. Throughout 1942 he was managing editor of the magazine, and in 1943–1944 he was one of its combat correspondents. He reported campaigns all over the Pacific theater. He came back to Washington in 1945 and was again managing editor of *The Leatherneck*.

Tolbert has written more than a hundred short stories and articles for *The Saturday Evening Post, Look, The Reader's Digest, Esquire, True,* and other periodicals. His first novel, *Bigamy Jones,* about an 1870s cowboy who got married every payday, was selected by the *New York Times Book Review* as one of the best books of 1954, and his other books—*Neiman-Marcus, Texas,* published in 1953, and another novel, *The Staked Plain* (1958)—won considerable attention and critical acclaim.

Mr. Tolbert also writes a daily column, "Tolbert's Texas," for the *Dallas News.* He and his wife, Kathleen, and their children, Frank and Kathleen, now live in Dallas.

INDEX